S0-BKD-771

Health 12/13

Thirty-Third Edition

EDITOR

Eileen L. Daniel
SUNY at Brockport

Eileen Daniel, a registered dietitian and licensed nutritionist, is a Professor in the Department of Health Science and Associate Vice Provost for Academic Affairs at the State University of New York at Brockport. She received a BS in Nutrition and Dietetics from the Rochester Institute of Technology in 1977, an MS in Community Health Education from SUNY at Brockport in 1987, and a PhD in Health Education from the University of Oregon in 1986. A member of the American Dietetics Association and other professional and community organizations, Dr. Daniel has published more than 40 journal articles on issues of health, nutrition, and health education. She is also the editor of *Taking Sides: Clashing Views on Controversial Issues in Health and Society,* tenth edition (McGraw-Hill/Contemporary Learning Series, 2012).

ANNUAL EDITIONS: HEALTH, THIRTY-THIRD EDITION

Published by McGraw-Hill, a business unit of The McGraw-Hill Companies, Inc., 1221 Avenue
of the Americas, New York, NY 10020. Copyright © 2012 by The McGraw-Hill Companies, Inc.

Annual Editions is published by the **Contemporary Learning Series** group within the
McGraw-Hill Higher Education division.

1 2 3 4 5 6 7 8 9 0 QDB/QDB 1 0 9 8 7 6 5 4 3 2 1

ISBN: 978–0–07–805103–6
MHID: 0–07–805103–7
ISSN: 0278–4653 (print)
ISSN: 2162–5638 (online)

Managing Editor: *Larry Loeppke*
Developmental Editor II: *Debra A. Henricks*
Permissions Coordinator: *Lenny J. Behnke*
Senior Marketing Communications Specialist: *Alice Link*
Senior Project Manager: *Melissa Leick*
Design Coordinator: *Margarite Reynolds*
Cover Designer: *Kristine Jubeck*
Buyer: *Susan K. Culbertson*
Media Project Manager: *Sridevi Palani*

Compositor: Laserwords Private Limited
Cover Image Credits: © liquidlibrary/PictureQuest (inset); Janis Christie/Getty Images (background)

Editors/Academic Advisory Board

Members of the Academic Advisory Board are instrumental in the final selection of articles for each edition of ANNUAL EDITIONS. Their review of articles for content, level, and appropriateness provides critical direction to the editors and staff. We think that you will find their careful consideration well reflected in this volume.

ANNUAL EDITIONS: Health 12/13
33rd Edition

EDITOR

Eileen L. Daniel
SUNY at Brockport

ACADEMIC ADVISORY BOARD MEMBERS

Preface

In publishing ANNUAL EDITIONS we recognize the enormous role played by the magazines, newspapers, and journals of the public press in providing current, first-rate educational information in a broad spectrum of interest areas. Many of these articles are appropriate for students, researchers, and professionals seeking accurate, current material to help bridge the gap between principles and theories and the real world. These articles, however, become more useful for study when those of lasting value are carefully collected, organized, indexed, and reproduced in a low-cost format, which provides easy and permanent access when the material is needed. That is the role played by ANNUAL EDITIONS.

America is in the midst of a revolution that is changing the way millions of Americans view their health. Traditionally, most people delegated responsibility for their health to their physicians and hoped that medical science would be able to cure whatever ailed them. This approach to health care emphasized the role of medical technology and funneled billions of dollars into medical research. The net result of all this spending is the most technically advanced and expensive health care system in the world. In an attempt to rein in health care costs, the health care delivery system moved from privatized health care coverage to what is termed "managed care." While managed care has turned the tide regarding the rising cost of health care, it has done so by limiting reimbursement for many cutting edge technologies. Unfortunately, many people also feel that it has lowered the overall quality of care that is being given. Perhaps the saving grace is that we live at a time in which chronic illnesses rather than acute illnesses are our number one health threat, and many of these illnesses can be prevented or controlled by our lifestyle choices. The net result of these changes has prompted millions of individuals to assume more personal responsibility for safeguarding their own health. Evidence of this change in attitude can be seen in the growing interest in nutrition, physical fitness, dietary supplements, and stress management. If we as a nation are to capitalize on this new health consciousness, we must devote more time and energy to educate Americans in the health sciences, so that they will be better able to make informed choices about their health. Health is a complex and dynamic subject, and it is practically impossible for anyone to stay abreast of all the current research findings. In the past, most of us have relied on books, newspapers, magazines, and television as our primary sources for medical/health information, but today, with the widespread use of personal computers connected to the World Wide Web, it is possible to access vast amount of health information, any time of the day, without even leaving one's home. Unfortunately, quantity and availability does not necessarily translate into quality, and this is particularly true in the area of medical/health information. Just as the Internet is a great source for reliable timely information, it is also a vehicle for the dissemination of misleading and fraudulent information.

Currently there are no standards or regulations regarding the posting of health content on the Internet, and this has led to a plethora of misinformation and quackery in the medical/health arena. Given this vast amount of health information, our task as health educators is twofold: (1) To provide our students with the most up-to-date and accurate information available on major health issues of our time and (2) to teach our students the skills that will enable them to sort out facts from fiction, in order to become informed consumers. *Annual Editions: Health 12/13* was designed to aid this task. It offers a sampling of quality articles that represents the latest thinking on a variety of health issues, and it also serves as a tool for developing critical thinking skills.

The articles in this volume were carefully chosen on the basis of their quality and timeliness. Because this book is revised and updated annually, it contains information that is not generally available in any standard textbook. As such, it serves as a valuable resource for both teachers and students. This edition of *Annual Editions: Health* has been updated to reflect the latest thinking on a variety of contemporary health issues. We hope that you find this edition to be a helpful learning tool filled with information and the presentation user-friendly. The 10 topical areas presented in this edition mirror those that are normally covered in introductory health courses: Promoting Healthy Behavior Change, Stress and Mental Health, Nutritional Health, Exercise and Weight Management, Drugs and Health, Sexuality and Relationships, Preventing and Fighting Disease, Health Care and the Health Care System, Consumer Health, and Contemporary Health Hazards. Because of the interdependence of the various elements that constitute health, the articles selected were written by authors with diverse educational backgrounds and expertise including naturalists, environmentalists, psychologists, economists, sociologists, nutritionists, consumer advocates, and traditional health practitioners.

Annual Editions: Health 12/13 was designed to be one of the most useful and up-to-date publications currently available in the area of health. Please let us know what you think of it by filling out and returning the postage paid *article rating form* on the last page of this book. Any anthology can be improved. This one will be—annually.

Eileen L. Daniel
Editor

The Annual Editions Series

VOLUMES AVAILABLE

Adolescent Psychology

Aging

American Foreign Policy

American Government

Anthropology

Archaeology

Assessment and Evaluation

Business Ethics

Child Growth and Development

Comparative Politics

Criminal Justice

Developing World

Drugs, Society, and Behavior

Dying, Death, and Bereavement

Early Childhood Education

Economics

Educating Children with Exceptionalities

Education

Educational Psychology

Entrepreneurship

Environment

The Family

Gender

Geography

Global Issues

Health

Homeland Security

Human Development

Human Resources

Human Sexualities

International Business

Management

Marketing

Mass Media

Microbiology

Multicultural Education

Nursing

Nutrition

Physical Anthropology

Psychology

Race and Ethnic Relations

Social Problems

Sociology

State and Local Government

Sustainability

Technologies, Social Media, and Society

United States History, Volume 1

United States History, Volume 2

Urban Society

Violence and Terrorism

Western Civilization, Volume 1

Western Civilization, Volume 2

World History, Volume 1

World History, Volume 2

World Politics

Contents

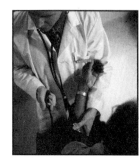

UNIT 1
Promoting Healthy Behavior Change

Unit Overview   xviii

UNIT 2
Stress and Mental Health

Unit Overview   10

The concepts in bold italics are developed in the article. For further expansion, please refer to the Topic Guide.

UNIT 3
Nutritional Health

UNIT 4
Exercise and Weight Management

The concepts in bold italics are developed in the article. For further expansion, please refer to the Topic Guide.

UNIT 5
Drugs and Health

UNIT 6
Sexuality and Relationships

The concepts in bold italics are developed in the article. For further expansion, please refer to the Topic Guide.

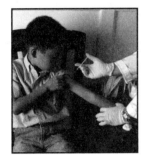

UNIT 7
Preventing and Fighting Disease

UNIT 8
Health Care and the Health Care System

The concepts in bold italics are developed in the article. For further expansion, please refer to the Topic Guide.

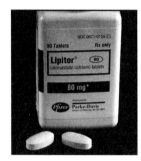

UNIT 9
Consumer Health

The concepts in bold italics are developed in the article. For further expansion, please refer to the Topic Guide.

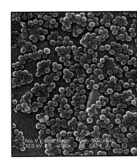

UNIT 10
Contemporary Health Hazards

The concepts in bold italics are developed in the article. For further expansion, please refer to the Topic Guide.

The concepts in bold italics are developed in the article. For further expansion, please refer to the Topic Guide.

Correlation Guide

The *Annual Editions* series provides students with convenient, inexpensive access to current, carefully selected articles from the public press. **Annual Editions: Health 12/13** is an easy-to-use reader that presents articles on important topics such as *consumer health, exercise, nutrition,* and many more. For more information on *Annual Editions* and other *McGraw-Hill Contemporary Learning Series* titles, visit www.mhhe.com/cls.

This convenient guide matches the units in **Annual Editions: Health 12/13** with the corresponding chapters in three of our best-selling McGraw-Hill Health textbooks by Hahn et al., Payne et al., and Insel/Roth.

Annual Editions: Health 12/13	Focus on Health, 11/e by Hahn et al.	Understanding Your Health, 12/e by Payne et al.	Core Concepts in Health, Brief, 12/e by Insel/Roth
Unit 1: Promoting Healthy Behavior Change	**Chapter 1:** Shaping Your Health	**Chapter 1:** Shaping Your Health	**Chapter 1:** Taking Charge of Your Health
Unit 2: Stress and Mental Health	**Chapter 2:** Achieving Psychological Health **Chapter 3:** Managing Stress	**Chapter 2:** Achieving Psychological Health **Chapter 3:** Managing Stress	**Chapter 2:** Stress: The Constant Challenge **Chapter 3:** Psychological Health
Unit 3: Nutritional Health	**Chapter 5:** Understanding Nutrition and Your Diet	**Chapter 5:** Understanding Nutrition and Your Diet	**Chapter 9:** Nutrition Basics
Unit 4: Exercise and Weight Management	**Chapter 4:** Becoming Physically Fit **Chapter 6:** Maintaining a Healthy Weight	**Chapter 4:** Becoming Physically Fit **Chapter 6:** Maintaining a Healthy Weight	**Chapter 10:** Exercise for Health and Fitness **Chapter 11:** Weight Management
Unit 5: Drugs and Health	**Chapter 7:** Making Decisions about Drug and Alcohol Use **Chapter 8:** Rejecting Tobacco Use	**Chapter 7:** Making Decisions about Drug Use **Chapter 8:** Taking Control of Alcohol Use **Chapter 9:** Rejecting Tobacco Use	**Chapter 7:** The Use and Abuse of Psychoactive Drugs **Chapter 8:** Alcohol and Tobacco
Unit 6: Sexuality and Relationships	**Chapter 12:** Understanding Sexuality **Chapter 13:** Managing Your Fertility	**Chapter 14:** Exploring the Origins of Sexuality **Chapter 15:** Understanding Sexual Behavior and Relationships **Chapter 16:** Managing Your Fertility **Chapter 17:** Becoming a Parent	**Chapter 4:** Intimate Relationships and Communication **Chapter 5:** Sexuality, Pregnancy, and Childbirth **Chapter 6:** Contraception and Abortion
Unit 7: Preventing and Fighting Disease	**Chapter 9:** Reducing Your Risk of Cardiovascular Disease **Chapter 10:** Living with Cancer and Chronic Conditions **Chapter 11:** Preventing Infectious Diseases	**Chapter 10:** Enhancing Your Cardiovascular Health **Chapter 11:** Living with Cancer **Chapter 12:** Managing Chronic Conditions **Chapter 13:** Preventing Infectious Diseases	**Chapter 12:** Cardiovascular Health and Cancer **Chapter 13:** Immunity and Infection
Unit 8: Health Care and the Health Care System	**Chapter 14:** Becoming an Informed Health Care Consumer	**Chapter 18:** Becoming an Informed Health Care Consumer	**Chapter 15:** Conventional and Complementary Medicine **Chapter 17:** The Challenge of Aging
Unit 9: Consumer Health	**Chapter 15:** Protecting Your Safety	**Chapter 19:** Protecting Your Safety	**Chapter 16:** The Environment and Your Health
Unit 10: Contemporary Health Hazards	**Chapter 16:** The Environment and Your Health	**Chapter 20:** The Environment and Your Health	**Chapter 14:** Environmental Health

Topic Guide

This topic guide suggests how the selections in this book relate to the subjects covered in your course. You may want to use the topics listed on these pages to search the Web more easily.

On the following pages a number of websites have been gathered specifically for this book. They are arranged to reflect the units of this Annual Editions reader. You can link to these sites by going to www.mhhe.com/cls.

All the articles that relate to each topic are listed below the bold-faced term.

Addiction
6. Internet Addiction
18. The New Quitter

AIDS
22. Sex, Drugs, Prisons, and HIV
24. Who Still Dies of AIDS, and Why
30. Incapacitated, Alone and Treated to Death
41. HIV Apathy

Alcoholism
2. The Perils of Higher Education
17. Caffeinated Alcohol in a Can, Four Loko Does the Job, Students Agree
18. The New Quitter

Antidepressants
4. The Depressing News about Antidepressants

Anxiety
5. "I Can't Let Anything Go": A Case Study with Psychological Testing of a Patient with Pathologic Hoarding
38. The Warrior's Brain

Behavior change
1. Crimes of the Heart
2. The Perils of Higher Education
3. Carrots, Sticks, and Health Care Reform—Problems with Wellness Incentives
18. The New Quitter

Birth control
26. Pharmacist Refusals: A Threat to Women's Health

Cancer
7. Antioxidants: Fruitful Research and Recommendations
13. Eat Like a Greek
23. New Mammogram Guidelines Raise Questions
25. A Mandate in Texas: The Story of a Compulsory Vaccination and What It Means
37. The Surprising Reason Why Heavy Isn't Healthy

Cholesterol
16. Great Drug, but Does It Prolong Life?

Consumer health
31. Vaccine Refusal, Mandatory Immunization, and the Risks of Vaccine-Preventable Diseases
32. Medical Tourism: What You Should Know
35. Hazardous Health Plans

Controversies
8. Keeping a Lid on Salt: Not So Easy
20. The Conservative Case for Gay Marriage
25. A Mandate in Texas: The Story of a Compulsory Vaccination and What It Means
26. Pharmacist Refusals: A Threat to Women's Health
28. Myth Diagnosis

Coronary heart disease
7. Antioxidants: Fruitful Research and Recommendations
13. Eat Like a Greek

Depression
4. The Depressing News about Antidepressants

Diabetes
13. Eat Like a Greek
36. The Rough Road to Dreamland

Dieting and weight loss
12. Defeating Childhood Obesity
13. Eat Like a Greek
14. Dieting on a Budget
15. In Obesity Epidemic, What's One Cookie?
18. The New Quitter

Drug use and abuse
2. The Perils of Higher Education
4. The Depressing News about Antidepressants
17. Caffeinated Alcohol in a Can, Four Loko Does the Job, Students Agree
18. The New Quitter

Environmental health hazards
33. Bed Bugs: The Pesticide Dilemma
40. Chemical in Plastic Bottles Fuels Science, Concern—and Litigation
43. Post-Earthquake Public Health in Haiti
44. Countering Radiation Fears with Just the Facts

Exercise and fitness
11. Phys Ed: Why Wii Fit Is Best for Grandparents

Food
9. Fruit Loopiness
10. F.D.A. Panel to Consider Warnings for Artificial Food Colorings
12. Defeating Childhood Obesity
34. Is Your Food Contaminated?

Food safety
10. F.D.A. Panel to Consider Warnings for Artificial Food Colorings
34. Is Your Food Contaminated?

Gender issues
19. The Thoroughly Modern Guide to Breakups
20. The Conservative Case for Gay Marriage
21. Is Pornography Adultery?
26. Pharmacist Refusals: A Threat to Women's Health

Health behavior
1. Crimes of the Heart
2. The Perils of Higher Education
18. The New Quitter

Internet References

The following Internet sites have been selected to support the articles found in this reader. These sites were available at the time of publication. However, because websites often change their structure and content, the information listed may no longer be available. We invite you to visit www.mhhe.com/cls for easy access to these sites.

Annual Editions: Health 12/13

General Sources

National Institute on Aging (NIA)
www.nia.nih.gov

The NIA, one of the institutes of the U.S. National Institutes of Health, presents this home page to lead you to a variety of resources on health and lifestyle issues on aging.

U.S. Department of Agriculture (USDA)/Food and Nutrition Information Center (FNIC)
www.nal.usda.gov/fnic

Use this site to find nutrition information provided by various USDA agencies, to find links to food and nutrition resources on the Internet, and to access FNIC publications and databases.

U.S. Department of Health and Human Services
www.os.dhhs.gov

This site has extensive links to information on such topics as the health benefits of exercise, weight control, and prudent lifestyle choices.

U.S. National Institutes of Health (NIH)
www.nih.gov

Consult this site for links to extensive health information and scientific resources. Comprising 24 separate institutes, centers, and divisions, the NIH is one of eight health agencies of the Public Health Service, which, in turn, is part of the U.S. Department of Health and Human Services.

U.S. National Library of Medicine
www.nlm.nih.gov

This huge site permits a search of a number of databases and electronic information sources such as MEDLINE. You can learn about research projects and programs and peruse the national network of medical libraries here.

World Health Organization
www.who.int/en

This home page of the World Health Organization will provide links to a wealth of statistical and analytical information about health around the world.

UNIT 1: Promoting Healthy Behavior Change

Columbia University's Go Ask Alice!
www.goaskalice.columbia.edu/index.html

This interactive site provides discussion and insight into a number of personal issues of interest to college-age people and often those younger and older. Many questions about physical and emotional health and well-being are answered.

The Society of Behavioral Medicine
www.sbm.org

This site provides listings of major, general health institutes and organizations as well as discipline-specific links and resources in medicine, psychology, and public health.

UNIT 2: Stress and Mental Health

The American Institute of Stress
www.stress.org

This site provides comprehensive information on stress: its dangers, the beliefs that build helpful techniques for overcoming stress, and so on. This easy-to-navigate site has good links to information on anxiety and related topics.

National Mental Health Association (NMHA)
www.nmha.org/index.html

The NMHA is a citizen volunteer advocacy organization that works to improve the mental health of all individuals. The site provides access to guidelines that individuals can use to reduce stress and improve their lives in small, yet tangible, ways.

Self-Help Magazine
www.selfhelpmagazine.com/index.html

Reach lots of links to self-help resources on the Net at this site, including resources on stress, anxiety, fears, and more.

UNIT 3: Nutritional Health

The American Dietetic Association
www.eatright.org

This organization, along with its National Center of Nutrition and Dietetics, promotes optimal nutrition, health, and well-being. This easy-to-navigate site presents FAQs about nutrition and dieting, nutrition resources, and career and member information.

Center for Science in the Public Interest (CSPI)
www.cspinet.org

CSPI is a nonprofit education and advocacy organization that focuses on improving the safety and nutritional quality of our food supply and on reducing the health problems caused by alcohol. This agency also evaluates the nutritional composition of fast foods, movie popcorn, and chain restaurants. There are also good links to related sites.

Food and Nutrition Information Center
www.nalusda.gov/fnic/index.html

This is an official Agriculture Network Information Center website. The FNIC is one of several information centers at the National Agriculture Library, the Agricultural Research Service, and the U.S. Department of Agriculture. The website has information on nutrition-related publications, an index of food and nutrition related Internet resources, and an online catalog of materials.

UNIT 4: Exercise and Weight Management

American Society of Exercise Physiologists (ASEP)
www.asep.org

The ASEP is devoted to promoting people's health and physical fitness. This extensive site provides links to publications related to exercise and career opportunities in exercise physiology.

Internet References

Cyberdiet
www.cyberdiet.com

This site, maintained by a registered dietician, offers Cyberdiet's interactive nutritional profile, food facts, menus and meal plans, and exercise and food-related sites.

Shape Up America!
www.shapeup.org

At the Shape Up America! website you will find the latest information about safe weight management, healthy eating, and physical fitness.

UNIT 5: Drugs and Health

Food and Drug Administration (FDA)
www.fda.gov

This site includes FDA news, information on drugs, and drug toxicology facts.

National Institute on Drug Abuse (NIDA)
www.nida.nih.gov

Use this site index for access to NIDA publications and communications, information on drugs of abuse, and links to other related websites.

UNIT 6: Sexuality and Relationships

Planned Parenthood
www.plannedparenthood.org

This home page provides links to information on contraceptives (including outercourse and abstinence) and to discussions of other topics related to sexual health.

Sexuality Information and Education Council of the United States (SIECUS)
www.siecus.org

SIECUS is a nonprofit, private advocacy group that affirms that sexuality is a natural and healthy part of living. This home page offers publications, what's new, descriptions of programs, and a listing of international sexuality education initiatives.

UNIT 7: Preventing and Fighting Disease

American Cancer Society
www.cancer.org

Open this site and its various links to learn the concerns and lifestyle advice of the American Cancer Society. It provides information on tobacco and alternative cancer therapies.

American Diabetes Association Home Page
www.diabetes.org

This site offers information on diabetes including treatment, diet, and insulin therapy.

American Heart Association
www.amhrt.org

This award-winning, comprehensive site of the American Heart Association offers information on heart disease, prevention, patient facts, eating plans, what's new, nutrition, smoking cessation, and FAQs.

National Institute of Allergy and Infectious Diseases (NIAID)
www3.niaid.nih.gov

Open this site and its various links to learn the concerns and lifestyle advice of the National Institute of Allergy and Infectious Diseases.

UNIT 8: Health Care and the Health Care System

American Medical Association (AMA)
www.ama-assn.org

The AMA offers this site to find up-to-date medical information, peer-review resources, discussions of such topics as HIV/AIDS and women's health, examination of issues related to managed care, and important publications.

MedScape: The Online Resource for Better Patient Care
www.medscape.com

For health professionals and interested consumers, this site offers peer-reviewed articles, self-assessment features, medical news, and annotated links to Internet resources. It also contains the Morbidity & Mortality Weekly Report, which is a publication of the Centers for Disease Control and Prevention.

UNIT 9: Consumer Health

FDA Consumer Magazine
www.fda.gov/fdac

This site offers articles and information that appears in the FDA Consumer Magazine.

Global Vaccine Awareness League
www.gval.com

This site addresses side effects related to vaccination. Its many links are geared to provide copious information.

National Sleep Foundation
www. sleep foundation.org

The goal of this site is to improve public health and safety through an understanding of sleep and sleep disorders, and through the support of sleep-related education, research, and advocacy.

UNIT 10: Contemporary Health Hazards

Centers for Disease Control: Flu
www.cdc.gov/flu

This CDC site provides updates, information, key facts, questions and answers, and ways to prevent influenza (the flu). Updated regularly during the flu season.

Environmental Protection Agency
www.epa.gov

Use this site to find environmental health information provided by various EPA agencies.

Food and Drug Administration
www.fda.gov

This site includes FDA news, information on drugs, and drug toxicology facts.

World Health Organization
www.who.org

This site offers information on health issues throughout the world. For data specific to Haiti, click www.who.int/countries/hti/en

UNIT 1

Promoting Healthy Behavior Change

Unit Selections

1. **Crimes of the Heart,** Walter C. Willett and Anne Underwood
2. **The Perils of Higher Education,** Steven Kotler
3. **Carrots, Sticks, and Health Care Reform—Problems with Wellness Incentives,** Harald Schmidt, Kristin Voigt, and Daniel Wikler

Learning Outcomes

After reading this unit, you should be able to:

- Describe why people continue to engage in behaviors that negatively affect their health even when they know about the ill effects these behaviors have on their well-being.

- Describe some programs/policies that could be pursued to help prevent heart disease.

- Explain how the negative behaviors practiced by college students contribute to academic difficulties.

- Discuss the role of incentives in promoting healthy behaviors.

- Describe the factors that contribute to a successful lifestyle change.

- Describe the relationship between health care reform and positive health behaviors.

Student Website

www.mhhe.com/cls

Internet References

Columbia University's Go Ask Alice!
www.goaskalice.columbia.edu/index.html
The Society of Behavioral Medicine
www.sbm.org

"Those of us who protect our health daily and those of us who put our health in constant jeopardy have exactly the same mortality: 100 percent. The difference, of course, is the timing." This quotation from Elizabeth M. Whelan, Sc.D., M.P.H., reminds us that we must all face the fact that we are going to die sometime. The question that is decided by our behavior is when and, to a certain extent, how. This book, and especially this unit, is designed to assist students to develop the cognitive skills and knowledge that, when put to use, help make the moment of our death come as late as possible in our lives and to maintain our health as long as possible. While we cannot control many of the things that happen to us, we must all strive to accept personal responsibility for, and make informed decisions about, things that we can control. This is no minor task, but it is one in which the potential reward is life itself. Perhaps the best way to start this process is by educating ourselves on the relative risks associated with the various behaviors and lifestyle choices we make. To minimize all the risks to life and health would significantly limit the quality of our lives, and while this might be a choice that some would make, it certainly is not the goal of health education. A more logical approach to risk reduction would be to educate the public on the relative risks associated with various behaviors and lifestyle choices, so that they are capable of making informed decisions. While it may seem obvious that certain behaviors, such as smoking, entail a high level of risk, the significance of others such as toxic waste sites and food additives are frequently blown out of proportion to the actual risks involved. The net result of this type of distortion is that many Americans tend to minimize the dangers of known hazards such as tobacco and alcohol and focus attention, instead, on potentially minor health hazards over which they have little or no control.

Educating the public on the relative risk of various health behaviors is only part of the job that health educators must tackle in order to assist individuals in making informed choices regarding their health. They must also teach the skills that will enable people to evaluate the validity and significance of new information as it becomes available. Just how important informed decision making is in our daily lives is evidenced by the numerous health-related media announcements and articles that fill our newspapers, magazines, and television broadcasts. Rather than informing and enlightening the public on significant new medical discoveries, many of these announcements do little more than add to the level of confusion or exaggerate or sensationalize health issues. "Crimes of the Heart" by Walter Willett and Anne Underwood discusses major health behavior improvements among residents of a small town in Minnesota. The changes were based on the city's decision to become involved in a project to help support healthy behavior change.

Let's assume for a minute that the scientific community is in general agreement that certain behaviors clearly promote our health while others damage our health. Given this information, are you likely to make adjustments to your lifestyle to comply with the findings? Logic would suggest that of course you

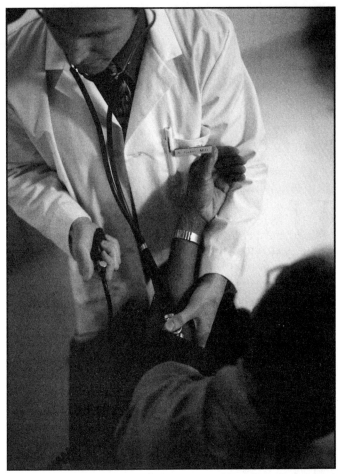

© Ryan McVay/Getty Images

would, but experience has taught us that information alone isn't enough to bring about behavioral change in many people. Why is it that so many people continue to make bad choices regarding their health behaviors when they are fully aware of the risks involved?

We can take vows to try and undo or minimize the negative health behaviors of our past. While strategies such as these may work for those who feel they are at risk, how do we help those who do not feel that they are at risk, or those who feel that it is too late in their lives for the changes to matter? In "The Perils of Higher Education," the Steven Kotler maintains that while college is a place to learn and grow, for many students it becomes four years of bad diet, too little sleep, and too much alcohol. These negative health behaviors affect not only the students' health, but their grades too. In "Carrots, Sticks, and Health Care Reform—Problems with Wellness Incentives," the authors address the issue of using incentives to influence positive health behaviors.

Crimes of the Heart

It's time society stopped reinforcing the bad behavior that leads to heart disease—and pursued policies to prevent it.

WALTER C. WILLETT AND ANNE UNDERWOOD

Until last year, the residents of Albert Lea, Minn., were no healthier than any other Americans. Then the city became the first American town to sign on to the AARP/Blue Zones Vitality Project—the brainchild of writer Dan Buettner, whose 2008 book, *The Blue Zones,* detailed the health habits of the world's longest-lived people. His goal was to bring the same benefits to middle America—not by forcing people to diet and exercise, but by changing their everyday environments in ways that encourage a healthier lifestyle.

What followed was a sort of townwide makeover. The city laid new sidewalks linking residential areas with schools and shopping centers. It built a recreational path around a lake and dug new plots for community gardens. Restaurants made healthy changes to their menus. Schools banned eating in hallways (reducing the opportunities for kids to munch on snack food) and stopped selling candy for fundraisers. (They sold wreaths instead.) More than 2,600 of the city's 18,000 residents volunteered, too, selecting from more than a dozen heart-healthy measures—for example, ridding their kitchens of supersize dinner plates (which encourage larger portions) and forming "walking schoolbuses" to escort kids to school on foot.

The results were stunning. In six months, participants lost an average of 2.6 pounds and boosted their estimated life expectancy by 3.1 years. Even more impressive, health-care claims for city and school employees fell for the first time in a decade—by 32 percent over 10 months. And benefits didn't accrue solely to volunteers. Thanks to the influence of social networks, says Buettner, "even the curmudgeons who didn't want to be involved ended up modifying their behaviors."

Isn't it time we all followed Albert Lea's example? Diet and exercise programs routinely fail not for lack of willpower, but because the society in which we live favors unhealthy behaviors. In 2006, cardiovascular disease cost $403 billion in medical bills and lost productivity. By 2025 an aging population is expected to drive up the total by as much as 54 percent. But creative government programs could help forestall the increases—and help our hearts, too. A few suggestions:

Require graphic warnings on cigarette packages. It's easy to disregard a black-box warning that smoking is "hazardous to your health." It's not so easy to dismiss a picture of gangrenous limbs, diseased hearts, or chests sawed open for autopsy. These are exactly the types of images that the law now requires on cigarette packages in Brazil. In Canada, such warning images must cover at least half the wrapping. In 2001, the year after the Canadian law took effect, 38 percent of smokers who tried to quit cited the images. Think of it as truth in advertising.

Sponsor "commitment contracts" to quit smoking. Yale economist Dean Karlan spearheaded a test program in the Philippines in which smokers who wanted to quit deposited the money they would have spent on cigarettes into a special bank account. After six months those who had succeeded got their money back, while those who had failed lost it. Such a program could be run here by public-health clinics and offer greater incentives, such as letting winners divvy up the money forfeited by losers. Even without such an enhancement, says Karlan, "Filipino participants were 39 percent more likely to quit than those who were not offered the option."

Subsidize whole grains, fruits, and vegetables in the food-stamp program. The underprivileged tend to have disastrously unhealthy diets, and no wonder: $1 will buy 100 calories of carrots—or 1,250 calories of cookies and chips. The government should offer incentives for buying produce. The Wholesome Wave Foundation has shown the way in 12 states, providing vouchers redeemable at farmers' markets to people in the SNAP program (the official name for food stamps). "We've seen purchases of fruits and vegetables double and triple among recipients," says president and CEO Michel Nischan.

Set targets for salt reduction. The average American consumes twice the recommended daily maximum of sodium, most of it from processed foods. The result: high blood pressure, heart attacks, and strokes. But New York City is leading a campaign to encourage food manufacturers to reduce added sodium over the next five years. Consumers will barely notice the changes because they will occur so gradually. The FDA should follow New York's lead.

One urban-planning expert advocates a "road diet" in which towns eliminate a lane or two of traffic and substitute sidewalks. "When roads slim down, so do people," he says.

Incorporate physical education into No Child Left Behind. American children may be prepping like crazy for standardized tests, but they're seriously lagging in physical fitness. Regular exercise improves mood, concentration, and academic achievement. It can also help reverse the growing trend toward type 2 diabetes and early heart disease in children and teenagers.

Require that sidewalks and bike lanes be part of every federally funded road project. The government already spends 1 percent of transportation dollars on such projects. It should increase the level to 2 to 3 percent. When sidewalks are built in neighborhoods and downtowns, people start walking. "The big win for city government is that anything built to a walkable scale leases out for three to five times more money, with more tax revenue on less infrastructure," says Dan Burden, executive director of the Walkable and Livable Communities Institute. He recommends a "road diet" in which towns eliminate a lane or two of downtown traffic and substitute sidewalks. "When roads slim down, so do people," he says.

It's all reasonable. But Dan Buettner isn't waiting for any of these measures to surmount the inevitable industry hurdles. This year he's looking to scale up the Blue Zones Vitality Project to a city of 100,000 or more. "If this works, it could provide a template for the government that's replicable across the country," says his colleague Ben Leedle, CEO of Healthways, which is developing the next phase of the project. The challenges will be much steeper in large cities. But with measures like these, we could one day find ourselves growing fitter without specifically dieting or exercising. Finally, a New Year's resolution we can all keep.

Critical Thinking

1. What behaviors are linked to a healthy heart?
2. What type of programs/policies could be pursued to help prevent heart disease?

WALTER C. WILLETT is a physician, chair of the department of nutrition at the Harvard School of Public Health, and coauthor of *The Fertility Diet*. **ANNE UNDERWOOD** is a Newsweek contributor.

The Perils of Higher Education

Can't remember the difference between declensions and derivatives? Blame college. The undergrad life is a blast, but it may lead you to forget everything you learn.

STEVEN KOTLER

We go to college to learn, to soak up a dazzling array of information intended to prepare us for adult life. But college is not simply a data dump; it is also the end of parental supervision. For many students, that translates into four years of late nights, pizza banquets and boozy weekends that start on Wednesday. And while we know that bad habits are detrimental to cognition in general—think drunk driving—new studies show that the undergrad urges to eat, drink and be merry have devastating effects on learning and memory. It turns out that the exact place we go to get an education may in fact be one of the worst possible environments in which to retain anything we've learned.

Dude, I Haven't Slept in Three Days!

Normal human beings spend one-third of their lives asleep, but today's college students aren't normal. A recent survey of undergraduates and medical students at Stanford University found 80 percent of them qualified as sleep-deprived, and a poll taken by the National Sleep Foundation found that most young adults get only 6.8 hours a night.

All-night cramfests may seem to be the only option when the end of the semester looms, but in fact getting sleep—and a full dose of it—might be a better way to ace exams. Sleep is crucial to declarative memory, the hard, factual kind that helps us remember which year World War I began, or what room the French Lit class is in. It's also essential for procedural memory, the "know-how" memory we use when learning to drive a car or write a five-paragraph essay. "Practice makes perfect," says Harvard Medical School psychologist Matt Walker, "but having a night's rest after practicing might make you even better."

Walker taught 100 people to bang out a series of nonsense sequences on a keyboard—a standard procedural memory task. When asked to replay the sequence 12 hours later, they hadn't improved. But when one group of subjects was allowed to sleep overnight before being retested, their speed and accuracy improved by 20 to 30 percent. "It was bizarre," says Walker. "We were seeing people's skills improve just by sleeping."

For procedural memory, the deep slow-wave stages of sleep were the most important for improvement—particularly during the last two hours of the night. Declarative memory, by contrast, gets processed during the slow-wave stages that come in the first two hours of sleep. "This means that memory requires a full eight hours of sleep," says Walker. He also found that if someone goes without sleep for 24 hours after acquiring a new skill, a week later they will have lost it completely. So college students who pull all-nighters during exam week might do fine on their tests but may not remember any of the material by next semester.

Walker believes that the common practice of back-loading semesters with a blizzard of papers and exams needs a rethink. "Educators are just encouraging sleeplessness," says Walker. "This is just not an effective way to force information into the brain."

Who's up for Pizza?

Walk into any college cafeteria and you'll find a smorgasbord of French fries, greasy pizza, burgers, potato chips and the like. On top of that, McDonald's, Burger King, Wendy's and other fast-food chains have been gobbling up campus real estate in recent years. With hectic schedules and skinny budgets, students find fast food an easy alternative. A recent Tufts University survey found that 50 percent of students eat too much fat, and 70 to 80 percent eat too much saturated fat.

But students who fuel their studies with fast food have something more serious than the "freshman 15" to worry about: They may literally be eating themselves stupid. Researchers have known since the late 1980s that bad eating habits contribute to the kind of cognitive decline found in diseases like Alzheimer's. Since then, they've been trying to find out exactly how a bad diet might be hard on the brain. Ann-Charlotte Granholm, director of the Center for Aging at the Medical University of South Carolina, has recently focused on trans fat, widely used in fast-food cooking because it extends the shelf life of foods. Trans fat is made by bubbling hydrogen through unsaturated fat, with copper or zinc added to speed the chemical reaction along. These metals are frequently found in the brains of people with Alzheimer's, which sparked Granholm's concern.

To investigate, she fed one group of rats a diet high in trans fat and compared them with another group fed a diet that was just as greasy but low in trans fat. Six weeks later, she tested the animals in a water maze, the rodent equivalent of a final exam in organic chemistry. "The trans-fat group made many more errors," says Granholm, especially when she used more difficult mazes.

When she examined the rats' brains, she found that trans-fat eaters had fewer proteins critical to healthy neurological function. She also saw inflammation in and around the hippocampus, the part of the brain responsible for learning and memory. "It was alarming," says Granholm. "These are the exact types of changes we normally see at the onset of Alzheimer's, but we saw them after six weeks," even though the rats were still young.

Students who fuel their studies with fast food have something serious to worry about: They may literally be eating themselves stupid.

Her work corresponds to a broader inquiry conducted by Veerendra Kumar Madala Halagaapa and Mark Mattson of the National Institute on Aging. The researchers fed four groups of mice different diets—normal, high-fat, high-sugar and high-fat/high-sugar. Each diet had the same caloric value, so that one group of mice wouldn't end up heavier. Four months later, the mice on the high-fat diets performed significantly worse than the other groups on a water maze test.

The researchers then exposed the animals to a neurotoxin that targets the hippocampus, to assess whether a high-fat diet made the mice less able to cope with brain damage. Back in the maze, all the animals performed worse than before, but the mice who had eaten the high-fat diets were the most seriously compromised. "Based on our work," says Mattson, "we'd predict that people who eat high-fat diets and high-fat/high-sugar diets are not only damaging their ability to learn and remember new information, but also putting themselves at much greater risk for all sorts of neurodegenerative disorders like Alzheimer's."

Welcome to Margaritaville State University

It's widely recognized that heavy drinking doesn't exactly boost your intellect. But most people figure that their booze-induced foolishness wears off once the hangover is gone. Instead, it turns out that even limited stints of overindulgence may have long-term effects.

Less than 20 years ago, researchers began to realize that the adult brain wasn't just a static lump of cells. They found that stem cells in the brain are constantly churning out new neurons, particularly in the hippocampus. Alcoholism researchers, in turn, began to wonder if chronic alcoholics' memory problems had something to do with nerve cell birth and growth.

In 2000, Kimberly Nixon and Fulton Crews at the University of North Carolina's Bowles Center for Alcohol Studies subjected lab rats to four days of heavy alcohol intoxication. They gave the rats a week to shake off their hangovers, then tested them on and off during the next month in a water maze. "We didn't find anything at first," says Nixon. But on the 19th day, the rats who had been on the binge performed much worse. In 19 days, the cells born during the binge had grown to maturity—and clearly, the neurons born during the boozy period didn't work properly once they reached maturity. "[The timing] was almost too perfect," says Nixon.

While normal rats generated about 2,500 new brain cells in three weeks, the drinking rats produced only 1,400. A month later, the sober rats had lost about half of those new cells through normal die-off. But all of the new cells died in the brains of the binge drinkers. "This was startling," says Nixon. "It was the first time anyone had found that alcohol not only inhibits the birth of new cells but also inhibits the ones that survive." In further study, they found that a week's abstinence produced a twofold burst of neurogenesis, and a month off the sauce brought cognitive function back to normal.

What does this have to do with a weekend keg party? A number of recent studies show that college students consume far more alcohol than anyone previously suspected. Forty-four percent of today's collegiates drink enough to be classified as binge drinkers, according to a nationwide survey of 10,000 students done at Harvard University. The amount of alcohol consumed by Nixon's binging rats far exceeded intake at a typical keg party—but other research shows that the effects of alcohol work on a sliding scale. Students who follow a weekend of heavy drinking with a week of heavy studying might not forget everything they learn. They just may struggle come test time.

Can I Bum a Smoke?

If this ledger of campus menaces worries you, here's something you really won't like: Smoking cigarettes may actually have some cognitive benefits, thanks to the power of nicotine. The chemical improves mental focus, as scientists have known since the 1950s. Nicotine also aids concentration in people who have ADHD and may protect against Alzheimer's disease. Back in 2000, a nicotine-like drug under development by the pharmaceutical company Astra Arcus USA was shown to restore the ability to learn and remember in rats with brain lesions similar to those found in Alzheimer's patients. More recently Granholm, the scientist investigating trans fats and memory, found that nicotine enhances spatial memory in healthy rats. Other researchers have found that nicotine also boosts both emotional memory (the kind that helps us *not* put our hands back in the fire after we've been burned) and auditory memory.

There's a catch: Other studies show that nicotine encourages state-dependent learning. The idea is that if, for example, you study in blue sweats, it helps to take the exam in blue sweats. In other words, what you learn while smoking is best recalled while smoking. Since lighting up in an exam room might cause problems, cigarettes probably aren't the key to getting on the dean's list.

Nonetheless, while the number of cigarette smokers continues to drop nationwide, college students are still lighting up: As many as 30 percent smoke during their years of higher education. The smoking rate for young adults between the ages of 18 and 24 has actually risen in the past decade.

All this news makes you wonder how anyone's ever managed to get an education. Or what would happen to GPAs at a vegetarian university with a 10 P.M. curfew. But you might not need to go to such extremes. While Granholm agrees that the excesses of college can be "a perfect example of what you shouldn't do to yourself if you are trying to learn," she doesn't recommend abstinence. "Moderation," she counsels, "just like in everything else. Moderation is the key to collegiate success."

Critical Thinking

1. Why do so many college students engage in negative health behaviors? What negative behaviors impact grades?
2. Discuss the relationship between fast food and the brain.

Steven Kotler, based in Los Angeles, has written for *The New York Times Magazine*, *National Geographic*, *Details*, *Wired* and *Outside*.

From *Psychology Today*, vol. 38, no. 2, March/April 2005, pp. 66, 68, 70. Copyright © 2005 by Sussex Publishers, LLC. Reprinted by permission.

Carrots, Sticks, and Health Care Reform—Problems with Wellness Incentives

HARALD SCHMIDT, MA, KRISTIN VOIGT, DPHIL, AND DANIEL WIKLER, PHD

Chronic conditions, especially those associated with overweight, are on the rise in the United States (as elsewhere). Employers have used both carrots and sticks to encourage healthier behavior.

The current health care reform bills seek to expand the role of incentives, which promise a win–win bargain: employees enjoy better health, while employers reduce health care costs and profit from a healthier workforce.

However, these provisions cannot be given an ethical free pass. In some cases, the incentives are really sticks dressed up as carrots. There is a risk of inequity that would further disadvantage the people most in need of health improvements, and doctors might be assigned watchdog roles that might harm the therapeutic relationship. We believe that some changes must be made to reconcile incentive use with ethical norms.

Under the 1996 Health Insurance Portability and Accountability Act (HIPAA), a group health plan may not discriminate among individuals on the basis of health factors by varying their premiums. But HIPAA does not prevent insurers from offering reimbursements through "wellness programs." These include what could be called participation incentives, which offer a premium discount or other reimbursement simply for participating in a health-promotion program, and attainment incentives, which provide reimbursements only for meeting targets—for example, a particular body-mass index or cholesterol level. Subsequent regulations specified that attainment incentives must not exceed 20% of the total cost of an employee's coverage (i.e., the combination of the employer's and employee's contributions).[1]

The health care reform measures currently before Congress would substantially expand these provisions (see box). However, ethical analysis and empirical research suggest that the current protections are inadequate to ensure fairness.

Attainment incentives provide welcome rewards for employees who manage to comply but may be unfair for those who struggle, particularly if they fail. The law demands the provision of alternative standards for those who cannot or should not participate because of medical conditions, but those categories are narrowly defined. For all others, the implicit assumption is that they can achieve targets if they try. This assumption is hard to reconcile with what we know about lifestyle change. Most diets, for example, do not result in long-lasting weight reduction, even though participants want and try to lose weight. Attainment-incentive programs make no distinction between those who try but fail and those who do not try.

Proponents of attainment incentives typically do not view this situation as inequitable. Steven Burd, the chief executive officer of Safeway, whose "Healthy Measures" program offers reimbursements for meeting weight, blood-pressure, cholesterol, and tobacco-use targets, compared his company's program to automobile insurance, in which for decades "driving behavior has been correlated with accident risk and has therefore translated into premium differences among drivers." In other words, says Burd, "the auto-insurance industry has long recognized the role of personal responsibility. As a result, bad behaviors (like speeding, tickets for failure to follow the rules of the road, and frequency of accidents) are considered when establishing insurance premiums. Bad driver premiums are not subsidized by the good driver premiums."[2]

If people could lose weight, stop smoking, or reduce cholesterol simply by deciding to do so, the analogy might be appropriate. But in that case, few would have had weight, smoking, or cholesterol problems in the first place. Moreover, there is a social gradient. A law school graduate from a wealthy family who has a gym on the top floor of his condominium block is more likely to succeed in losing weight if he

Summary of Wellness Incentives in the Current Legislation

The "Affordable Health Care for America Act" (House of Representatives), section 112, requires that qualifying programs:

- Be evidence-based and certified by the Department of Health and Human Services.
- Provide support for populations at risk for poor health outcomes.
- Include designs that are "culturally competent [and] physically and programmatically accessible (including for individuals with disabilities)."
- Be available to all employees without charge.
- Not link financial incentives to premiums.
- Entail no cost shifting.

The "Patient Protection and Affordable Care Act" (Senate), section 2705, proposes to increase reimbursement levels to 30% of the cost of employee-only coverage, or up to 50% with government approval. In part restating provisions for current wellness programs, it also requires that qualifying programs:

- Be "available to all similarly situated individuals."
- Have "a reasonable chance of improving the health of, or preventing disease in, participating individuals."
- Not be "overly burdensome, [be] a subterfuge for discriminating based on a health status factor, [or be] highly suspect in the method chosen to promote health or prevent disease."
- Provide an alternative standard for employees whose medical condition—as certified by a physician—precludes participation in attainment-incentive programs.
- Not pose an "undue burden for individuals insured in the individual insurance market."
- Entail no cost shifting.
- Be evaluated in pilot studies and a 10-state demonstration project.

tries than is a teenage mother who grew up and continues to live and work odd jobs in a poor neighborhood with limited access to healthy food and exercise opportunities. And he is more likely to try. In Germany, where both participation and attainment incentives have been offered since 2004, participation rates among people in the top socioeconomic quintile are nearly double the rates among those in the poorest quintile.[3]

Incentive schemes are defended on the grounds of personal responsibility, but as Kant observed, "ought" implies "can." Although alternative standards must be offered to employees for whom specific targets are medically inappropriate, disadvantaged people with multiple coexisting conditions may refrain from making such petitions, seeing them as degrading or humiliating. These potential problems are important in view of the proposed increases in reimbursement levels.

The reform proposals prohibit cost shifting, but provisions in the Senate bill could result in a substantial increase in financial burden on employees who do not meet targets (or alternative standards). On the basis of the average cost of $4700 for employee-only coverage, a 20% incentive amounts to $940; 30% would equal $1410 and 50%, $2350. In practice, insurers may stay below the maximum levels. Some may elect to absorb the full cost of reimbursements, in part because some or all of these costs may be offset by future savings from a healthier workforce. Alternatively, however, insurers might recoup some or all of the costs by increasing insurance contributions from insurance holders. In the extreme case, the incentive might then simply consist of being able to return to the previous level of contributions. Similar effects can be achieved by varying applicable copayments or deductibles.[4] Direct and indirect increases would disproportionately hurt lower-paid workers, who are generally less healthy than their higher-paid counterparts and thus in greater need of health care, less likely to meet the targets, and least likely to be able to afford higher costs. Some employees might decide to opt out of employer-based health insurance—and indeed, one wellness consulting firm, Benicomp, implies in its prospectus that such a result might be desirable, pointing out that employees who do not comply might be "motivated to consider other coverage options" and highlighting the savings that would result for employers.[4]

Proponents emphasize that wellness incentives are voluntary. But the scenarios above show that voluntariness can become dubious for lower-income employees, if the only way to obtain affordable insurance is to meet the targets. To them, programs that are offered as carrots may feel more like sticks. It is worth noting that countries such as Germany generally use far lower reimbursements ($45 to $130 per year, or a maximum of 6% of an employee's contribution) and often use in-kind incentives (such as exercise equipment, heart-rate monitors, or vouchers contributing to the cost of a "wellness holiday") rather than cash.[3]

There are also questions about the effect on the therapeutic relationship. When the German Parliament passed a law making lower copayments conditional on patients' undergoing certain cancer screenings and complying with therapy, medical professionals rejected it, partly out of concern about being put in a policing position.[3] American physicians expressed concern when West Virginia's Medicaid program charged participating doctors with monitoring patients' adherence to the requirements set out in the member agreement.[5] Requiring physicians to certify an employee's medical unsuitability for an incentive scheme or to attest to their achievement of a target might similarly introduce an adversarial element into the doctor–patient relationship.

Incentives for healthy behavior may be part of an effective national response to risk factors for chronic disease. Wrongly implemented, however, they can introduce substantial inequity into the health insurance system. It is a problem if the people who are less likely to benefit from the programs are those who may need them more. The proposed increases in reimbursement levels threaten to further exacerbate inequities. Reform legislation should therefore not raise the incentive cap. Attainment incentives that primarily benefit the well-off and healthy should be phased out, and the focus should shift to participation-incentive schemes tailored to the abilities and needs of lower-paid employees. Moreover, it is crucial that the evaluation of pilots include an assessment of the socioeconomic and ethnic backgrounds of both users and nonusers to ascertain the equitability of programs.

Notes

1. Mello MM, Rosenthal MB. Wellness programs and lifestyle discrimination—the legal limits. *N Engl J Med* 2008;359:192–9.

2. Burd SA. How Safeway is cutting health-care costs. *Wall Street Journal.* June 12, 2009.

3. Schmidt H, Stock S, Gerber A. What can we learn from German health incentive schemes? *BMJ* 2009;339:b3504.

4. Detailed overview, 2009. Ft. Wayne, IN: BeniComp Advantage. (Accessed December 22, 2009, at www.benicompadvantage.com/products/overview.htm.)

5. Bishop G, Brodkey A. Personal responsibility and physician responsibility—West Virginia's Medicaid plan. *N Engl J Med* 2006;355:756–8.

Critical Thinking

1. What motivates people to engage in healthy behaviors?
2. What role do incentives play in promoting wellness?
3. Distinguish between the carrot-and-stick approach to health practices

Financial and other disclosures provided by the authors are available with the full text of this article at NEJM.org.

From the Harvard School of Public Health and the Harvard University Program in Ethics and Health, Boston.

UNIT 2

Stress and Mental Health

Unit Selections

Learning Outcomes

After reading this unit, you should be able to:

- Explain why antidepressants may not be the best choice for all patients.

- Describe the behaviors of pathologic hoarders.

- Explain the causes of obsessive compulsive disorder.

- Describe the major stressors in life.

- Explain how stressors have changed over the last 5,000 years.

- Contrast positive and negative stressors in shaping one's life.

- Explain the risks and causes of Internet addiction.

Student Website

www.mhhe.com/cls

Internet References

The American Institute of Stress
www.stress.org
National Mental Health Association (NMHA)
www.nmha.org/index.html
Self-Help Magazine
www.selfhelpmagazine.com/index.html

The brain is one organ that still mystifies and baffles the scientific community. While more has been learned about this organ in the last decade than in all the rest of recorded history, our understanding of the brain is still in its infancy. What has been learned, however, has spawned exciting new research and has contributed to the establishment of new disciplines, such as psychophysiology and psychoneuroimmunology (PNI).

Traditionally, the medical community has viewed health problems as either physical or mental and has treated each type separately. This dichotomy between the psyche (mind) and soma (body) is fading in the light of scientific data that reveal profound physiological changes associated with mood shifts. What are the physiological changes associated with stress? Hans Selye, the father of stress research, described stress as a nonspecific physiological response to anything that challenges the body. He demonstrated that this response could be elicited by both mental and physical stimuli. Stress researchers have come to regard this response pattern as the "flight-or-fight" response, perhaps an adaptive throwback to our primitive ancestors. Researchers now believe that repeated and prolonged activation of this response can trigger destructive changes in our bodies and contribute to the development of several chronic diseases. So profound is the impact of emotional stress on the body that current estimates suggest that approximately 90 percent of all doctor visits are for stress-related disorders. If emotional stress elicits a generalized physiological response, why are there so many different diseases associated with it? Many experts believe that the answer may best be explained by what has been termed "the weak-organ theory." According to this theory, every individual has one organ system that is most susceptible to the damaging effects of prolonged stress.

Mental illness, which is generally regarded as a dysfunction of normal thought processes, has no single identifiable etiology. One may speculate that this is due to the complex nature of the organ system involved. There is also mounting evidence to suggest that there is an organic component to the traditional forms of mental illness such as schizophrenia, chronic depression, and manic depression. The fact that certain mental illnesses tend to occur within families has divided the mental health community into two camps: those who believe that there is a genetic factor operating and those who see the family tendency as more of a learned behavior. In either case, the evidence supports mental illness as another example of the weak-organ theory. The reason one person is more susceptible to the damaging effects of stress than another may not be altogether clear, but evidence is mounting that one's perception or attitude plays a key role in the stress equation. A prime example demonstrating this relationship comes from the research that relates cardiovascular disease to stress. The realization that our attitude has such a significant impact on our health has led to a burgeoning new movement in psychology termed "positive psychology." Dr. Martin Seligman, professor of psychology at the University of Pennsylvania and father of the positive psychology movement, believes that optimism is a key factor in maintaining not only our mental health, but our physical health as well. Dr. Seligman notes that while some people are naturally more optimistic than others, optimism can be learned.

One area in particular that appears to be influenced by the positive psychology movement is the area of stress management.

© Jules Frazier/Getty Images

Traditionally, stress management programs have focused on the elimination of stress, but that is starting to change as new strategies approach stress as an essential component of life and a potential source of health. It is worth noting that this concept, of stress serving as a positive force in a person's life, was presented by Dr. Hans Selye in 1974 in his book *Stress Without Distress.* Dr. Selye felt that there were three types of stress: negative stress (distress), normal stress, and positive stress (eustress). He maintained that positive stress not only increases a person's self-esteem but also serves to inoculate the person against the damaging effects of distress. Only time will tell if this change of focus in the area of stress management makes any real difference in patient outcome.

The causes of stress are many, but for some individuals, the coming of winter is a very difficult time. Many of these folks experience periods of depression during the shorter days of winter. Workplace stress is another form of distress that causes the economy billions of dollars per year due to sick leave and thereby loss of productivity. Researchers have made significant strides in their understanding of the mechanisms that link emotional stress to physical ailments, but they are less clear on the mechanisms by which positive emotions bolster one's health. Although significant gains have been made in our understanding of the relationship between body and mind, much remains to be learned. What is known indicates that perception and one's attitude are the key elements in shaping our responses to stressors.

Two articles in this section address mental health issues. "I Can't Let Anything Go': A Case Study with Psychological Testing of a Patient with Pathologic Hoarding" by Janna Koretz and Thomas G. Gutheil describes pathologic hoarding and obsessive compulsive disorder. While many of us use the Internet as a source of information and entertainment, some individuals become addicted. Author Greg Beato discusses how addiction to the Internet affects the balance of people's lives in "Internet Addiction."

There are many approaches to treating mental health issues, including the use of antidepressants. However, studies suggest that for some patients, a placebo may be more effective. Sharon Begley discusses this issue in "The Depressing News about Antidepressants."

The Depressing News about Antidepressants

Studies suggest that the popular drugs are no more effective than a placebo. In fact, they may be worse.

SHARON BEGLEY

Although the year is young, it has already brought my first moral dilemma. In early January a friend mentioned that his New Year's resolution was to beat his chronic depression once and for all. Over the years he had tried a medicine chest's worth of antidepressants, but none had really helped in any enduring way, and when the side effects became so unpleasant that he stopped taking them, the withdrawal symptoms (cramps, dizziness, headaches) were torture. Did I know of any research that might help him decide whether a new antidepressant his doctor recommended might finally lift his chronic darkness at noon?

The moral dilemma was this: oh, yes, I knew of 20-plus years of research on antidepressants, from the old tricyclics to the newer selective serotonin reuptake inhibitors (SSRIs) that target serotonin (Zoloft, Paxil, and the granddaddy of them all, Prozac, as well as their generic descendants) to even newer ones that also target norepinephrine (Effexor, Wellbutrin). The research had shown that antidepressants help about three quarters of people with depression who take them, a consistent finding that serves as the basis for the oft-repeated mantra "There is no question that the safety and efficacy of antidepressants rest on solid scientific evidence," as psychiatry professor Richard Friedman of Weill Cornell Medical College recently wrote in *The New York Times*. But ever since a seminal study in 1998, whose findings were reinforced by landmark research in *The Journal of the American Medical Association* last month, that evidence has come with a big asterisk. Yes, the drugs are effective, in that they lift depression in most patients. But that benefit is hardly more than what patients get when they, unknowingly and as part of a study, take a dummy pill—a placebo. As more and more scientists who study depression and the drugs that treat it are concluding, that suggests that antidepressants are basically expensive Tic Tacs.

Hence the moral dilemma. The placebo effect—that is, a medical benefit you get from an inert pill or other sham treatment—rests on the holy trinity of belief, expectation,

and hope. But telling someone with depression who is being helped by antidepressants, or who (like my friend) hopes to be helped, threatens to topple the whole house of cards. Explain that it's all in their heads, that the reason they're benefiting is the same reason why Disney's Dumbo could initially fly only with a feather clutched in his trunk—believing makes it so—and the magic dissipates like fairy dust in a windstorm. So rather than tell my friend all this, I chickened out. Sure, I said, there's lots of research showing that a new kind of antidepressant might help you. Come, let me show you the studies on PubMed.

It seems I am not alone in having moral qualms about blowing the whistle on antidepressants. That first analysis, in 1998, examined 38 manufacturer-sponsored studies involving just over 3,000 depressed patients. The authors, psychology researchers Irving Kirsch and Guy Sapirstein of the University of Connecticut, saw—as everyone else had—that patients did improve, often substantially, on SSRIs, tricyclics, and even MAO inhibitors, a class of antidepressants that dates from the 1950s. This improvement, demonstrated in scores of clinical trials, is the basis for the ubiquitous claim that antidepressants work. But when Kirsch compared the improvement in patients taking the drugs with the improvement in those taking dummy pills—clinical trials typically compare an experimental drug with a placebo—he saw that the difference was minuscule. Patients on a placebo improved about 75 percent as much as those on drugs. Put another way, three quarters of the benefit from antidepressants seems to be a placebo effect. "We wondered, what's going on?" recalls Kirsch, who is now at the University of Hull in England. "These are supposed to be wonder drugs and have huge effects."

The study's impact? The number of Americans taking antidepressants doubled in a decade, from 13.3 million in 1996 to 27 million in 2005.

To be sure, the drugs have helped tens of millions of people, and Kirsch certainly does not advocate that patients suffering from depression stop taking the drugs. On the contrary. But they are not necessarily the best first choice. Psychotherapy, for instance, works for moderate, severe, and even very severe depression. And although for some patients, psychotherapy in combination with an initial course of prescription antidepressants works even better, the question is, *how* do the drugs work? Kirsch's study and, now, others conclude that the lion's share of the drugs' effect comes from the fact that patients expect to be helped by them, and not from any direct chemical action on the brain, especially for anything short of very severe depression.

As the inexorable rise in the use of antidepressants suggests, that conclusion can't hold a candle to the simplistic "antidepressants work!" (unstated corollary: "but don't ask how") message. Part of the resistance to Kirsch's findings has been due to his less-than-retiring nature. He didn't win many friends with the cheeky title of the paper, "Listening to Prozac but Hearing Placebo." Nor did it inspire confidence that the editors of the journal *Prevention & Treatment* ran a warning with his paper, saying it used meta-analysis "controversially." Although some of the six invited commentaries agreed with Kirsch, others were scathing, accusing him of bias and saying the studies he analyzed were flawed (an odd charge for defenders of antidepressants, since the studies were the basis for the Food and Drug Administration's approval of the drugs). One criticism, however, could not be refuted: Kirsch had analyzed only some studies of antidepressants. Maybe if he included them all, the drugs would emerge head and shoulders superior to placebos.

Kirsch agreed. Out of the blue, he received a letter from Thomas Moore, who was then a health-policy analyst at George Washington University. You could expand your data set, Moore wrote, by including everything drug companies sent to the FDA—published studies, like those analyzed in "Hearing Placebo," but also unpublished studies. In 1998 Moore used the Freedom of Information Act to pry such data from the FDA. The total came to 47 company-sponsored studies—on Prozac, Paxil, Zoloft, Effexor, Serzone, and Celexa—that Kirsch and colleagues then pored over. (As an aside, it turned out that about 40 percent of the clinical trials had never been published. That is significantly higher than for other classes of drugs, says Lisa Bero of the University of California, San Francisco; overall, 22 percent of clinical trials of drugs are not published. "By and large," says Kirsch, "the unpublished studies were those that had failed to show a significant benefit from taking the actual drug.") In just over half of the published and unpublished studies, he and colleagues reported in 2002, the drug alleviated depression no better than a placebo. "And the extra benefit of antidepressants was even less than we saw when we analyzed only published studies," Kirsch recalls. About 82 percent of the response to antidepressants—not the 75 percent he had calculated from examining only published studies—had also been achieved by a dummy pill.

Only in patients with very severe symptoms was there a clinically meaningful drug benefit, the *JAMA* study found.

The extra effect of real drugs wasn't much to celebrate, either. It amounted to 1.8 points on the 54-point scale doctors use to gauge the severity of depression, through questions about mood, sleep habits, and the like. Sleeping better counts as six points. Being less fidgety during the assessment is worth two points. In other words, the clinical significance of the 1.8 extra points from real drugs was underwhelming. Now Kirsch was certain. "The belief that antidepressants can cure depression chemically is simply wrong," he told me in January on the eve of the publication of his book *The Emperor's New Drugs: Exploding the Antidepressant Myth.*

The 2002 study ignited a furious debate, but more and more scientists were becoming convinced that Kirsch—who had won respect for research on the placebo response and who had published scores of scientific papers—was on to something. One team of researchers wondered if antidepressants were "a triumph of marketing over science." Even defenders of antidepressants agreed that the drugs have "relatively small" effects. "Many have long been unimpressed by the magnitude of the differences observed between treatments and controls," psychology researcher Steven Hollon of Vanderbilt University and colleagues wrote—"what some of our colleagues refer to as 'the dirty little secret.'" In Britain, the agency that assesses which treatments are effective enough for the government to pay for stopped recommending antidepressants as a first-line treatment, especially for mild or moderate depression.

But if experts know that antidepressants are hardly better than placebos, few patients or doctors do. Some doctors have changed their prescribing habits, says Kirsch, but more "reacted with anger and incredulity." Understandably. For one thing, depression is a devastating, underdiagnosed, and undertreated disease. Of course doctors recoiled at the idea that such drugs might be mirages. If that were true, how were physicians supposed to help their patients?

Two other factors are at work in the widespread rejection of Kirsch's (and, now, other scientists') findings about antidepressants. First, defenders of the drugs scoff at the idea that the FDA would have approved ineffective drugs. (Simple explanation: the FDA requires two well-designed clinical trials showing a drug is more effective than a placebo. That's two, period—even if many more studies show no such effectiveness. And the size of the "more effective" doesn't much matter, as long as it is statistically significant.) Second, doctors see with their own eyes, and feel with their hearts, that the drugs lift the black cloud from many of their depressed patients. But since doctors are not exactly in the habit of prescribing dummy pills, they have no experience comparing how their patients do on them, and therefore never see that a placebo would be almost as effective as a $4 pill. "When they prescribe a treatment and it works," says Kirsch, "their natural tendency is to attribute the cure to the treatment." Hence the widespread "antidepressants work" refrain that persists to this day.

Drug companies do not dispute Kirsch's aggregate statistics. But they point out that the average is made up of some patients in whom there is a true drug effect of antidepressants and some in whom there is not. As a spokesperson for Lilly (maker of Prozac) said, "Depression is a highly individualized illness," and "not all patients respond the same way to a particular treatment." In addition, notes a spokesperson for GlaxoSmithKline (maker of Paxil), the studies analyzed in the *JAMA* paper differ from studies GSK submitted to the FDA when it won approval for Paxil, "so it is difficult to make direct comparisons between the results. This study contributes to the extensive research that has helped to characterize the role of antidepressants," which "are an important option, in addition to counseling and lifestyle changes, for treatment of depression." A spokesperson for Pfizer, which makes Zoloft, also cited the "wealth of scientific evidence documenting [antidepressants'] effects," adding that the fact that antidepressants "commonly fail to separate from placebo" is "a fact well known by the FDA, academia, and industry." Other manufacturers pointed out that Kirsch and the *JAMA* authors had not studied their particular brands.

Even Kirsch's analysis, however, found that antidepressants are a little more effective than dummy pills—those 1.8 points on the depression scale. Maybe Prozac, Zoloft, Paxil, Celexa, and their cousins do have some non-placebo, chemical benefit. But the small edge of real drugs compared with placebos might not mean what it seems, Kirsch explained to me one evening from his home in Hull. Consider how research on drugs works. Patient volunteers are told they will receive either the drug or a placebo, and that neither they nor the scientists will know who is getting what. Most volunteers hope they get the drug, not the dummy pill. After taking the unknown meds for a while, some volunteers experience side effects. Bingo: a clue they're on the real drug. About 80 percent guess right, and studies show that the worse side effects a patient experiences, the more effective the drug. Patients apparently think, this drug is so strong it's making me vomit and hate sex, so it must be strong enough to lift my depression. In clinical-trial patients who figure out they're receiving the drug and not the inert pill, expectations soar.

That matters because belief in the power of a medical treatment can be self-fulfilling (that's the basis of the placebo effect). The patients who correctly guess that they're getting the real drug therefore experience a stronger placebo effect than those who get the dummy pill, experience no side effects, and are therefore disappointed. That might account for antidepressants' slight edge in effectiveness compared with a placebo, an edge that derives not from the drugs' molecules but from hopes and expectations that patients in studies feel when they figure out they're receiving the real drug.

The boy who said the emperor had no clothes didn't endear himself to his fellow subjects, and Kirsch has fared little better. A nascent collaboration with a scientist at a medical school ended in 2002 when the scientist was warned not to submit a grant proposal with Kirsch if he ever wanted to be funded again. Four years later, another scientist wrote a paper questioning the effectiveness of antidepressants, citing Kirsch's work. It was published in a prestigious journal. That ordinarily brings accolades. Instead, his department chair dressed him down and warned him not to become too involved with Kirsch.

But the question of whether antidepressants—which in 2008 had sales of $9.6 billion in the U.S., reported the consulting firm IMS Health—have any effect other than through patients'

belief in them was too important to scare researchers off. Proponents of the drugs have found themselves making weaker and weaker claims. Their last stand is that antidepressants are more effective than a placebo in patients suffering the most severe depression.

So concluded the *JAMA* study in January. In an analysis of six large experiments in which, as usual, depressed patients received either a placebo or an active drug, the true drug effect—that is, in addition to the placebo effect—was "nonexistent to negligible" in patients with mild, moderate, and even severe depression. Only in patients with very severe symptoms (scoring 23 or above on the standard scale) was there a statistically significant drug benefit. Such patients account for about 13 percent of people with depression. "Most people don't need an active drug," says Vanderbilt's Hollon, a coauthor of the study. "For a lot of folks, you're going to do as well on a sugar pill or on conversations with your physicians as you will on medication. It doesn't matter what you do; it's just the fact that you're doing something." But people with very severe depression are different, he believes. "My personal view is the placebo effect gets you pretty far, but for those with very severe, more chronic conditions, it's harder to knock down and placebos are less adequate," says Hollon. Why that should be remains a mystery, admits coauthor Robert DeRubeis of the University of Pennsylvania.

Like every scientist who has stepped into the treacherous waters of antidepressant research, Hollon, DeRubeis, and their colleagues are keenly aware of the disconnect between evidence and public impression. "Prescribers, policy makers, and consumers may not be aware that the efficacy of [antidepressants] largely has been established on the basis of studies that have included only those individuals with more severe forms of depression," something drug ads don't mention, they write. People with anything less than very severe depression "derive little specific pharmacological benefit from taking medications. Pending findings contrary to those reported here . . . efforts should be made to clarify to clinicians and prospective patients that . . . there is little evidence to suggest that [antidepressants] produce specific pharmacological benefit for the majority of patients."

Right about here, people scowl and ask how anti depressants—especially those that raise the brain's levels of serotonin—can possibly have no direct chemical effect on the brain. Surely raising serotonin levels should right the synapses' "chemical imbalance" and lift depression. Unfortunately, the serotonin-deficit theory of depression is built on a foundation of tissue paper. How that came to be is a story in itself, but the basics are that in the 1950s scientists discovered, serendipitously, that a drug called iproniazid seemed to help some people with depression. Iproniazid increases brain levels of serotonin and norepinephrine. Ergo, low levels of those neurotransmitters must cause depression. More than 50 years on, the presumed effectiveness of antidepressants that act this way remains the chief support for the chemical-imbalance theory of depression. Absent that effectiveness, the theory hasn't a leg to stand on. Direct evidence doesn't exist. Lowering people's serotonin levels does not change their mood. And a new drug, tianeptine,

The Placebo Effect

In addition to depression, many illnesses show a strong response to placebo treatments. These tend to be conditions for which the body's own biochemicals, such as opiates and dopamine, act as natural medications. Because placebos trigger the production of these compounds, dummy pills can be almost as effective as real ones. Among the conditions that have been successfully treated with placebos:

Hypertension pain parkinson's disease psoriasis rheumatoid arthritis ulcers

Illnesses that do not respond to the body's natural opiates and other compounds show little to no placebo response either. These include:

Atherosclerosis cancer growth-hormone deficiency high cholesterol infertility obsessive-compulsive disorder

which is sold in France and some other countries (but not the U.S.), turns out to be as effective as Prozac-like antidepressants that keep the synapses well supplied with serotonin. The mechanism of the new drug? It *lowers* brain levels of serotonin. "If depression can be equally affected by drugs that increase serotonin and by drugs that decrease it," says Kirsch, "it's hard to imagine how the benefits can be due to their chemical activity."

Perhaps antidepressants would be more effective at higher doses? Unfortunately, in 2002 Kirsch and colleagues found that high doses are hardly more effective than low ones, improving patients' depression-scale rating an average of 9.97 points vs. 9.57 points—a difference that is not statistically significant. Yet many doctors increase doses for patients who do not respond to a lower one, and many patients report improving as a result. There's a study of that, too. When researchers gave such nonresponders a higher dose, 72 percent got much better, their symptoms dropping by 50 percent or more. The catch? Only half the patients really got a higher dose. The rest, unknowingly, got the original, "ineffective" dose. It is hard to see the 72 percent who got much better on ersatz higher doses as the result of anything but the power of expectation: the doctor upped my dose, so I believe I'll get better.

Something similar may explain why some patients who aren't helped by one antidepressant do better on a second, or a third. This is often explained as "matching" patient to drug, and seemed to be confirmed by a 2006 federal study called STAR*D. Patients still suffering from depression after taking one drug were switched to a second; those who were still not better were switched to a third drug, and even a fourth. No placebos were used. At first blush, the results offered a ray of hope: 37 percent of the patients got better on the first drug, 19 percent more on their second, 6 percent more improved on their third try, and 5 percent more on their fourth. (Half of those who recovered relapsed within a year, however.)

So does STAR*D validate the idea that the key to effective treatment of depression is matching the patient to the drug?

Maybe. Or maybe people improved in rounds two, three, and four because depression sometimes lifts due to changes in people's lives, or because levels of depression tend to rise and fall over time. With no one in STAR*D receiving a placebo, it is not possible to conclude with certainty that the improvements in rounds two, three, and four were because patients switched to a drug that was more effective for them. Comparable numbers might have improved if they had switched to a placebo. But STAR*D did not test for that, and so cannot rule it out.

It's tempting to look at the power of the placebo effect to alleviate depression and stick an "only" in front of it—as in, the drugs work *only* through the placebo effect. But there is nothing "only" about the placebo response. It can be surprisingly enduring, as a 2008 study found: "The widely held belief that the placebo response in depression is short-lived appears to be based largely on intuition and perhaps wishful thinking," scientists wrote in the *Journal of Psychiatric Research.* The strength of the placebo response drives drug companies nuts, since it makes showing the superiority of a new drug much harder. There is a strong placebo component in the response to drugs for pain, asthma, irritable-bowel syndrome, skin conditions such as contact dermatitis, and even Parkinson's disease. But compared with the placebo component of antidepressants, the placebo response accounts for a smaller fraction of the benefit from drugs for those disorders—on the order of 50 percent for analgesics, for instance.

Which returns us to the moral dilemma. In any year, an estimated 13.1 million to 14.2 million American adults suffer from clinical depression. At least 32 million will have the disease at some point in their life. Many of the 57 percent who receive treatment (the rest do not) are helped by medication. For that benefit to continue, they need to believe in their pills. Even Kirsch warns—in boldface type in his book, which is in stores this week—that patients on antidepressants not suddenly stop taking them. That can cause serious withdrawal symptoms, including twitches, tremors, blurred vision, and nausea—as well as depression and anxiety. Yet Kirsch is well aware that his book may have the same effect on patients as the crows did on Dumbo when they told him the "magic feather" wasn't really giving him the power of flight: the little elephant began crashing to earth. Friends and colleagues who believe Kirsch is right ask why he doesn't just shut up, since publicizing the finding that the effectiveness of antidepressants is almost entirely due to people's hopes and expectations will undermine that effectiveness.

If placebos can make people better, then depression can be treated without drugs that come with serious side effects, not to mention costs.

It's all well and good to point out that psychotherapy is more effective than either pills or placebos, with dramatically lower relapse rates. But there's the little matter of reality. In the U.S., most patients with depression are treated by primary-care doctors, not psychiatrists. The latter are in short supply, especially outside cities and especially for children and adolescents. Some insurance plans discourage such care, and some psychiatrists do not accept insurance. Maybe keeping patients in the dark about the ineffectiveness of antidepressants, which for many are their only hope, is a kindness.

Or maybe not. As shown by the explicit criticism of drug companies by the authors of the recent *JAMA* paper, more and more scientists believe it is time to abandon the "don't ask, don't tell" policy of not digging too deeply into the reasons for the effectiveness of antidepressants. Maybe it is time to pull back the curtain and see the wizard for what he is. As for Kirsch, he insists that it is important to know that much of the benefit of antidepressants is a placebo effect. If placebos can make people better, then depression can be treated without drugs that come with serious side effects, not to mention costs. Wider recognition that antidepressants are a pharmaceutical version of the emperor's new clothes, he says, might spur patients to try other treatments. "Isn't it more important to know the truth?" he asks. Based on the impact of his work so far, it's hard to avoid answering, "Not to many people."

Critical Thinking

1. What is "the placebo effect?"
2. Why aren't antidepressants the best choice for all patients?

"I Can't Let Anything Go": A Case Study with Psychological Testing of a Patient with Pathologic Hoarding

Pathologic hoarding is a symptom generally recognized as related to obsessional dynamics (Gutheil, 1959). The hoarder cannot, without great anxiety, tolerate separation from or dispose of his possessions. Thus the hoarder accumulates vast amount of possessions, often in such amounts as to compromise freedom of movement in the residence. Popular in tabloid reportage, such news items portray persons found dead among floor-to-ceiling piles of old newspapers and similar detritus, while in actual clinical practice such dramatic cases are not common (Bryk, 2005; Duenwald, 2004). More importantly, such individuals are rarely available for psychological intervention or testing both because of social isolation and injury or death caused by the hoarded materials. Additionally, a majority of the current literature regarding hoarding is linked with Obsessive Compulsive Disorder (OCD), though other major disorders have been noted.

This report describes a particular individual with characteristic features of hoarding which is explored through formal psychological testing.

JANNA KORETZ AND THOMAS G. GUTHEIL

Hoarding—Definition

Frost and Hard (1996) define hoarding as follows:

a. The acquisition of, and failure to, discard a large number of possessions that appear to be useless or of limited value.

b. Living spaces sufficiently cluttered so as to preclude activities for which these spaces were designed.

c. Significant distress or impairment in functioning caused by the hoarding.

d. Reluctance or inability to return borrowed items. As boundaries blur, impulsive acquisitiveness could lead to kleptomania or stealing (p. 341).

Case Examples in Literature

The small but striking literature on hoarding contains a number of dramatic case examples, such as that of a 32 year old singer, which captures some of the classic features of hoarding dynamics (Gutheil, 1959).

> The patient's separation anxiety included . . . separation from objects. The patient was unable to throw away or discard anything. The result was that her apartment, in the course of time, resembled a huge garbage bin.

The patient considered all objects in her possession, even the most insignificant ones, such as burnt out matchsticks, cigarette butts, or candy wrappers, as parts of her ego, and discarding them as tantamount to weakening of her ego integration. Giving them away was like giving away parts of herself (p. 799).

Perhaps the most famous example of hoarding was that of the Collyer brothers (Lidz, 2003). Set in the later 1940s, two brothers Homer and Langley lived a highly reclusive hermit-like existence in a Harlem brownstone, which at the time of their death contained over 100 tons of trash that they had collected over a lifetime. The material in the house included:

> baby carriages, rusted bicycles, old food, potato peelers, guns, glass chandeliers, bowling balls, camera equipment, the folding top of a horsedrawn carriage, a saw horse, three dressmaking dummies, painted portraits, pinup girl photos, plaster busts, Mrs. Collyer's hope chests, rusty bedsprings, a kerosene stove, a child's chair . . . , more than 25,000 books, human organs pickled in jars, eight live cats, the chassis of [a model T Ford], tapestries, hundreds of yards of unused silks and fabric, clocks, fourteen pianos . . . , a clavichord, two organs, banjos, violins, bugles, accordions, a gramophone and records and countless bundles of newspapers and magazines, some of them decades old (p. 5).

Based on their expressed fears of intruders, both realistic and paranoid, the brothers had rigged a number of booby traps within their residence. Langley, who had been crawling through tunnels in the debris to bring food to his blind and paralyzed brother, was caught in one of his own traps and killed. Then Homer starved to death. The stench of Langleys' decaying corpses led the police to attempt to break into their house, only to find infinite piles of objects blocking their way. Police confronted rat-infested piles of detritus stacked to the ceilings in rooms and stairwells. While Homer was found dead in his chair shortly after the police entered, Langley was not found until nearly a month later, a short distance away from his brother, but concealed under debris from the trap (Lidz, 2003).

Discover Magazine Online (Duenwald, 2004) provides another succinct case of hoarding:

[For years] . . . Patrice Moore received . . . load[s] of mail—newspapers, magazines, book, catalogs and random solicitations. Each day the 43-year-old recluse piled the new with the old, until floor-to-ceiling stacks of disorganized paper nearly filled his windowless 10-by-10-foot apartment in New York City. In late December, the avalanche came, and Moore was buried standing up. He stood alone for two days, until neighbors heard his muffled moaning. The landlord broke in with a crowbar; it took another hour for neighbors and firefighters to dig Moore out and get him medical help (p. 1).

New avenues of understanding about hoarding have opened through brain imaging and cortical function studies (Saxena et al., 2008; Anonymous, 2008; Steller, 1943). However, our focus here is on the psychological aspects of hoarding.

Report of the Case
Prelude to Admission

Michael (identifying data in this case report have been altered to preclude recognition) is a middle-aged, white, unmarried male who attended two years of community college and briefly worked as a box cutter until 1992, after which he subsisted solely on Social Security income. He is a tall, balding man with hair grown out on the sides of his head to his shoulders; he refuses to cut his hair and nails. He wears thick glasses, which magnify his eyes, and tends to stare intensely at others, sometimes without speaking.

Michael was brought to the hospital after being evicted from his apartment for causing disturbances, playing music very loudly, calling the police with allegations of the neighbors' making noise, and knocking on neighbors' doors late at night. His landlord had offered to let him stay if he engaged in treatment, but Michael was very erratic about attending therapy: During conversation he was agreeable to the plan but then did not appear. Eventually, when his landlord took him to court, he was ordered to attend a treatment program if he wanted to leave his possessions in his apartment. As treatment, Michael entered a daytime partial hospital program and resided in the evenings in the adjacent shelter.

At the point of his planned eviction, the landlord, without informing Michael, entered his apartment in order to clean it. There he encountered piles of magazines, trash, sheet music, and many other items stacked all over the apartment's floor space up to the ceiling. Ultimately, a cleaning team required two weeks to clear out the apartment contents sufficiently to open fully the front door.

On an unauthorized visit home, Michael arrived at the apartment while the landlord and his team were cleaning it. Upon seeing his things being thrown away, he became acutely anxious and defecated on himself. He returned, in great distress, to the partial hospital program shelter.

Family and Social History

Michael has no known living relatives or friends and had interpersonal difficulties throughout his life. His mother died of cancer when he was in early grade school, and his father died when Michael was in his mid-thirties, and his stepmother died roughly around the same time. During this time, Michael's stepfamily pushed him from his father's house so that they could sell it, and Michael moved to the above-mentioned apartment mentioned. Some of the items from his stepfamily's house were of high emotional significance to Michael and were part of the hoarded materials.

The diagnoses for the current hospitalization included Major Depressive Disorder (MDD) with psychotic features and paranoid personality disorder with a history of treatment noncompliance. Michael had a significant depressive history. He had been hospitalized five times for suicidal ideation and attempts, the most recent of which was 12 years before this admission, though he experienced a waxing and waning depressive mood throughout that time.

Mental Status

At the time of the interview, Michael was oriented to person, place, and time. He had an unusual cadence of speech, but did maintain a regular rate. His thought form was goal oriented, and he was preoccupied with relational difficulties with others, primarily women. Michael denied any current or past auditory and visual hallucinations.

Psychological Testing
Instruments Used

Interview, Wechsler Adult Intelligence Scale (WAIS-III), Rorschach, Thematic Apperception Test (TAT), Minnesota Multiphasic Personality Inventory (MMPI-2)

Behavioral Observations

Michael appeared on time for each of the four sessions of the evaluation, and was cooperative and pleasant throughout. He stated repeatedly that he enjoyed the testing process very much. Michael, who had previously displayed only a flat affect with the examiner, smiled and laughed a few times during the testing sessions. Michael did not appear to be anxious, except during the inquiry section of the Rorschach when the question, "What made it look like that?" was repeated. He became visibly

Table 1 Full Scale IQ

76/5th Percentile			
Verbal IQ (Left Brain) 79/8th Percentile		**Performance IQ (Right Brain) 77/6th Percentile**	
Verbal Comprehension (CVI) 93/32nd percentile	Working Memory Index (WMI) 61/. 5th percentile	Perceptual Organization Index (POI) 82/12th percentile	Processing Speed Index (PSI) 66/1st percentile
Digit Span-5	Information-12	Picture Completion-6	Symbol Search-I
Lemer Number Sequencing-2	Comprehension-4	Block Design-7	Coding-5
Arithmetic-4	Similarities-7	Matrix Reasoning-8	
	Vocabulary-7	Object Assembly-5	
		Picture Arrangement-6	

agitated. These observations were confirmed by Michael's verbal acknowledgment of his anxiety during that particular time as well as his denial of anxiety during any other tests. His speech was perfunctory but appropriate, and his affect was usually flat with intermittent episodes of more appropriate affect.

Michael's thinking appeared confused, as many of his answers were not appropriate to the questions asked. For example, on the vocabulary section of the WAIS-III, when asked the definition of breakfast, Michael gave elements of what could be considered breakfast, such as "eggs, food," but also included "energy and vitamins," material not entirely appropriate to the definition. Although Michael's stated his mood was "good," he appeared to be somewhat morose.

Generally, Michael was very aware of his personal struggles and his differences compared to others. Cognitively, his dysregulation created an inability to change his behavior or cognitive sets. Because of this Michael appears to be somewhat lost in his world, which has increased his desire for self-harm, social isolation, and paranoid thought.

The following table describes the breakdown of Michael's full-scale IQ. In testing terms, "index scores" break down the categories of Verbal and Performance into slightly smaller subcategories that narrow the focus of the tasks tested. It is important to note that Michael's total Performance and Verbal IQ scores do not adequately describe the significant discrepancies *within* each of these categories. These discrepancies, seen through Michael's index scores in the VCI, WMI, POI and PSI cells shown above, much more accurately elucidate Michael's cognitive fingerprint.

Michael's profile reveals relative strengths and weaknesses in both his right and left hemispheres. Michael scored high on the Verbal Comprehension index in comparison to his other scores, showing that he retained a good base of knowledge from his formal education, which stayed with him throughout the years. In comparison to his other scores, Michael also scored high on the Perceptual Organization index, demonstrating that he was able to organize and work with data fairly well. Interestingly, Michael's answers to many items on the Information, Comprehension, and Vocabulary sections were not as integrated, as his scores indicate; though he received credit for many of his answers, they tended to be superficial and tangential.

Michael also showed weaknesses in his profile. He scored lowest on the Working Memory index, which primarily tests auditory memory. Michael's lowest subtest score within this index was on Letter-Number Sequencing, a task that requires the individual to remember numbers and letters while rearranging their order. Letter-Number Sequencing requires a high level of planning as well as flexibility. Michael is a concrete thinker, so that the complexity of this task may have been too difficult for him. Additionally, because of the concreteness of his thinking, Michael might not have had the ability to think flexibly enough to engage well in this task. Furthermore, this task can be highly influenced by anxiety; if the individual is experiencing anxiety, then the ability to remember numbers and letters while reorganizing their sequence is highly compromised.

Michael also had relative difficulty in the Processing Speed index, which falls under the Performance IQ composite score. Michael received a scaled score of 1, a very low score, on the Symbol Search subtest, a test that requires an individual to determine whether a series of symbols contains any symbols presented in another group. This task also requires quick visual-motor speed, efficiency, and graphomotor output. Michael might not have these skills, partially due to his poor working memory; thus it would be nearly impossible for Michael to hold the figure designs in his mind while searching for them in a new location. An alternative explanation would be that Michael might have had an obsessive concern with detail, which would prevent him from moving quickly through the task. This reason is plausible given Michael's history with hoarding and its obsessional roots.

In the emotional realm, the results from the Rorschach, MMPI-2, and TAT are convergent in many regards. Michael's awareness of his own differences can be seen through his high level of dependency and narcissistic defenses as shown by his responses on the Rorschach, which indicate that he may rely on others for direction and support and may believe that people will be more tolerant of his demands than they may actually be. Michael appears to be experiencing more needs for closeness than are being met; he is, therefore, likely to feel lonely, emotionally deprived, and interpersonally needy. This also is observed in Michael's responses on the TAT, which were primarily about family and loss. One of the cards indicated that, when fear is evoked in Michael, he becomes extremely disorganized and confused.

This disorganization leads Michael to become cognitively rigid. Michael's Rorschach responses show an avoidant style in which he tends to view himself in an overly narrow focus of attention. This was seen in the multitude of solely form-determinant responses on the Rorschach and his refusal to use the whole card in many of his responses. This rigidity and confusion about events in his daily life would likely cause Michael to feel depressed and trigger him to isolate from others.

Michael's cognitive rigidity, in combination with his impairment in reality testing, leads him to have an unusual and incorrect perception of reality. Michael's adaptation is compromised by instances of arbitrary and circumstantial reasoning and moments in which loose and scattered ideation confuses him. Although his insight is limited, Michael is able to recognize that his confusion and perception do not fit into the world in which he lives. This awareness significantly contributes to his low self-esteem, desire for self-harm, social isolation, and paranoid thinking. This is confirmed on the MMPI-2, where Michael scores extremely high on the sections outlining paranoid thinking and schizophrenia characteristics, and he endorses such ideas as "It is safer to trust no one," and "If people had not had it in for me, I would have been much more successful."

Michael's feelings of social isolation can be surmised from his answers to Card 13 B on the TAT, in which it seems that Michael projects his feelings of being different. He states: "A boy is sitting outside his house . . . watching the world go by . . . he is wondering 'Why can't I go to school? Why can't I do what they're doing?' " This response illustrates that Michael feels different from the world he lives in and that he knows he is not fully incorporated into the world around him.

Michael's responses on the Rorschach also show that he tends to overvalue his personal worth and to become preoccupied with his own needs as a defense against the continual rejection he feels in his world. Michael exhibits narcissistic tendencies such as entitlement and externalization of blame and responsibility as defenses against his substantial self-doubt and low self-esteem.

An example of Michael's low self-esteem and sadness can be seen in his response to Card 3 BM on the TAT where Michael says:

> Woman that is crying. She is very sad and depressed . . . she just lost her house, case, and family . . . she is homeless and doesn't know what to do. Fragile. She has lost everything . . . lost her family too.

This response captures Michael's apparent feeling that he is upset about the substantial loss in his life.

Michael's hoarding behaviors can be connected to these neuropsychological findings. Although hoarding can be understood in terms of obsessive and compulsive symptoms, it can also be seen through the lens of loss. Michael's history shows that he has suffered many losses throughout his life, leading to anxiety around separation, which he viewed as equivalent to death. This explains why Michael refused to get rid of a

multitude of items. As in the literature excerpts at the start of this article illustrate about those who hoard, Michael might have experienced objects as being a part of his ego and therefore, a loss of these items would feel to him like a loss of a part of himself. Similarly, if Michael suffered a loss through rejection, he might overcompensate his own feelings of rejection by refusing to reject anything.

Discussion

Michael is a 50-year-old man with a diagnosis of recurrent MDD, with psychotic features, ruling out anxiety disorder and paranoid personality disorder. Michael suffers from significant depression and suicidal ideation, anxiety, coping deficiencies, disordered thinking, social isolation, paranoia, hoarding behaviors, and a possible history of trauma. Michael is also painfully aware of his lack of connectedness and deficits in fitting in with his peers. Although Michael has a borderline IQ, he has some relative strength in both verbal competence as well as perceptual organization. Despite experiencing high anxiety, Michael is somewhat willing to engage in situations that increase his anxiety level. Michael would likely benefit from a psychopharmacological evaluation to clarify whether his medication suits his needs, continued individual therapy, and continued group therapy aimed at practicing social and therapeutic skills.

Hoarding behaviors, though usually connected with OCD dynamics, have been linked to major depression, information processing deficits, problems with emotional attachment, decision-making deficits, and behavioral avoidance (all of which Michael experiences), as well as schizophrenia and other disorders. As in the case of the Collyer brothers, death can result from physical dangers associated with hoarding; death may also occur following separation from the hoarded objects.

Hoarders tend to view their possessions as extensions of themselves, "with objects valued as safety signals because of the sense of security derived from them . . . hoarders often report that discarding possessions becomes akin to losing a loved one" (Kyrios et al., 2004, p. 244). This distorted view of their processions may bring a sense of safety to hoarders because they lack an appropriate alternative attachment (Kyrios et al., 2004). Previous studies have indicated the correlation between ambivalent attachments and low self-worth. A family environment characterized by overprotective, yet highly demanding parenting styles, not only leads an individual to seek security elsewhere, but also strengthens their alternative attachments to objects as a compensation for the high levels of perceived parental criticism that the individual received (Kyrios et al., 2004). Although not much is known about Michael's past, it is possible that he possessed this kind of attachment style and similar familial environment, possibly leading him to develop hoarding behaviors.

Michael was discharged from the partial hospital program to a day program in the area. Michael's attendance has been nearly nonexistent, and he declined group or congregate housing options. Michael has also been inconsistent in making his appointments with any of his outpatient treaters.

Conclusion

Our case report with psychological testing has illuminated some of the underlying dynamics of hoarding behavior. Although hoarding is a recognized aspect of mental illness, hoarding unrelated to OCD has been given very little attention. In cases such as Michael's, treatment plans would likely be more effective with a deeper understanding of the origin of his hoarding. Future research is needed to understand hoarding in a broader context and in relation to mental disorders beyond OCD.

References

Anonymous. Secret of compulsive hoarding revealed (New Scientist, 15 November, 2003, magazine issue 2421 (www.newscientist.com/article/mgl8024212.800.html) retrieved 8/1/09.

Bryk, W. (2005, April 13). The Collyer Brothers. *The New York Sun.* Retrieved 3/12/09 from www.nysun.com/on-the-town/collyer-brothers/12165

Duenwald, M. (2004, October). The psychology of . . . hoarding. What lies beneath the pathological desire to hoard tons of stuff [Electronic version]. *Discover Magazine.* Retrieved 3/17/09 (http://discovermagazine.com/2004/oct/psychology-of-hoarding)

Frost, R.O. & Hard, T.L. (1996). A cognitive behavioral model of compulsive hoarding. *Behavior Research and Therapy,* 34:341–350.

Gutheil, E.A. (1959). Problems of therapy in obsessive-compulsive neurosis. *American Journal of Psychotherapy,* 13:793–808.

Kyrios, M., Frost, R.O., & Steketee, G. (2004). Cognitions in compulsive buying and acquisition. *Cognitive Therapy and Research,* 28:241–258.

Lidz, F: The paper chase. *New York Times:* October 26, 2003. Retrieved 8/1/09 from www.nytimes.com/2003/10/26/nyregion/26feat.html

Saxena, S., Brody, A.L., Maidment, K.M., Smith, E.C., Zohrabi, N., Katz, E., Baker, S.K., Baxter, Lewis R., Jr. (2004). Cerebral Glucose Metabolism in Obsessive-Compulsive Hoarding. *American Journal of Psychiatry,* 161:1038–1048. Retrieved 8/1/09 from Psychiatry Online (http://ajp.psychiatryonline.org/cgi/content/full/161/6/1038)

Steller, E. The effect of epinephrine, insulin, and glucose upon hoarding in rats. Brown University: January 28, 1943.

Critical Thinking

1. What are the signs and symptoms of pathological hoarding?
2. Distinguish between clutter and pathological hoarding.

Acknowledgments—The authors thank June Wolf, PhD for the review of the psychological testing.

Internet Addiction

What once was parody may soon be diagnosis.

GREG BEATO

In 1995, in an effort to parody the way the American Psychiatric Association's hugely influential *Diagnostic and Statistical Manual of Mental Disorders* medicalizes every excessive behavior, psychiatrist Ivan Goldberg introduced on his website the concept of "Internet Addiction Disorder." Last summer Ben Alexander, a 19-year-old college student obsessed with the online multiplayer game *World of Warcraft,* was profiled by CBS News, NPR, the Associated Press, and countless other media outlets because of his status as client No. 1 at reSTART, the first residential treatment center in America for individuals trying to get themselves clean from Azeroth, iPhones, and all the other digital narcotics of our age.

At reSTART's five-acre haven in the woods near Seattle, clients pay big bucks to detox from pathological computer use by building chicken coops, cooking hamburgers, and engaging in daily therapy sessions with the program's two founders, psychologist Hilarie Cash and clinical social worker and life coach Cosette Rae. With room for just six addicts at a time and a $14,500 program fee, reSTART isn't designed for the masses, and so far it seems to have attracted more reporters than paying clients. When I spoke with Rae in May, she said "10 to 15" people had participated in the 45-day program to date.

Still, the fact that reSTART exists at all shows how far we've progressed in taking Dr. Goldberg's spoof seriously. You may have been too busy monitoring Kim Kardashian's every passing thought-like thing on Twitter to notice, but Digital Detox Week took place in April, and Video Game Addiction Awareness Week followed on its heels in June. Internet addiction disorder has yet to claim a Tiger Woods of its own, but the sad, silly evidence of our worldwide cyber-bingeing mounts on a daily basis. A councilman in the Bulgarian city of Plovdiv is ousted from his position for playing *Farmville* during budget meetings. There are now at least three apps that use the iPhone's camera to show the world right in front of you so you can keep texting while walking down the street, confident in your ability to avoid sinkholes, telephone poles, and traffic. Earlier this year, 200 students taking a class in media literacy at the University of Maryland went on a 24-hour media fast for a group study, then described how "jittery," "anxious," "miserable," and "crazy" they felt without Twitter, Facebook, iPods, and laptops.

"I clearly am addicted," one student concluded, "and the dependency is sickening."

In the early days of the Web, dirty talk was exchanged at the excruciatingly slow rate of 14.4 bits per second, connectivity charges accrued by the hour instead of the month, and the only stuff for sale online was some overpriced hot sauce from a tiny store in Pasadena. It took the patience of a Buddhist monk, thousands of dollars, and really bad TV reception to overuse the Web in a self-destructive manner. Yet even then, many people felt Ivan Goldberg's notes on Internet addiction worked better as psychiatry than comedy. A year before Goldberg posted his spoof, Kimberly Young, a psychologist at the University of Pittsburgh, had already begun conducting formal research into online addiction. By 1996 the Harvard-affiliated McLean Hospital had established a computer addiction clinic, a professor at the University of Maryland had created an Internet addiction support group, and *The New York Times* was running op-eds about the divorce epidemic that Internet addiction was about to unleash.

Fifteen years down the line, you'd think we'd all be introverted philanderers by now, isolating ourselves in the virtual Snuggie of *World of Warcraft* by day and stepping out at night to destroy our marriages with our latest hook-ups from AshleyMadison.com. But the introduction of flat monthly fees, online gaming, widespread pornography, MySpace, YouTube, Facebook, WiFi, iPhones, netbooks, and free return shipping on designer shoes with substantial markdowns does not seem to have made the Internet any more addictive than it was a decade ago.

In 1998 Young told the Riverside *Press-Enterprise* that "5 to 10 percent of the 52 million Internet users [were] addicted or 'potentially addicted.'" Doctors today use similar numbers when estimating the number of online junkies. In 2009 David Greenfield, a psychiatrist at the University of Connecticut, told the *San Francisco Chronicle* that studies have shown 3 percent to 6 percent of Internet users "have a problem." Is it possible that the ability to keep extremely close tabs on Ashton Kutcher actually has reduced the Internet's addictive power?

Granted, 3 percent is an awful lot of people. Argue all you like that a real addiction should require needles, or spending time in seedy bars with people who drink vodka through their eyeballs, or at least the overwhelming and nihilistic urge to invest thousands of dollars in a broken public school system through the purchase of lottery tickets. Those working on the front lines of technology overuse have plenty of casualties to point to. In our brief conversation, Cosette Rae tells me about a Harvard student who lost a scholarship because he spent too much time playing games, a guy who spent so many sedentary hours at his computer that he developed blood clots in his leg and had to have it amputated, and an 18-year-old who chose homelessness over gamelessness when his parents told him he either had to quit playing computer games or move out.

A few minutes on Google yields even more lurid anecdotes. In 2007 an Ohio teenager shot his parents, killing his mother and wounding his father, after they took away his Xbox. This year a South Korean couple let their real baby starve to death because they were spending so much time caring for their virtual baby in a role-playing game called *Prius Online*.

On a pound-for-pound basis, the average *World of Warcraft* junkie undoubtedly represents a much less destructive social force than the average meth head. But it's not extreme anecdotes that make the specter of Internet addiction so threatening; it's the fact that Internet overuse has the potential to scale in a way that few other addictions do. Even if Steve Jobs designed a really cool-looking syringe and started distributing free heroin on street corners, not everyone would try it. But who among us doesn't already check his email more often than necessary? As the Internet weaves itself more and more tightly into our lives, only the Amish are completely safe.

As early as 1996, Kimberly Young was promoting the idea that the American Psychiatric Association (APA) should add Internet addiction disorder to the *Diagnostic and Statistical Manual of Mental Disorders* (*DSM*). In February, the APA announced that its coming edition of the *DSM*, the first major revision since 1994, will for the first time classify a behavior-related condition—pathological gambling—as an "addiction" rather than an "impulse control disorder." Internet addiction disorder is not being included in this new category of "behavioral addictions," but the APA said it will consider it as a "potential addition . . . as research data accumulate."

If the APA does add excessive Internet use to the *DSM*, the consequences will be wide-ranging. Health insurance companies will start offering at least partial coverage for treatment programs such as reSTART. People who suffer from Internet addiction disorder will receive protection under the Americans With Disabilities Act if their impairment "substantially limits one or more major life activities." Criminal lawyers will use their clients' online habits to fashion diminished capacity defenses.

Which means that what started as a parody in 1995 could eventually turn more darkly comic than ever imagined. Picture a world where the health care system goes bankrupt because insurers have to pay for millions of people determined to kick their Twitter addictions once and for all. Where employees who view porn at work are legally protected from termination. Where killing elves in cyberspace could help absolve you for killing people in real life. Is it too late to revert to our older, healthier, more balanced ways of living and just spend all our leisure hours watching *Love Boat* reruns?

Critical Thinking

1. What is the difference between Internet use and Internet addiction?

2. Should Internet addiction be classified as a disorder? Explain your answer.

From *Reason Magazine*, August/September 2010, pp. 16–17. Copyright © 2010 by Reason Foundation, 3415 S. Sepulveda Blvd., Suite 400, Los Angeles, CA 90034. www.reason.com

UNIT 3

Nutritional Health

Unit Selections

Learning Outcomes

After reading this unit, you should be able to:

- List the four nutrients that function as antioxidants. Identify the best food sources of these nutrients in foods that you commonly eat.

- Identify the four groups that should pay particular attention to sodium content of foods and consume no more than 1,500 mg of sodium per day, as recommended in the Dietary Guidelines for Americans.

- Address why, despite ample health information, the number of adults who eat adequate servings of healthy foods such as vegetables is declining.

- Explain the possible link between food coloring and behavior change in children.

Student Website

www.mhhe.com/cls

Internet References

The American Dietetic Association
   www.eatright.org
Center for Science in the Public Interest (CSPI)
   www.cspinet.org
Food and Nutrition Information Center
   www.nalusda.gov/fnic/index.html

For years, the majority of Americans paid little attention to nutrition, other than to eat three meals a day and, perhaps, take a vitamin supplement. While this dietary style was generally adequate for the prevention of major nutritional deficiencies, medical evidence began to accumulate linking the American diet to a variety of chronic illnesses. In an effort to guide Americans in their dietary choices, the U.S. Dept. of Agriculture and the U.S. Public Health Service review and publish Dietary Guidelines every five years. The year 2000 Dietary Guidelines' recommendations are no longer limited to food choices; they include advice on the importance of maintaining a healthy weight and engaging in daily exercise. In addition to the Dietary Guidelines, the Department of Agriculture developed the Food Guide Pyramid to show the relative importance of food groups.

Despite an apparent ever-changing array of dietary recommendations from the scientific community, five recommendations remain constant: (1) eat a diet low in saturated fat, (2) eat whole grain foods, (3) drink plenty of fresh water daily, (4) limit your daily intake of sugar and salt, and (5) eat a diet rich in fruits and vegetables. These recommendations, while general in nature, are seldom heeded and in fact many Americans don't eat enough fruits and vegetables and eat too much sugar and saturated fat.

Of all the nutritional findings, the link between dietary fat and coronary heart disease remains the most consistent throughout the literature. Current recommendations suggest that the types of fats consumed may play a much greater role in disease processes than the total amount of fat consumed. As it currently stands, most experts agree that it is prudent to limit our intake of trans fat, which appears to raise LDLs, the bad cholesterol, and lower HDLs, the good cholesterol, thus increasing the risk of heart disease. There's also evidence that trans fats increase the risk of diabetes.

Although the basic advice on eating healthy remains fairly constant, many Americans are still confused about exactly what to eat. Should their diet be low carbohydrate, high protein, or low fat? When people turn to standards such as the Food Guide Pyramid, even here there is some confusion. The pyramid, designed by the Department of Agriculture over 20 years ago, recommends a diet based on grains, fruits, and vegetables with several servings of meats and dairy products. It also restricts the consumption of fats, oils, and sweets. While the pyramid offers guidelines as to food groups, individual nutrients are not emphasized. One mineral, sodium, is vital to life, but too much sodium has been linked to high blood pressure among sensitive individuals. In "Keeping a Lid on Salt: Not So Easy" Nanci Hellmich addresses the challenges of restricting sodium in the current U.S. food environment. Food coloring is another additive that may need to be restricted. Gardiner Harris explores the possible link between behavioral problems and food coloring in "F.D.A. Panel to Consider Warnings for Artificial Food Colorings."

The media continues to bombard us with articles and television segments on nutrition-related issues, adding to the confusion

© Harrison Eastwood/Getty Images

about which foods are healthy. "Antioxidants: Fruitful Research and Recommendations" by Pamela Brummit discusses antioxidants and the best food sources for these naturally occurring promoters of health.

Of all the topic areas in health, food and nutrition is certainly one of the most interesting, if for no other reason than the rate at which dietary recommendations change. One constant piece of advice is to eat plenty of fruits and vegetables. Though this information is widely disseminated, a surprisingly number of children and adults don't eat the recommended number of servings. As described in "Fruit Loopiness," Katherine Schreiber believes that education about nutrition is important, but understanding the underlying issues that lead people to eat unhealthy food is equally vital. Despite all the controversy and conflict, the one message that seems to remain constant is the importance of balance and moderation in everything we eat.

Antioxidants: Fruitful Research and Recommendations

PAMELA S. BRUMMIT, MA, RD/LD

Free radicals, which are produced during food metabolism and by external factors such as radiation and smog, can damage cells and may contribute to some diseases—notably heart disease and cancer—and many experts believe antioxidants can help prevent this damage.

The body's immune system helps defend against oxidative stress. As we age, this defense becomes less effective, which contributes to poor health. Clinical studies hypothesize that when we consume antioxidants, we provide our bodies with protection and health benefits.

Antioxidants Defined

The USDA identifies beta-carotene (vitamin A), selenium, vitamin C, vitamin E, lutein, and lycopene as antioxidant substances.

Lycopene is a pigment that gives vegetables and fruits such as tomatoes, pink grapefruit, and watermelon their red hue. Several studies suggest that consuming foods rich in lycopene is associated with a lower risk of prostate cancer and cardiovascular disease. Lycopene is better absorbed when consumed in processed tomato products rather than in fresh tomatoes.

Selenium is a trace mineral that is essential to good health but required only in small amounts. Its antioxidant properties help prevent cellular damage from free radicals. Plant foods are the major dietary sources of selenium, but the content in a particular food depends on the selenium content of the soil where it's grown. Soils in the high plains of northern Nebraska and the Dakotas have very high levels of selenium.

Lutein is found in large amounts in the lens and retina of our eyes and is recognized for its eye health benefits. It may also protect against damage caused by UVB light and is a critical component to overall skin health. Lutein is found naturally in foods such as dark green, leafy vegetables and egg yolks.

The antioxidant function of beta-carotene (precursor to vitamin A) is its ability to reduce free radicals and protect the cell membrane lipids from the harmful effects of oxidation. In addition, beta-carotene may provide some synergism to vitamin E.

As a water-soluble antioxidant, vitamin C reduces free radicals before they can damage the lipids. These antioxidant properties fight free radicals that can promote wrinkles, age spots, cataracts, and arthritis. Also, the antioxidants in vitamin C have been found to fight free radicals that prey on organs and blood vessels.

As an antioxidant, vitamin E may help prevent or delay cardiovascular disease and cancer and has been shown to play a role in immune function. DNA repair, and other metabolic processes.

Fruits and vegetables, nuts, grains, poultry, and fish are major sources of antioxidants.

Research

Researchers have studied antioxidants and disease processes for years. Some studies have found that an increased intake of beta-carotene is associated with decreased cardiovascular mortality in older adult populations. Studies on the effects of vitamin E on aging have shown potential relationships between the vitamin and the prevention of atherosclerosis, cancer, cataracts, arthritis, central nervous system disorders such as Parkinson's disease, Alzheimer's disease, and impaired glucose tolerance. Studies on vitamin C suggest that it may help protect against vascular dementia, and studies on selenium point to its potential role in cancer prevention. Beta-carotene, vitamin C, and vitamin E showed a positive improvement in muscle strength and may improve physical performance in older adults.

One lycopene study found that eating 10 or more servings per week of tomato products was associated with up to a 35% reduced risk of prostate cancer. Another study suggested that men who had the highest amount of lycopene in their body fat were one half as likely to suffer a heart attack as those with the least amount. Numerous studies correlate a high intake of lycopene-containing foods or high lycopene serum levels with reduced incidence of cancer, cardiovascular disease, and macular degeneration. However, estimates of lycopene consumption have been based on reported tomato intake, not on the use of lycopene supplements. Since tomatoes are sources of other nutrients, including vitamin C, folate, and potassium, it is unclear whether lycopene itself is beneficial.

Some researchers suggest that eliminating free radicals may actually interfere with a natural defense mechanism within the body. Large doses of antioxidants may keep immune systems from fighting off invading pathogens.

Three out of four intervention trials using high-dose beta-carotene supplements did not show protective effects against cancer or cardiovascular disease. Rather, the high-risk population (smokers and asbestos workers) showed an increase in cancer and angina cases. It appears that beta-carotene can promote health when taken at dietary levels but may have adverse effects when taken in high doses by subjects who smoke or who have been exposed to asbestos.

Results from one study indicate that antioxidant supplementation may not be beneficial for disease prevention. This study showed no consistent, clear evidence for health effects. However, the preliminary studies suggest antioxidants may block the heart-damaging effects of oxygen on arteries and the cell damage that might encourage some kinds of cancer.

There remains a lack of knowledge regarding the safety of long-term mega-doses of vitamins. Research continues to be inconclusive and the data incomplete. Research has not been able to validate a link between oxidative stress and chronic disease. As with all research, the studies have been too diverse to provide conclusions.

Recommendations

The American Dietetic Association and the American Heart Association (AHA) recommend that people eat a variety of nutrient-rich foods from all of the food groups on a daily basis because this provides necessary nutrients, including antioxidants. Some researchers believe antioxidants are effective only when they are consumed in foods that contain them.

The recognized beneficial roles that fruits and vegetables play in the reduced risk of disease has led health organizations to develop programs encouraging consumers to eat more antioxidant-rich fruits and vegetables. The AHA and the American Cancer Society recommend that healthy adults eat five or more servings per day. The World Cancer Research Fund and the American Institute for Cancer Research report that "evidence of dietary protection against cancer is strongest and most consistent for diets high in vegetables and fruits."

Given the high degree of scientific consensus regarding the benefits of a diet high in fruits and vegetables—particularly those that contain dietary fiber and vitamins A and C—the FDA released a health claim for fruits and vegetables in relation to cancer. Food packages that meet FDA criteria may now carry the claim, "Diets low in fat and high in fruits and vegetables may reduce the risk of some cancers." The FDA also released a dietary guidance message for consumers: "Diets rich in fruits and vegetables may reduce the risk of some types of cancer and other chronic diseases." The 2005 Dietary Guidelines for Americans states, "Increased intakes of fruits, vegetables, whole grains, and fat-free or low-fat milk and milk products are likely to have important health benefits for most Americans."

Antioxidant research continues to grow and emerge as researchers discover new, beneficial components of food. Reinforced by current research, the message remains that antioxidants obtained from food sources, including fruits, vegetables, and whole grains, may reduce disease risk and can benefit human health.

Using the latest research technologies, USDA nutrition scientists measured the antioxidant levels in more than 100 different foods, including fruits, vegetables, nuts, dried fruits, spices, and cereals. The top 20 ranked foods that interfere with or prevent damage from free radicals are artichokes (cooked), black beans, black plums, blackberries, cranberries, cultivated blueberries, Gala apples, Granny Smith apples, pecans, pinto beans, plums, prunes, raspberries, Red Delicious apples, red kidney beans, Russet potatoes (cooked), small red beans, strawberries, sweet cherries, and wild blueberries.

How can we encourage older adults to eat more fruits and vegetables, especially those high in antioxidants? Share this helpful list with your older adult clients and patients.

1. Try one new fruit or vegetable per week. Variety is key!
2. Keep washed, ready-to-eat fruits and vegetables on hand and easily accessible. On the run? Take a bag of fruits or vegetables with you to munch on.
3. Serve fruits and vegetables with other favorite foods.
4. Add vegetables to casseroles, stews, and soups and puréed fruits and vegetables to sauces. Include vegetables in sandwiches and pastas.
5. Sprinkle vegetables with Parmesan cheese or top with melted low-fat cheese or white sauce made with low-fat milk.
6. Experiment with different methods of cooking fruits and vegetables.
7. Enjoy vegetables with low-fat dip for a snack.
8. Try commercial prepackaged salads and stir-fry mixes to save time.
9. Drink 100% fruit juice instead of fruit-flavored drinks or soda.
10. Serve fruit for dessert.
11. Keep a bowl of apples, bananas, and/or oranges on the dining room table.
12. Choose a side salad made with a variety of leafy greens.
13. Bake with raisin, date, or prune purée to reduce fat intake and increase fiber consumption.
14. Order vegetable toppings on your pizza.
15. Sip fruit smoothies for breakfast or snacks. Blend papaya with pineapple for a cool afternoon treat, or sip on a glass of fresh tomato juice at dinner.
16. Make a fruit salad to try many different types of fruit at once.
17. Learn to recognize a serving of fruits and vegetables: a medium-sized piece of fruit or ½ cup of most fresh, canned, or cooked fruits and vegetables.
18. Start your day with fruit. For example, add fruit to cereal or yogurt or pile on waffles. Or add vegetables—tomatoes, onions, potatoes—to an omelet or scrambled eggs.
19. Top meat and fish with salsa made from tomatoes, onions, corn, mangos, or other fruits and vegetables.
20. Try vegetarian choices: Vegetable stir fry, bean burrito, etc.

Critical Thinking

1. What diseases have been linked to free radical damage? What is the relationship of free radicals and antioxidants?

2. Identify three vitamins, one mineral, and two bioactive compounds that function as antioxidants.

3. Classify the top 20 foods that prevent damage from free radicals by food group (fruit, vegetable, or legumes).

Pamela S. Brummit, MA, RD/LD, is the founder and president of Brummit & Associates, Inc, a dietary consulting firm. She has held more than 20 board positions in local, state, and national dietetic associations and is past chair of Consultant Dietitians in Health Care Facilities dietetic practice group.

Keeping a Lid on Salt: Not So Easy

Known as a silent killer, it's part of how we live.

NANCI HELLMICH

For years, Americans have been advised to consume less sodium, and they've taken that advice with a grain of salt.

Even many health-conscious consumers figured it was the least of their worries, especially compared with limiting their intake of calories, saturated fat, trans fat, cholesterol and sugar.

All that changed last week when a report from the Institute of Medicine urged the government to gradually reduce the maximum amount of sodium that manufacturers and restaurants can add to foods, beverages and meals. The report put a spotlight on what doctors and nutritionists have argued is a major contributor to heart disease and stroke.

More than half of Americans have either high blood pressure or pre-hypertension, says cardiologist Clyde Yancy, president of the American Heart Association and medical director at the Baylor Heart and Vascular Institute in Dallas.

"That puts a lot of us in the bucket of people who need to be on a lower sodium diet. Sodium contributes to most people's high blood pressure, and for some it may be the primary driver."

Cutting back on sodium could save thousands of people from early deaths caused by heart attacks and strokes each year, and it could save billions of dollars in health care costs, he says.

Others second that. "Salt is the single most harmful element in our food supply, silently killing about 100,000 people each year," says Michael Jacobson, executive director of the Washington, D.C.-based Center for Science in the Public Interest. "That's like a crowded jetliner crashing every single day. But the food industry has fended off government action for more than three decades."

Now salt has our attention.

But reducing it in the American diet is easier said than done. "We have, in essence, ignored the advice because we are driven by convenience, and sodium makes a fast-food lifestyle very easy," Yancy says. "To change, we would need to live and eat differently."

Very differently.

Americans now consume an average of about 3,400 milligrams of sodium a day, or about 1½ teaspoons, government data show. Men consume more than women.

But most adults—including those with high blood pressure, African Americans, the middle-aged and the elderly—should consume no more than 1,500 milligrams a day, according to the dictary guidelines from the U.S. Department of Agriculture. Others should consume less than 2,300 milligrams, or less than a teaspoon, the guidelines say.

And yet it's virtually impossible to limit yourself to such amounts if you often eat processed foods, prepared foods or restaurant fare, including fast food. Most Americans' sodium intake comes from those sources, not the salt shaker on the table.

Some restaurant entrees have 2,000 milligrams or more in one dish. Fast-food burgers can have more than 1,000 milligrams. Many soups are chock-full of sodium. So are many spaghetti sauces, broths, lunch meats, salad dressings, cheeses, crackers and frozen foods.

Can't see it, can't taste it.

Salt serves many functions in products. Besides adding to a food's taste, it is a preservative. "You can't see it," Yancy says. "You can't even taste it because you are so accustomed to it. If you want the freedom to make healthy choices, you are limited by today's foods. That's a problem."

To change that, food companies and restaurants will have to come up with new ways to formulate products and recipes to help consumers gradually lower their salt levels, which would wean them off the taste.

That's a huge challenge, but nutritionists and public health specialists say it can be done and will be worth it. "There is no health benefit to a high-sodium diet, and there is considerable risk," says Linda Van Horn, a professor of preventive medicine at Northwestern University Feinberg School of Medicine.

Even those whose blood pressure is in the normal range should watch their intake, Yancy says. "Here's a wake-up call: Every American who is age 50 or older has a 90% chance of developing hypertension. That increases the risk of heart disease and stroke. This is a preventable process, and it's preventable with sodium reduction, weight control and physical activity."

Why It Can Be Harmful

There are several theories for why sodium increases blood pressure, Yancy says, "but the most obvious one is that it makes us retain fluids, and that retention elevates blood pressure," which injures blood vessels and leads to heart disease and stroke. "It's a connect-the-dots phenomenon."

Some people, especially some African Americans, are more salt-sensitive than others, Yancy says.

"When they are exposed to sodium, they retain more fluid, and because of the way their kidneys handle sodium, they may have a greater proportional rise in blood pressure," he says.

The cost of this damage? An analysis by the Rand Corp. found that if the average sodium intake of Americans was reduced to 2,300 milligrams a day, it might decrease the cases of high blood pressure by 11 million, improve quality of life for millions of people and save about $18 billion in annual health care costs.

The estimated value of improved quality of life and living healthier longer: $32 billion a year. Greater reductions in sodium consumption in the population would save more lives and money, says Roland Sturm, a senior economist with Rand.

Yancy says the country doesn't just need health care reform, "we need health reform. If we don't adjust the demand part of the equation, no system will work. Remarkably, people might be overall healthier by simply reducing sodium."

But Yancy says people need to keep in mind that sodium is just one of the factors that increase the risk of heart disease and stroke. Others include obesity, consuming too much sugar and too few fruits and vegetables, lack of physical activity and smoking.

Salt Industry Disagrees

Leaders in the salt industry say their product is being unfairly maligned. The Institute of Medicine report and the government "are focusing on one small aspect of health, which is a small increase in blood pressure in a small segment of population," says Lori Roman, president of the Salt Institute, an industry group.

Some of the research that ties salt to health risks is based on faulty assumptions and extrapolations, Roman says. She says a recent worldwide study indicated there is no country where people eat an average of less than 1,500 milligrams a day. "That's way below the normal range," Roman says. The Italians eat more sodium than Americans, but their cardiovascular health is better than Americans', and the reason is they eat a lot of fruits and vegetables, she says.

"This is the real story that the government is missing," Roman says. "It is the secret to good health."

She says people may end up following a less healthy diet if they cut back on sodium. "Have you ever bought a can of low-sodium string beans and then tried to season it to taste good? It's impossible," Roman says. "Here's one of the unintended consequences of this recommendation: People will eat fewer vegetables, and by eating fewer vegetables, they will be less healthy."

Yancy says the first step for many people is making the decision to cut back on salt intake. He knows from experience that it can be done.

An African American, Yancy, 52, has high blood pressure and a family history of heart disease and stroke. He's lean and exercises for an hour a day, but still he has to take medication for hypertension. Before he started watching his sodium intake a few years ago, Yancy says, he was consuming more than 4,000 milligrams a day, partly because he grew up in southern Louisiana and was used to a salty, high-fat diet.

But he has weaned himself off the taste. He doesn't have a salt shaker in his house, and he reads the labels on grocery store items and doesn't buy any that have more than 100 milligrams of sodium in a serving.

"I taste the salt in items and put them aside. I find it difficult to enjoy prepared soups. I can taste the salt in prepared meals. I've learned to make my own soups."

When he eats out, he orders salads and asks for his fish and meat to be grilled. "Typically, I eat fish with lemon juice and pepper."

Even so, he believes his sodium intake is probably higher than it should be because he often eats in restaurants and cafeterias, and many foods have hidden sodium.

Changes in food products need to be made over time as the Institute of Medicine report suggests, says Van Horn, a research nutritionist at Northwestern. "If we drop the sodium overnight, people will be desperately seeking salt shakers."

So how hard is it going to be to reduce the salt in processed and prepared foods?

"We've been trying to reduce the sodium in foods for more than 30 years. If this were easy, it would have been accomplished," says Roger Clemens, a professor of pharmacology at the University of Southern California and a spokesman for the Institute of Food Technologists.

The primary dietary source of sodium is sodium chloride, also known as table salt, he says. There are other sodium salts, such as sodium bicarbonate (baking soda) in baking and sodium benzoate (preservative) in bread and beverages. And there are potassium salts that are used in foods—as emulsifiers in cheese and buffers in beverages, he says.

"Salt is a natural preservative. It has been used in the food supply to ensure food safety for centuries," Clemens says. "It's critical for preserving bacon, olives, lunch meats, fish and poultry."

"Some foods, such as cheese, can only be produced with salt. No other compound allows the proteins to knit together to become cheese."

If It Doesn't Taste Good...

To make cheese that is lower in sodium, foodmakers must put the cheese through a special procedure that basically extracts some of the sodium. "It's a very long, tedious process," he says.

Salt also is crucial for making most breads. To get dough to rise, manufacturers use sodium chloride and sodium bicarbonate, Clemens says. "If you were to eat a sodium-free product, the texture and flavor would be markedly different. It would be more compressed. I don't think you'd like it at first."

He says some manufacturers have experimented with low-sodium items, and in some cases consumers have turned up their noses. "If it doesn't taste good, consumers won't buy it."

Melissa Musiker, a nutrition spokeswoman for the Grocery Manufacturers Association, agrees. "You can't get ahead of consumers," she says. "You work on the recipes, test them, see how consumers respond and go back and tweak."

There is no one single alternative for replacing it in various foods, she says. "It has to be replaced on an ingredient-by-ingredient basis."

Clemens says food companies will continue to try to develop new technologies to lower the sodium.

"It has taken us 30 years to get this far, and it will probably take us another decade to get a significant difference in the intake. If we can lower sodium in our diet, we'll have a huge health impact on generations to come."

Critical Thinking

1. Which groups of people should consume less than 1,500 mg of sodium per day, as recommended in the Dietary Guidelines for Americans?

2. What is the largest source of sodium in the typical Western diet?

3. How does dietary sodium increase blood pressure in someone who is salt sensitive?

Fruit Loopiness

When it comes to eating fruits and veggies, we're talking about it more but doing it less. It just might be a case of TMI.

KATHERINE SCHREIBER

Chances are, someone has told you to eat your vegetables. If it wasn't Grandma, then it was probably the government. From newsstands to iPhone apps, federal dietary guidelines are more accessible than ever. Nevertheless, chances are even greater that you haven't heeded the advice.

A mere 26.3 percent of American adults consumed three or more vegetable servings a day in 2009, according to the Centers for Disease Control and Prevention—about the same as in 2000, despite a rising tide of information about healthy eating. Some 32.5 percent of us got in two or more daily fruit servings—a decline from 2000, when 34.4 percent of us consumed a couple of pieces of fruit a day. But both numbers fall far short of targets set by our nutritional keepers, the Department of Agriculture and the Department of Health and Human Services.

"These reports are disappointing," declares CDC physician Jennifer Foltz, noting that a diet rich in fruits and veggies can help reduce the risk for many leading causes of death. "We wanted to double fruit and vegetable consumption in 2000. A decade later, we're seeing a 2 percent decrease in fruit intake and no change in vegetable consumption."

Is a cup of spinach really that hard to stomach? Apparently it is—although Foltz hopes that the newly revised *Dietary Guidelines for Americans* might help it go down. They emphasize consumption of plants over grains, more nutrition education for schoolchildren, and fresher foods in school and workplace cafeterias.

The law of unintended consequences takes some twists in the nutrition realm.

Americans got their first taste of dietary guidelines in 1980, when officials laid out the nutritional elements shown to reduce the growing toll of chronic diseases. They boiled down to favoring fruits, vegetables, and whole grains—while shunning refined sugars, saturated fats, cholesterol, and sodium. The recommendations have since been revised every five years to incorporate the latest research.

Although the 2005 guidelines set off changes to food labels detailing nutritional content and spawned interactive food pyramids, they did little to stir up fruit and veggie enthusiasm. In fact, in a stunning example of the law of unintended consequences, which takes unique twists in the food realm, they might have inadvertently driven us away from the good stuff.

Our eating behaviors are particularly sensitive to "the ironic effect of external controls," contends University of Chicago psychologist Stacey Finkelstein. In one set of studies, she recruited college students to rate their hunger levels after taste-testing several protein bars. The nutritional content of the bars was identical; some, however, were described as "healthy" while others were said to be "tasty." Overwhelmingly, the "healthier" samples proved the least satisfying and left subjects wanting to consume more; their "tastier" counterparts satisfied more.

Finkelstein then explored how perceptions of our own control influence how hungry we think we are. Half of the 53 subjects were *invited* to *try* the protein bars before rating their hunger, and half were *told* that doing so was their *job*. Those who felt they had been denied a choice proved hungrier after their nosh.

Impose healthy eating and such are the consequences, Finkelstein insists. "Not only do many of us fail to associate healthier foods with satiation, most of us find nothing as fulfilling as free will. We experience a rebound in hunger and consumption when others make our food healthier for us," she explains.

Blame biology. "We're designed to be easily overwhelmed by high-fat and high-sugar foods," says Leah Olson, a biology professor at Sarah Lawrence College. "They provide the quickest route to fueling our brains and our bodies."

Of course, whatever fuel we don't end up using we store as fat. To our forever-foraging ancestors living at the edge of famine, this was an advantage. Modern Americans are still just as drawn to energy-rich foods although we're far less physically active. Enter obesity, diabetes, cardiovascular disease, and other maladies.

Ironically, the cure for our dietary woes might be a little less information. "More nutritional labeling doesn't get at the heart of the problem," observes Gavan Fitzsimons, professor of marketing and psychology at Duke University. "Instead of providing more information, we need to address the underlying motivational issues." Our surroundings play an enormous role in governing our behavior; sights, smells, and sounds commonly coerce us into unhealthy behaviors.

Simply surrounding ourselves with healthy foods could go a long way to getting them into our mouths. "When you're distracted, hungry, or fatigued, you act on what's physically salient," says behavioral neuroeconomist Baba Shiv of Stanford University. "You're focused on what's in front of you." Unfortunately, calorie-dense processed products are most likely to be within arms reach; they're marketed far more aggressively than produce.

Brian Wansink, Cornell University food behavior scientist and author of *Mindless Eating: Why We Eat More Than We Think,* hopes to change this. He's come up with new designs for school lunchrooms that outsmart our nutritional quirks. He'd place healthier options strategically to increase their chances of being chosen.

"Basic behavioral principles can be applied to making lunchrooms smarter," Wansink says. Like moving the salad bar so that kids bump into it en route to the cash register. Placing chocolate milk behind the white milk. Labeling healthy foods "delicious" or "awesome." Giving kids a choice between celery and carrots, rather than just providing carrots, ups their carrot quotient by 30 percent.

"People taste what they think they're going to taste," he explains. "Telling a kid, 'Hey, eat this, it's healthy' is a really dumb way to approach the problem. The better and smarter way is to say something like, 'Hey, try this, it's really creamy.'"

Culinary Contradictions

SCRATCH A CONSUMER and you'll expose lots of contradictions in their food consumption patterns. It's part of the human condition, says Finnish researcher Hanna Leipämaa-Leskinen. She asked 257 people ages 18 to 64 to cite their top impediments to leading a healthier lifestyle.

28 percent didn't have enough time
20 percent found healthy items too costly
20 percent preferred to indulge
13 percent didn't want to violate the (unhealthy) eating habits of friends and family
12 percent were confused about which foods are healthy
4 percent preferred to stick to habitual eating patterns
3 percent didn't respond, and odds are they weren't off in the kitchen cooking cabbage

---

Critical Thinking

1. Why do people continue to eat unhealthy food?
2. What is the difference between "healthy" and "tasty" with regard to satisfaction?
3. What strategies can be used to help kids make healthier choices?

F.D.A. Panel to Consider Warnings for Artificial Food Colorings

GARDINER HARRIS

Washington—After staunchly defending the safety of artificial food colorings, the federal government is for the first time publicly reassessing whether foods like Jell-O, Lucky Charms cereal and Minute Maid Lemonade should carry warnings that the bright artificial colorings in them worsen behavior problems like hyperactivity in some children.

The Food and Drug Administration concluded long ago that there was no definitive link between the colorings and behavior or health problems, and the agency is unlikely to change its mind any time soon. But on Wednesday and Thursday, the F.D.A. will ask a panel of experts to review the evidence and advise on possible policy changes, which could include warning labels on food.

The hearings signal that the growing list of studies suggesting a link between artificial colorings and behavioral changes in children has at least gotten regulators' attention—and, for consumer advocates, that in itself is a victory.

In a concluding report, staff scientists from the F.D.A. wrote that while typical children might be unaffected by the dyes, those with behavioral disorders might have their conditions "exacerbated by exposure to a number of substances in food, including, but not limited to, synthetic color additives."

Renee Shutters, a mother of two from Jamestown, N.Y., said in a telephone interview on Tuesday that two years ago, her son Trenton, then 5, was having serious behavioral problems at school until she eliminated artificial food colorings from his diet. "I know for sure I found the root cause of this one because you can turn it on and off like a switch," Ms. Shutters said.

But Dr. Lawrence Diller, a behavioral pediatrician in Walnut Creek, Calif., said evidence that diet plays a significant role in most childhood behavioral disorders was minimal to nonexistent. "These are urban legends that won't die," Dr. Diller said.

There is no debate about the safety of natural food colorings, and manufacturers have long defended the safety of artificial ones as well. In a statement, the Grocery Manufacturers Association said, "All of the major safety bodies globally have reviewed the available science and have determined that there is no demonstrable link between artificial food colors and hyperactivity among children."

In a 2008 *petition* filed with federal food regulators, the Center for Science in the Public Interest, a consumer advocacy group, argued that some parents of susceptible children do not know that their children are at risk and so "the appropriate public health approach is to remove those dangerous and unnecessary substances from the food supply."

The federal government has been cracking down on artificial food dyes for more than a century in part because some early ones were not only toxic but were also sometimes used to mask filth or rot. In 1950, many children became ill after eating Halloween candy containing Orange No. 1 dye, and the F.D.A. banned it after more rigorous testing suggested that it was toxic. In 1976, the agency banned Red No. 2 because it was suspected to be carcinogenic. It was then replaced by Red No. 40.

Many of the artificial colorings used today were approved by the F.D.A. in 1931, including Blue No. 1, Yellow No. 5 and Red No. 3. Artificial dyes were developed—just as aspirin was—from coal tar, but are now made from petroleum products.

In the 1970s, Dr. Benjamin Feingold, a pediatric allergist from California, had success treating the symptoms of hyperactivity in some children by prescribing a diet that, among other things, eliminated artificial colorings. And some studies, including one published in The Lancet medical journal in 2007, have found that artificial colorings might lead to behavioral changes even in typical children.

The consumer science group asked the government to ban the dyes, or at least require manufacturers to include prominent warnings that "artificial colorings in this food cause hyperactivity and behavioral problems in some children."

Citizen petitions are routinely dismissed by the F.D.A. without much comment. Not this time. Still, the agency is not asking the experts to consider a ban during their two-day meeting, and agency scientists in lengthy analyses expressed skepticism about the scientific merits of the Lancet study and others suggesting any definitive link between dyes and behavioral issues. Importantly, the research offers almost no clue about the relative risks of individual dyes, making specific regulatory actions against, say, Green No. 3 or Yellow No. 6 almost impossible.

The F.D.A. scientists suggested that problems associated with artificial coloring might be akin to a peanut allergy, or "a unique intolerance to these substances and not to any inherent neurotoxic properties" of the dyes themselves. As it does for peanuts and other foods that can cause reactions, the F.D.A. already requires manufacturers to disclose on food labels the presence of artificial colorings.

A spokeswoman for General Mills refused to comment. Valerie Moens, a spokeswoman for Kraft Foods Inc., wrote in an e-mail that all of the food colors the company used were approved and clearly labeled, but that the company was expanding its "portfolio to include products without added colors," like Kool-Aid Invisible, Capri Sun juices and Kraft Macaroni and Cheese Organic White Cheddar.

The panel will almost certainly ask that more research on the subject be conducted, but such calls are routinely ignored. Research on pediatric behaviors can be difficult and expensive to conduct since it often involves regular and subjective assessments of children by parents and teachers who should be kept in the dark about the specifics of the test. And since the patents on the dyes expired long ago, manufacturers have little incentive to finance such research themselves.

Popular foods that have artificial dyes include Cheetos snacks, Froot Loops cereal, Pop-Tarts and Hostess Twinkies, according to an extensive listing in the consumer advocacy group's petition. Some grocery chains, including Whole Foods Market and Trader Joe's, refuse to sell foods with artificial coloring.

Critical Thinking

1. Why should the F.D.A. continue to investigate the relationship between food color and behavior change in children?

UNIT 4
Exercise and Weight Management

Unit Selections

Learning Outcomes

After reading this unit, you should be able to:

- Explain why exergames such as Wii are better suited for older rather than younger exercisers.

- Address ways to combat childhood obesity.

- Identify seven steps to incorporating the Mediterranean lifestyle.

- Explain how one can lose weight on a limited budget.

- Explain why it is important to exercise to achieve optimal health.

- Discuss why eliminating one particular food item a day will not likely lead to permanent weight loss.

Student Website
www.mhhe.com/cls

Internet References

American Society of Exercise Physiologists (ASEP)
www.asep.org
Cyberdiet
www.cyberdiet.com/reg/index.html
Shape Up America!
www.shapeup.org

Recently, a new set of guidelines, dubbed "Exercise Lite," has been issued by the U.S. Centers for Disease Control and Prevention in conjunction with the American College of Sports Medicine. These guidelines call for 30 minutes of exercise, five days a week, which can be spread over the course of a day. The primary focus of this approach to exercise is improving health, not athletic performance. Examples of activities that qualify under the new guidelines are walking your dog, playing tag with your kids, scrubbing floors, washing your car, mowing the lawn, weeding your garden, and having sex. From a practical standpoint, this approach to fitness will likely motivate many more people to become active and stay active. Remember, since the benefits of exercise can take weeks or even months before they become apparent, it is very important to choose an exercise program that you enjoy so that you will stick with it. Gretchen Reynolds describes a fun activity suitable for older exercisers in "Phys Ed: Why Wii Fit Is Best for Grandparents."

While a good diet cannot compensate for the lack of exercise, exercise can compensate for a less than optimal diet. Exercise not only makes people physically healthier, it also keeps their brains healthy. While the connection hasn't been proven, there is evidence that regular workouts may cause the brain to better process and store information, which results in a smarter brain.

While exercise and a nutritious diet can keep people fit and healthy, many Americans are not heeding this advice. For the first time in our history, the average American is now overweight when judged according to the standard height/weight tables. In addition, more than 25 percent of Americans are clinically obese, and the number appears to be growing. Even more alarming, a large percentage of the children in America are overweight or obese. Tina Schwager suggests ways to combat this problem in "Defeating Childhood Obesity."

Why is this happening, given the prevailing attitude that Americans have toward fat? One theory that is currently gaining support suggests that while Americans have cut back on their consumption of fatty snacks and desserts, they have actually increased their total caloric intake by failing to limit their consumption of carbohydrates. The underlying philosophy goes something like this: Fat calories make you fat, but you can eat as many carbohydrates as you want and not gain weight. The truth is that all calories count when it comes to weight gain, and if cutting back on fat calories prevents you from feeling satiated, you will naturally eat more to achieve that feeling. While this position seems reasonable enough, some groups, most notably supporters of the Atkins diet, have suggested that eating a high-fat diet will actually help people lose weight because of fat's high satiety value in conjunction with the formation of ketones (which suppress appetite). Whether people limit fat or carbohydrates, they will not lose weight unless their total caloric intake is less than their energy expenditure.

America's preoccupation with body weight has given rise to a billion-dollar industry. When asked why people go on diets, the predominant answer is for social reasons such as appearance and group acceptance, rather than concerns regarding health. Why do diets and diet aids fail? One of the major reasons lies in the mindset of the dieter. Many dieters do not fully understand the biological and behavioral aspects of weight loss, and consequently they have unrealistic expectations regarding the process.

Being overweight not only causes health problems; it also carries with it a social stigma. Overweight people are often thought of as weak-willed individuals with little or no self-respect. The notion that weight control problems are the result of personality defects is being challenged by new research findings. Evidence is mounting that suggests that physiological and hereditary factors may play as great a role in obesity as do behavioral and environmental factors. Researchers now believe that genetics dictate the base number of fat cells an individual will have, as well as the location and distribution of these cells within the body. The study of fat metabolism has provided additional clues as to why weight control is so difficult. These

© Getty Images/Jonelle Weaver

metabolic studies have found that the body seems to have a "setpoint," or desired weight, and it will defend this weight through alterations in basal metabolic rate and fat-cell activities. While this process is thought to be an adaptive throwback to primitive times when food supplies were uncertain, today, with our abundant food supply, this mechanism only contributes to the problem of weight control.

It should be apparent by now that weight control is both an attitudinal and a lifestyle issue. Fortunately, a new, more rational approach to the problem of weight control is emerging. This approach is based on the premise that you can be perfectly healthy and good looking without being pencil-thin. The primary focus of this approach to weight management is the attainment of your body's "natural ideal weight" and not some idealized, fanciful notion of what you would like to weigh. The concept of achieving your natural ideal body weight suggests that we need to take a more realistic approach to both fitness and weight control and also serves to remind us that a healthy lifestyle is based on the concepts of balance and moderation. Moderation such as eating well but reducing one high-calorie food per day as a means of weight control is covered in "In Obesity Epidemic, What's One Cookie?" How to eat a healthy, low-calorie diet without spending a fortune is discussed in "Dieting on a Budget."

The Mediterranean diet is widely accepted as a healthy way of eating. This acceptance by the medical community and popular press are encouraging Americans to adopt principles and foods of the Mediterranean lifestyle. " Eat Like a Greek " from *Consumer Reports on Health* leads the reader through practical steps of how to incorporate the Mediterranean lifestyle into daily life.

Phys Ed: Why Wii Fit Is Best for Grandparents

GRETCHEN REYNOLDS

With the Christmas video-game-buying season in full swing, now seems the right time to ask, Are active video games being aimed, at least in part, at the wrong audience? Active video games refer, of course, to games that require you to be active. Often also called exergames, they include the Wii Fit, Dance Dance Revolution from Konami and the new Microsoft Xbox Kinect and Sony PlayStation Move systems, among others. Depending on the game, they exhort players to hop, wriggle, serve and volley, left-hook a virtual boxing opponent or, in some other fashion, move. The underlying premise of these games is that, unlike Madden NFL 11 or Super Street Fighter IV, playing them should improve people's fitness and health.

But the latest science suggests that that outcome, desirable as it may be, is rarely achieved by most players, particularly the young. In theory, active games should come close to replicating the energy demands and physiological benefits of playing the actual sports they imitate. But as most of us might guess, they don't. Studies consistently have found that active video games, although they require more energy than simply watching television or playing passive video games, are not nearly as physically demanding as real sports and physical activities. A study published earlier this year in Medicine and Science in Sports and Exercise found that when adults "exergamed" in a metabolic chamber that precisely measured their energy expenditure, only 22 of the 68 active video games tested resulted in moderately intense exercise, similar to brisk walking. The vast majority were light-intensity activities, which burned few calories and raised heart rates only slightly. None of the games were as vigorous as a run or an actual tennis match, and few lasted long.

Another issue with exergames is that they do not contain images of viscera, explosions, chase scenes or aliens. Parents might applaud that. But many gamers do not. Several recent studies have found that young people often grow bored with exergaming. Three months into a recent six-month study of the effects of a dance game, for instance, only 2 of the 21 children participating were still using the game at least twice a week.

The importance of these various findings is clear. "At this point, there is little scientific evidence to suggest that exergames can be used alone to meet current guidelines for physical activity in young people," said Elaine Biddiss, Ph.D., an assistant professor at the University of Toronto and co-author of a review article published this summer in *The Archives of Pediatric and Adolescent Medicine* about children and active video gaming. Exergaming can be an adjunct to other activities, she and other experts say. It can be worthwhile if it replaces time sitting on the couch. But by themselves, active video games do not result in enough energy expenditure to keep children and teenagers fit.

But there may be another, unexpected group for whom exergaming might be extremely beneficial: grandparents. The number of research studies examining elderly exergame users remains small (as does the number of elderly exergamers). But the available results are provocative. A representative case study published last year found that an 89-year-old woman with a balance disorder and a history of falls significantly improved her scores on a series of balance tests after six sessions of Wii Bowling, an encouraging outcome given that, as the study authors point out, falls remain the leading cause of injury-related deaths in the elderly.

A broader study presented last month at the annual meeting of the Society for Neuroscience in San Diego produced similar results. For that experiment, researchers at Elon University in North Carolina recruited 11 healthy elderly volunteers (average age 75), and 15 undergraduates. The older group was, on the whole, notably healthy. Each lived on his or her own and exercised for about an hour a day. The young adults also were fit. The scientists asked both groups to complete several gaming sessions with the Wii Fit, receiving ready agreement. (There are worse ways to benefit science.)

The sessions began with balance tests, on either one or both legs. Everyone balanced well on two legs, but to the surprise of both subjects and scientists, the elderly volunteers "performed rather poorly" during the single-legged tests, said Caroline Ketcham, Ph.D., an assistant professor at Elon University and lead author of the study. "They thought they were in good shape and had good balance. It scared them a bit, frankly, to see how awful their balance really was."

After only a few sessions with the Wii Fit, though, the older volunteers improved their balance scores significantly, lowering their supposed "Wii age" (a score assigned by the game system, based primarily on balance tests) by about eight years. The young people improved by only about one year. The results suggest, Dr. Ketcham wrote, "that older adults would greatly benefit from balance training in their daily routines, and Wii Fit is an affordable and effective tool to use in their homes."

So perhaps we should consider redirecting those newly purchased Wii Fit or Kinect systems? Maybe we should be giving them to our parents, and having our children visit to set them up and stay to bowl or box with their grandparents.

Critical Thinking

1. For young athletes, are exergames the best option for fitness? Explain your answer.
2. What is the best type of fitness program for senior adults?

Defeating Childhood Obesity

Are you ready to step up to the challenge?

TINA SCHWAGER

There was a time when we, as kids, could ask our moms, "Can we go outside and play?" And they would respond, "OK, just be back by dinner time." Then we'd hop on our bikes and off we'd go. And we would play outside . . . all day long. In those days, we didn't have computers, or video games, or cell phones. Every kid knew how to throw and kick a ball, play a game of tag that could last for hours, and find things to keep busy until it was time to head home.

Things are different now. Today, kids can "play" with friends in a virtual world, and going outside simply to goof around is a rarity. An overabundance of conveniences makes most everything we do easier, faster and more connected with the mere push of a button. But those conveniences are a part of what is helping to destroy our kids.

To be blunt, a large percentage of kids in America are fat and unhealthy. In the past 20 years, "the prevalence of obesity among children ages 6 to 11 years has more than doubled," and more than tripled in adolescents ages 12 to 19.[2] Organizations such as the Centers for Disease Control and Prevention (CDC) and the American Obesity Association (AOA) have amassed the numbers on this disturbing epidemic: 30.3% of kids ages 6 to 11 are overweight, 15.3% are classified as obese, and for adolescents, 30.4% are estimated to be overweight and 15.5% obese.[5] The tendency toward overweight is slightly greater in boys than girls (32.7% to 27.8%[5]) and is an even bigger problem among lower-income and ethnic minority families where African-American, Hispanic and Native-American kids ". . . have a particularly high obesity prevalence."[5]

The American Obesity Association (AOA) defines overweight as being at or above 85% of one's Body Mass Index (BMI), and obesity as 95% of BMI.[5]

So, who or what is to blame? Unfortunately, multiple factors come into play, making ultimate victory over this problem something that demands a multifaceted attack.

Heredity

Several generations ago, a "chunky" kid was often attributed to some hefty relative, and the family gene pool took the hit. The unspoken assumption was that there is nothing one can do about heredity. But heredity alone is not responsible, since ". . . genetic characteristics of the human population have not changed in the last three decades, but the prevalence of obesity has tripled . . . ."[8] Combining poor dietary habits and lack of physical activity with a family history is what truly increases the risk for overweight and obesity.

Media

Call it entertainment, or a learning tool . . . it doesn't matter what you call it. Media tools such as computers, cell phones, video games, high-tech TVs and hand-held media devices (like music and movie players) are helping make young people fat. In 2007, the national Youth Risk Behavior Survey done by the Department of Health and Human Services, Centers for Disease Control and Prevention, found that 25% of high school kids played ". . . video or computer games or used a computer for something that was not school work for 3 or more hours per day on an average school day." And as for TV, 35% watched 3 or more hours a day.[6]

Sitting in front of a screen and watching others do things that grown-ups used to get out and actually do; playing with virtual friends or against foes instead of running around outside; texting instead of riding bikes together—all these tools of convenience lead to a reduction in physical activity and lots of mindless snacking. Studies like those done at Stanford Prevention Research Center indicate that kids snack more on unhealthy foods while involved in media activities, and ". . . may not stop eating when they are full because of the distraction."[4] Watching TV has been found to contribute to poor food choices in several ways—the ads often tout unhealthy or high-fat foods; passively watching robs kids of physical play time; and TV watching was actually found to lower kids' metabolic rates.[8]

What Is BMI?

There are many methods that try and determine fitness and health levels. The simplest and most practical way to screen for overweight and obesity is Body Mass Index, or BMI. It addresses the issue based solely on someone's weight in relation to their height. According to the CDC, BMI is the most widely accepted method to screen for overweight and obesity in kids and teens because:

- It is easy to obtain height and weight measurements
- It is noninvasive
- It correlates with body fatness.[7]

Less Physical Activity

For many kids, getting outside and playing has been replaced by technological interaction. While being at school used to guarantee at least a little bit of physical activity via recess and PE classes, funds to support physical education programs are, in many cases, simply not there. So unless a kid plays in a sports league or can afford to work with a pro of some type, their sports experience tends to be limited, and so does their overall level of physical exertion.

In addition, it simply isn't as safe as it used to be for kids to go outside and play. "Today's youth are considered the most inactive generation in history, caused in part by reduction in school physical education programs and unavailable or unsafe community recreation facilities."[5] Statistically, as of a 2007 study, 65% of high school students didn't meet recommended levels of physical activity and 70% didn't attend PE classes daily.[6] The CDC reports that daily PE participation among adolescents dropped from 42% in 1991 to 28% in 2003.[8]

Poor Nutrition

Everything is big these days—big TVs, big cars and big food portions. The airwaves show commercial after commercial advertising unhealthy foods and giant portions. And you can bet the mindless snacking that comes with too much media exposure doesn't include carrot sticks and hummus. Media driven snacking undoubtedly consists of empty calories that do nothing to contribute to growth and development while preventing kids from putting something nutritious into their bodies. High-fat, high-sodium, high-calorie snacks are everywhere. Media overload puts those items right in front of their hungry little faces.

According to the CDC, ". . . large portion sizes for food and beverages, eating meals away from home, [and] frequent snacking on energy-dense foods . . ."[8] are all factors in our kids' high-calorie world. And unlike a calorie conscious adult, kids don't know to change their intake at meals to balance the extra snack calories.

Another ticket to poor nutrition is the on-the-go lifestyle most families lead. The family schedule is often so jam-packed that meals are frequently eaten on the run. And, "when schedules get hectic, busy families turn to fast food."[4]

The Future Outlook

While multiple factors are responsible for the obesity epidemic among children, it's the fallout for the future that is undeniably frightening. Excess fat and body weight are directly linked to what are termed "diseases of excess," chronic conditions that used to be the burden of adults who overdid it by eating too much fatty, fried, salty and generally unhealthy food—coronary heart disease, high blood pressure, diabetes and certain forms of cancer. But now those conditions are showing up in our kids. Check out these statistics from the CDC and the AOA:

- Type 2 diabetes, formerly known as adult onset diabetes, accounted for 2 to 4% of childhood diabetics prior to 1992, but by 1994 that number jumped to 16%.[5]
- Type 2 diabetes has become so prevalent that it is estimated one in three American children born in 2000 will develop it in their lifetime.[1]
- Children who become obese by age 8 are found to be more severely obese as adults.[2]
- Eighty percent of kids who were overweight at age 10 to 15 were obese adults at age 25.[3]
- Early indicators of atherosclerosis are being seen in childhood and adolescence.[2]
- Elevated blood pressure levels occurred nine times more often in obese kids and adolescents.[5]
- Since developing bones and cartilage can't bear excess weight, orthopedic problems frequently develop in overweight kids, or lead to degenerative conditions in adulthood.[5]

So Now What?

The picture looks pretty grim. But government efforts through committees such as the CDC's Division of Adolescent and School Health are attempting to educate families and school personnel and create policies that help monitor and improve nutrition and activity habits at school. For example, the Coordinated School Health Program consists of eight components addressing the problem: health education, physical education, health services, nutrition services, counseling and social services, health promotion for staff, and community involvement.[1]

Outside of school, hope may lie in the hands of fitness professionals trained to reach out and educate young people. Some suggestions include:

- Create a basic level or specialty program just for kids and teens
- Offer seminars or other community outreach activities to teach kids strategies for taking control of their own well-being (nutrition classes, boot camp for teens, yoga for kids and dance-infused aerobics)
- Create a newsletter for your clients that is also available at local businesses or nearby schools to market your programs that help local youth.

Knowing the magnitude of this problem may inspire your facility to create something that could change not only the present, but the future of young lives. One at a time, a difference can be made.

References

1. "Addressing childhood obesity through nutrition and physical activity." U.S. Department of health and human services, centers for disease control and prevention. www.cdc.gov (Accessed Jun 29, 2010).
2. www.allergan.com/assets/pdf/obesity_fact_sheet.pdf (Accessed Jul 19, 2010).
3. "Childhood obesity: A growing problem." Stanford prevention research center. prevention.standford.Edu (Accessed Jun 29, 2010).
4. "Childhood overweight and obesity," 3/31/10. Centers for disease control and prevention. www.cdc.gov (Accessed Jun 29, 2010).
5. Overweight and obesity. www.cdc.gov/obesity/childhood/causes.html (Accessed Jul 19, 2010).
6. "Defining childhood overweight and obesity," 10/20/09. Centers for disease control and prevention. www.cdc.gov/obesity/childhood/defining.html (Accessed Jul 19, 2010).
7. "Nutrition and the health of young people," Nov 2008. U.S. Department of Health and Human Services, Centers for Disease Control and Prevention. www.cdc.gov/healthyouth/nutrition/facts.htm (Accessed Jul 20, 2010).
8. "The obesity epidemic and united states students." Department of health and human services, centers for disease control and prevention. www.cdc.gov/healthyyouth/yrbs/pdf/us_obesity-combo.pdk (Accessed Jul 19, 2010).

Critical Thinking

1. How important is exercise to achieving optimal health? Explain your answer.
2. Why should exercise be included in any weight control program?

TINA SCHWAGER, ATC, PTA, *is a certified Athletic Trainer and Physical Therapy Assistant with over 20 years' experience in outpatient orthopedic rehabilitation and sports conditioning. She is also the author of three self-help books for teenage girls, published by Free Spirit Publishing:* The Right Moves: A Girl's Guide to Getting Fit and Feeling Good, Gutsy Girls: Young Women Who Dare, *and* Cool Women, Hot Jobs. *Schwager has written extensively on topics related to fitness, sports medicine and motivation; created an informative online newsletter covering issues related to health, sports medicine and nutrition; and continues to publish articles nationally, both online and in print.*

From *American Fitness*, November/December 2010, pp. 18–20. Copyright © 2010 by Tina Schwager.

Eat Like a Greek

Want flavor plus good health? The Mediterranean style of dining has it all.

Diets are often doomed to fail because they focus more on what you can't eat than what you can. Don't eat bread. Don't eat sugar. Don't eat fat. On some diets, even certain fruits and vegetables are forbidden. After a few weeks of being told "no," our inner toddler throws a tantrum and runs screaming to Krispy Kreme.

That's what is so appealing about the Mediterranean diet, which isn't really a diet at all but a style of eating that focuses on an abundance of delicious, hearty, and nutritious food. Just looking at the pyramid at right, developed by Oldways Preservation Trust, a nonprofit organization that encourages healthy food choices, may be enough to make you look forward to the next meal.

"What I like about this approach to food is that it's very easy," says Sara Baer-Sinnott, executive vice president of Oldways. "It's not a fancy way of eating, but you'll never feel deprived because the foods have so much flavor."

The best part is that eating like a Greek not only satisfies your need to say yes to food, but has been scientifically proven to be good for your health. Decades of research has shown that traditional Mediterranean eating patterns are associated with a lower risk of several chronic diseases, including the big three—cancer, heart disease, and type 2 diabetes. Most recently, a systematic review of 146 observational studies and 43 randomized clinical trials published in the April 13, 2009, issue of the *Archives of Internal Medicine* found strong evidence that a Mediterranean diet protects against cardiovascular disease. Other recent research has linked the eating style to a lower risk of cognitive decline and dementia.

So, where do you start? Your next meal is as good a place as any. Just walk through our guide for menu planning.

Stepping into a Mediterranean Lifestyle

Although a trip to southern Italy or Greece would be nice, you needn't go farther than your local supermarket. If your menu planning usually begins with a meat entrée, then adds a starch and a vegetable side dish as an afterthought, you'll want to reprioritize your food choices. "Think about designing a plate where a good half of it is taken up with vegetables, another one-quarter is healthy grains—whole-grain pasta, rice, couscous, quinoa—and the remaining quarter is

lean protein," says Katherine McManus, R.D., director of nutrition at Brigham and Women's Hospital in Boston and a consultant on the most recent version of the Mediterranean pyramid. "Of course, you needn't physically separate your foods in that fashion, but it gives you a good idea of the proportions to aim for."

STEP 1: Start with plant foods. Build your menus around an abundance of fruits and vegetables (yes, even potatoes); breads and grains (at least half of the servings should be whole grains); and beans, nuts, and seeds. To maximize the health benefits, emphasize a variety of minimally processed and locally grown foods.

STEP 2: Add some lean protein. The Mediterranean diet draws much of its protein from the sea, reflecting its coastal origins. Fish is not only low in saturated fat but can also be high in heart-healthy omega-3 fatty acids. Aim for two servings of fish a week, especially those, such as salmon and sardines, that are high in omega-3s but lower in mercury. You can also include moderate amounts of poultry and even eggs.

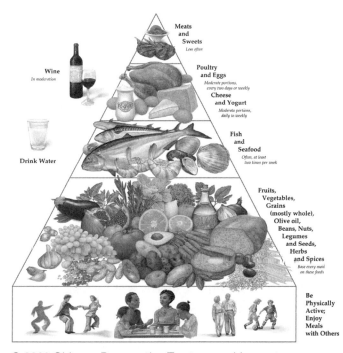

© 2009 Oldways Preservation Trust, www.oldwayspt.org

A Day in the Mediterranean Life

Breakfast

It's hard to go wrong with whole-grain cereal, fruit, and low-fat milk. Variations on the theme include low-fat yogurt with fresh berries and granola, or meaty steel-cut oats topped with fresh fruit, applesauce, whipped yogurt, or a sprinkle of nuts. Enjoy eggs? Try sautéing vegetables or greens in a bit of olive oil until soft and then scramble in a beaten egg. Go Greek with chopped olives and feta, or top with salsa and avocado for a Tex-Mex flair.

Lunch

Whether you're at home or brown-bagging, a Mediterranean lunch is tastier and healthier than drive-through fare and often faster and cheaper, too. Bagged salad greens provide a base for whatever you have on hand—fruit, vegetables, nuts, cheese, or a bit of leftover grilled chicken or fish. Consider topping it with a low-fat ranch dressing, an olive-oil vinaigrette, or just a drizzle of flavorful oil and a squeeze of fresh lemon. Or fill a whole-wheat pita pocket with hummus and as much fresh lettuce, peppers, cucumbers, and tomatoes as you can stuff in. If you're really pressed for time, heat up a can of low-sodium lentil, minestrone, or vegetable soup.

Snack Time

Keep a ready supply of fruit and veggies on hand so you'll grab them at snack time. Hummus, low-fat yogurt, and salad dressings pair nicely with them. If you don't want to invest the prep time, buy pre-cut. It's also a good idea to keep some nonperishable snacks at your desk or in your car—raisins or other dried fruit, nuts, and whole-grain crackers or pretzels.

Dinner

This is when many of us lose sight of nutrition goals because it's so easy after a long day to fall into old, comfortable habits. Fortunately, Mediterranean-style dining emphasizes simple foods and cooking methods.

While your pasta boils, for example, you can sauté a variety of vegetables in olive oil and garlic, then toss in a few shrimp and cook until they turn pink. Mix it all with a sprinkle of cheese, pour yourself a glass of wine, and you're sitting down to a relaxing dinner in less than 20 minutes.

In much the same manner, you can put together a quick stir-fry with slices of chicken breast, vegetables, and rice. Fresh fish is the simplest of entrées because it cooks quickly and doesn't take much dressing up. Spritz it with olive oil and your favorite seasonings and broil it, or coat it in bread crumbs and pan fry in a bit of olive oil. Squeeze on fresh lemon juice and adorn with parsley just before serving.

Two things you should have on hand for your evening meal: frozen vegetables, which are usually just as nutritious as fresh, and a plastic container of salad, preferably filled with a variety of greens. It's also a good idea to stock your crisper with seasonal fruit. A bowl of ripe berries, a chunk of melon, or a soft, farm-fresh peach is a delicious and satisfying end to any meal.

Oldways Preservation Trust, a nonprofit organization that promotes healthful eating, has more recipes and menu ideas on the two websites it sponsors: www.oldwayspt.org and www.mediterraneanmark.org.

Or substitute with vegetarian sources of protein, such as beans, nuts, or soy products. Limit red meat to a couple of servings a month, and minimize consumption of processed meats.

STEP 3: Say cheese. Include some milk, yogurt, or cheese in your daily meal. While low-fat versions are preferable, others are fine in small amounts. A sprinkle of high-quality Romano or Parmesan, for example, adds a spark to vegetables and pasta. Soy-based dairy products are fine, too, if you prefer them or are lactose intolerant.

STEP 4: Use oils high in "good" fats. Canola oil is a good choice, but many Mediterranean recipes call for olive oil. Both are high in unsaturated fat. Minimize artery-clogging saturated fat, which comes mainly from animal sources, and avoid the even more heart-harming trans fat, which comes from partially hydrogenated vegetable oil.

STEP 5: End meals with the sweetness of fruit. Make sugary and fatty desserts just an occasional indulgence.

STEP 6: Drink to your health. A moderate amount of alcohol—especially red wine—may help protect your heart. But balance that against the increased risks from drinking alcohol, including breast cancer in women. A moderate amount is one drink a day for women, two for men.

STEP 7: Step out. "The Mediterranean lifestyle is built around daily activity," McManus says. Go for a walk after dinner. And choose leisure activities that keep you moving.

Critical Thinking

1. Why do the authors support the use of the term Mediterranean lifestyle rather than Mediterranean diet?
2. Following a Mediterranean lifestyle has been associated with lower risk of several chronic diseases. What are five chronic diseases that are positively correlated with following the Mediterranean lifestyle?
3. An easy guide to Mediterranean meal planning is a meal of vegetables, whole grains, and lean protein. What proportions of the plate should each of these food groups make up in the meal?

Dieting on a Budget

Plus the secrets of thin people, based on our survey of 21,000 readers.

With jobs being cut and retirement accounts seemingly shrinking by the day, it's too bad our waistlines aren't dwindling, too. We can't rectify that cosmic injustice, but in this issue we aim to help you figure out the most effective, least expensive ways to stay trim and fit.

Though most Americans find themselves overweight by middle age, an enviable minority stay slim throughout their lives. Are those people just genetically gifted? Or do they, too, have to work at keeping down their weight?

To find out, the Consumer Reports National Research Center asked subscribers to *Consumer Reports* about their lifetime weight history and their eating, dieting, and exercising habits. And now we have our answer:

People who have never become overweight aren't sitting in recliners with a bowl of corn chips in their laps. In our group of always-slim respondents, a mere 3 percent reported that they never exercised and that they ate whatever they pleased. The eating and exercise habits of the vast majority of the always-slim group look surprisingly like those of people who have successfully lost weight and kept it off.

Both groups eat healthful foods such as fruits, vegetables, and whole grains and eschew excessive dietary fat; practice portion control; and exercise vigorously and regularly. The only advantage the always-slim have over the successful dieters is that those habits seem to come a bit more naturally to them.

"When we've compared people maintaining a weight loss with controls who've always had a normal weight, we've found that both groups are working hard at it; the maintainers are just working a little harder," says Suzanne Phelan, Ph.D., an assistant professor of kinesiology at California Polytechnic State University and co-investigator of the National Weight Control Registry, which tracks people who have successfully maintained a weight loss over time. For our respondents, that meant exercising a little more and eating with a bit more restraint than an always-thin person—plus using more monitoring strategies such as weighing themselves or keeping a food diary.

A total of 21,632 readers completed the 2007 survey. The always thin, who had never been overweight, comprised 16 percent of our sample. Successful losers made up an additional 15 percent. We defined that group as people who, at the time of the survey, weighed at least 10 percent less than they did at their heaviest, and had been at that lower weight for at least three years. Failed dieters, who said they would like to slim down yet still weighed at or near their lifetime high, were, sad to say, the largest group: 42 percent. (The remaining 27 percent of respondents, such as people who had lost weight more recently, didn't fit into any of the categories.)

An encouraging note: More than half of our successful losers reported shedding the weight themselves, without aid of a commercial diet program, a medical treatment, a book, or diet pills. That confirms

Price vs. Nutrition: Making Smart Choices

Although healthful foods often cost more than high-calorie junk such as cookies and soda, we unearthed some encouraging exceptions. As illustrated below, two rich sources of nutrients, black beans and eggs, cost mere pennies per serving—and less than plain noodles, which supply fewer nutrients. And for the same price as a doughnut, packed with empty calories, you can buy a serving of broccoli.

- **Cooked black beans**
  - Serving size 1/2 cup
  - Calories per serving 114
  - Cost per serving 74¢
- **Hard-boiled egg**
  - Serving size one medium
  - Calories per serving 78
  - Cost per serving 94¢
- **Cooked noodles**
  - Serving size 3/4 cup
  - Calories per serving 166
  - Cost per serving 134¢
- **Glazed doughnut**
  - Serving size 1 medium
  - Calories per serving 239
  - Cost per serving 324¢
- **Cooked broccoli**
  - Serving size 1/2 cup chopped
  - Calories per serving 27
  - Cost per serving 334¢
- **Chicken breast**
  - Serving size 4 oz.
  - Calories per serving 142
  - Cost per serving 364¢

Sources: Adam Drewnowski, Ph.D., director of the Center for Public Health Nutrition, University of Washington; USDA Nutrient Database for Standard Reference.

what we found in our last large diet survey, in 2002, in which 83 percent of "superlosers"—people who'd lost at least 10 percent of their starting weight and kept it off for five years or more—had done it entirely on their own.

Stay-Thin Strategies

Successful losers and the always thin do a lot of the same things—and they do them more frequently than failed dieters do. For the dietary strategies below, numbers reflect those who said they are that way at least five days a week, a key tipping point, our analysis found. (Differences of less than 4 percentage points are not statistically meaningful.)

Lifetime Weight History

Failed dieters: overweight and have tried to lose, but still close to highest weight. **Always thin:** never overweight. **Successful losers:** once overweight but now at least 10 percent lighter and have kept pounds off for at least three years.

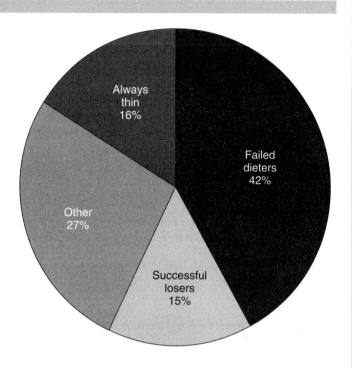

Strength Train at Least Once a Week

Always thin	31%
Successful loser	32%
Failed dieter	23%

Do Vigorous Exercise at Least Four Days a Week

Always thin	35%
Successful loser	41%
Failed dieter	27%

Eat Fruit and Vegetables at Least Five Times a Day

Always thin	49%
Successful loser	49%
Failed dieter	38%

Eat Whole Grains, Not Refined

Always thin	56%
Successful loser	61%
Failed dieter	49%

Eat Less Than 1/3 Calories from Fat

Always thin	47%
Successful loser	53%
Failed dieter	35%

Observe Portion Control at Every Meal

Always thin	57%
Successful loser	62%
Failed dieter	42%

Count Calories

Always thin	9%
Successful loser	47%
Failed dieter	9%

6 Secrets of the Slim

Through statistical analyses, we were able to identify six key behaviors that correlated the most strongly with having a healthy body mass index (BMI), a measure of weight that takes height into account. Always thin people were only slightly less likely than successful losers to embrace each of the behaviors—and significantly more likely to do so than failed dieters. By following the behaviors, you can, quite literally, live like a thin person.

Watch portions. Of all the eating behaviors we asked about, carefully controlling portion size at each meal correlated most strongly with having a lower BMI. Successful losers—even those who were still overweight—were especially likely (62 percent) to report practicing portion control at least five days per week. So did 57 percent of the always thin, but only 42 percent of failed dieters.

Portion control is strongly linked to a lower BMI.

Limit fat. Specifically, that means restricting fat to less than one-third of daily calorie intake. Fifty-three percent of successful losers and 47 percent of the always thin said they did that five or more days a week, compared with just 35 percent of failed dieters.

Eat fruits and vegetables. The more days that respondents ate five or more servings of fruits or vegetables, the lower their average BMI score. Forty-nine percent of successful losers and the always thin said they ate that way at least five days a week, while 38 percent of failed dieters did so.

Choose whole grains over refined. People with lower body weights consistently opted for whole-wheat breads, cereals, and other grains over refined (white) grains.

Eat at home. As the number of days per week respondents are restaurant or takeout meals for dinner increased, so did their weight. Eating at home can save a lot of money, too.

Exercise, exercise, exercise. Regular vigorous exercise—the type that increases breathing and heart rate for 30 minutes or longer—was strongly linked to a lower BMI. Although only about one quarter of respondents said they did strength training at least once a week, that practice was significantly more prevalent among successful losers (32 percent) and always thin respondents (31 percent) than it was among failed dieters (23 percent).

What Didn't Matter

One weight-loss strategy is conspicuously absent from the list: going low-carb. Of course we asked about it, and it turned out that limiting carbohydrates was linked to higher BMIs in our survey. That doesn't necessarily mean low-carb plans such as the Atkins or South Beach diets don't work. "If you go to the hospital and everyone there is sick, that doesn't mean the hospital made them sick," says Eric C. Westman, M.D., associate professor of medicine and director of the Lifestyle Medicine Clinic at Duke University Medical School. "Just as people go to hospitals because they're ill, people may go to carb restriction because they have a higher BMI, not the other way around." At the same time, the findings do suggest that cutting carbs alone, without other healthful behaviors such as exercise and portion control, might not lead to great results.

Eating many small meals, or never eating between meals, didn't seem to make much difference one way or another. Including lean protein with most meals also didn't by itself predict a healthier weight.

Realistic Expectations

Sixty-six percent of our respondents, all subscribers to *Consumer Reports,* were overweight as assessed by their body mass index; that's the same percentage as the population as a whole. One third of the overweight group, or 22 percent of the overall sample, qualified as obese.

Although that might seem discouraging, the survey actually contains good news for would-be dieters. Our respondents did much better at losing weight than published clinical studies would predict. Though such studies are deemed successful if participants are 5 percent lighter after a year, our successful losers had managed to shed an average of 16 percent of their peak weight, an average of almost 34 pounds. They had an impressive average BMI of 25.7, meaning they were just barely overweight.

One key to weight loss success is having realistic goals and our subscribers responses proved encouraging. A staggering 70 percent of them said they currently wanted to lose weight. But when we asked how many pounds they hoped to take off, we found that their goals were modest: The vast majority reported wanting to lose 15 percent or less of their overall body weight; 65 percent sought to lose between 1 and 10 percent. Keeping expectations in check might help dieters from becoming discouraged when they don't achieve, say, a 70-pound

---

Are You Overweight?

A body mass index under 25 is considered normal weight: from 25 to 29, overweight; and 30 or above, obese. To calculate your BMI, multiply your weight in pounds by 703, then divide by your height squared in inches.

---

weight loss or drop from a size 20 to a size 6—a common problem in behavioral weight loss studies.

Realistic goals are one key to weight loss.

What You Can Do

Weight loss is a highly individual process, and what matters most is finding the combination of habits that work for you. But our findings suggest that there are key behaviors common to people who have successfully lost weight and to those who have never gained it in the first place. By embracing some or all of those behaviors, you can probably increase your chances of weight-loss success, and live a healthier life in the process. In addition to following the steps above, consider these tips:

Don't get discouraged. Studies show that prospective dieters often have unrealistic ideas about how much weight they can lose. A 10 percent loss might not sound like much, but it significantly improves overall health and reduces risk of disease.

Ask for support. Though only a small minority of respondents overall reported that a spouse or family member interfered with their healthful eating efforts, that problem was much more likely among failed dieters, 31 percent of whom reported some form of spousal sabotage in the month prior to the survey. Ask housemates to help you stay on track by, for example, not pestering you to eat foods you're trying to avoid, or not eating those foods in front of you.

Get up and move. While regular vigorous exercise correlated most strongly with healthy body weight, our findings suggest that any physical activity is helpful, including activities you might not even consider exercise. Everyday activities such as housework, yard work, and playing with kids were modestly tied to lower weight. By contrast, hours spent sitting each day, whether at an office desk or at home watching television, correlated with higher weight.

Critical Thinking

1. Is it possible to diet on a limited food budget? Explain.
2. Why should exercise be included in any weight control program?

In Obesity Epidemic, What's One Cookie?

TARA PARKER-POPE

The basic formula for gaining and losing weight is well known: a pound of fat equals 3,500 calories.

That simple equation has fueled the widely accepted notion that weight loss does not require daunting lifestyle changes but "small changes that add up," as the first lady, Michelle Obama, put it last month in announcing a national plan to counter childhood obesity.

In this view, cutting out or burning just 100 extra calories a day—by replacing soda with water, say, or walking to school—can lead to significant weight loss over time: a pound every 35 days, or more than 10 pounds a year.

While it's certainly a hopeful message, it's also misleading. Numerous scientific studies show that small caloric changes have almost no long-term effect on weight. When we skip a cookie or exercise a little more, the body's biological and behavioral adaptations kick in, significantly reducing the caloric benefits of our effort.

Small caloric changes have almost no long-term effect on weight, studies show.

But can small changes in diet and exercise at least keep children from gaining weight? While some obesity experts think so, mathematical models suggest otherwise.

As a recent commentary in *The Journal of the American Medical Association* noted, the "small changes" theory fails to take the body's adaptive mechanisms into account. The rise in children's obesity over the past few decades can't be explained by an extra 100-calorie soda each day, or fewer physical education classes. Skipping a cookie or walking to school would barely make a dent in a calorie imbalance that goes "far beyond the ability of most individuals to address on a personal level," the authors wrote—on the order of walking 5 to 10 miles a day for 10 years.

This doesn't mean small improvements are futile—far from it. But people need to take a realistic view of what they can accomplish.

"As clinicians, we celebrate small changes because they often lead to big changes," said Dr. David Ludwig, director of the Optimal Weight for Life program at Children's Hospital Boston and a co-author of the JAMA commentary. "An obese adolescent who cuts back TV viewing from six to five hours each day may then go on to decrease viewing much more. However, it would be entirely unrealistic to think that these changes alone would produce substantial weight loss."

Why wouldn't they? The answer lies in biology. A person's weight remains stable as long as the number of calories consumed doesn't exceed the amount of calories the body spends, both on exercise and to maintain basic body functions. As the balance between calories going in and calories going out changes, we gain or lose weight.

But bodies don't gain or lose weight indefinitely. Eventually, a cascade of biological changes kicks in to help the body maintain a new weight. As the JAMA article explains, a person who eats an extra cookie a day will gain some weight, but over time, an increasing proportion of the cookie's calories also goes to taking care of the extra body weight. Eventually, the body adjusts and stops gaining weight, even if the person continues to eat the cookie.

Similar factors come into play when we skip the extra cookie. We may lose a little weight at first, but soon the body adjusts to the new weight and requires fewer calories.

Regrettably, however, the body is more resistant to weight loss than weight gain. Hormones and brain chemicals that regulate your unconscious drive to eat and how your body responds to exercise can make it even more difficult to lose the weight. You may skip the cookie but unknowingly compensate by eating a bagel later on or an extra serving of pasta at dinner.

"There is a much bigger picture than parsing out the cookie a day or the Coke a day," said Dr. Jeffrey M. Friedman, head of Rockefeller University's molecular genetics lab, which first identified leptin, a hormonal signal made by the body's fat cells that regulates food intake and energy expenditure. "If you ask anyone on the street, 'Why is someone obese?,' they'll say, 'They eat too much.'"

"That is undoubtedly true," he continued, "but the deeper question is why do they eat too much? It's clear now that there are many important drivers to eat and that it is not purely a conscious or higher cognitive decision."

This is not to say that the push for small daily changes in eating and exercise is misguided. James O. Hill, director of the Center for Human Nutrition at the University of Colorado Denver, says that while weight loss requires significant lifestyle changes, taking away extra calories through small steps can help slow and prevent weight gain.

In a study of 200 families, half were asked to replace 100 calories of sugar with a noncaloric sweetener and walk an extra 2,000 steps a day. The other families were asked to use pedometers to record their exercise but were not asked to make diet changes.

During the six-month study, both groups of children showed small but statistically significant drops in body mass index; the group that also cut 100 calories had more children who maintained or reduced body mass and fewer children who gained excess weight.

The study, published in 2007 in Pediatrics, didn't look at long-term benefits. But Dr. Hill says it suggests that small changes can keep overweight kids from gaining even more excess weight.

"Once you're trying for weight loss, you're out of the small-change realm," he said. "But the small-steps approach can stop weight gain."

While small steps are unlikely to solve the nation's obesity crisis, doctors say losing a little weight, eating more heart-healthy foods and increasing exercise can make a meaningful difference in overall health and risks for heart disease and diabetes.

"I'm not saying throw up your hands and forget about it," Dr. Friedman said. "Instead of focusing on weight or appearance, focus on people's health. There are things people can do to improve their health significantly that don't require normalizing your weight."

Dr. Ludwig still encourages individuals to make small changes, like watching less television or eating a few extra vegetables, because those shifts can be a prelude to even bigger lifestyle changes that may ultimately lead to weight loss. But he and others say that reversing obesity will require larger shifts—like regulating food advertising to children and eliminating government subsidies that make junk food cheap and profitable.

"We need to know what we're up against in terms of the basic biological challenges, and then design a campaign that will truly address the problem in its full magnitude," Dr. Ludwig said. "If we just expect that inner-city child to exercise self-control and walk a little bit more, then I think we're in for a big disappointment."

Critical Thinking

1. Can eliminating one food serving a day contribute to a lasting weight loss? Explain.

2. Should obesity be classified as a disease rather than the result of a lack of willpower? Explain.

UNIT 5

Drugs and Health

Unit Selections

Learning Outcomes

After reading this unit, you should be able to:

- Describe how statin drugs work.

- Distinguish between the risks versus benefits of statin drugs.

- Address the health risks associated with the use of caffeinated alcoholic beverages marketed to young people.

- Describe the process of overcoming an addiction and explain why relapsing is the rule rather than the exception.

Student Website

www.mhhe.com/cls

Internet References

Food and Drug Administration (FDA)
www.fda.gov
National Institute on Drug Abuse (NIDA)
www.nida.nih.gov

As a culture, Americans have come to rely on drugs not only as a treatment for disease but also as an aid for living normal, productive lives. This view of drugs has fostered a casual attitude regarding their use and resulted in a tremendous drug abuse problem. Drug use and abuse has become so widespread that there is no way to describe the typical drug abuser.

There is no simple explanation for why America has become a drug-taking culture, but there certainly is evidence to suggest some of the factors that have contributed to this development.

From the time that we are children, we are constantly bombarded by advertisements about how certain drugs can make us feel and look better. While most of these ads deal with proprietary drugs, the belief created is that drugs are a legitimate and effective way to help us cope with everyday problems. Certainly drugs can have a profound effect on how we feel and act, but research has also demonstrated that our mind plays a major role in the healing process. For many people, it's easier to take a drug than to adopt a healthier lifestyle. They are more willing to take statin drugs to lower their cholesterol than to change their diet, exercise, and lose weight. Tara Parker-Pope addresses this issue related to usage of one of the most commonly prescribed medicines in the United States in "Great Drug, but Does It Prolong Life?"

Growing up, most of us probably had a medicine cabinet full of prescription and over-the-counter (OTC) drugs, freely dispensed to family members to treat a variety of ailments. This familiarity with drugs, coupled with rising health care costs, has prompted many people to diagnose and medicate themselves with OTC medications without sufficient knowledge of the possible side effects. Though most of these preparations have little potential for abuse, it does not mean that they are innocuous. Generally speaking, OTC drugs are relatively safe if taken at the recommended dosage by healthy people, but the risk of dangerous side effects rises sharply when people exceed the recommended dosage. Another potential danger associated with the use of OTC drugs is the drug interactions that can occur when they are taken in conjunction with prescription medications. The gravest danger associated with the use of OTC drugs is that an individual may use them to control symptoms of an underlying disease and thus prevent its early diagnosis and treatment.

While OTC drugs can be abused, an increasing number of drug-related deaths over the past five years have been linked to prescription drugs. These drugs such as opiate-based painkillers include OxyContin, Darvon, and Vicodin and are often used as an alternative to an illicit high.

As a culture, we have grown up believing that there is, or should be, a drug to treat any malady or discomfort that befalls us. Would we have a drug problem if there was no demand for drugs? One drug that is used widely in the United States is alcohol, especially on college campuses. Every year over 1,000 students die from alcohol-related causes, mostly drinking and driving. In "Caffeinated Alcohol in a Can, Four Loko Does the Job, Students Agree," author Don Troop discusses risks associated with students drinking caffeinated alcoholic beverages including missed classes, falling behind in school work, damage

© Ingram Publishing / AGE Fotostock

to property, traffic accidents, and injuries that occur while under the influence of alcohol.

While alcohol abuse among college students is a serious issue, drinking among pregnant women is also a concern. Women who drink during their pregnancies risk delivering a baby who could suffer from a range of effects including physical, emotional, mental, behavioral, and cognitive abnormalities.

In addition to alcohol, another widely used legal drug is tobacco. Millions still smoke despite all the well-publicized health effects linked to smoking. Many Americans have quit and many others would like to quit. To facilitate this process, some companies have developed programs to help employees quit the habit. Since smoking and its related diseases cost approximately $150 billion dollars each year, the stakes are enormous. Kathleen McGowan discusses the frequency in which people relapse while trying to change harmful health behaviors in "The New Quitter."

Great Drug, but Does It Prolong Life?

Tara Parker-Pope

Statins are among the most prescribed drugs in the world, and there is no doubt that they work as advertised—that they lower not only cholesterol but also the risk for heart attack.

But in the fallout from the headline-making trial of Vytorin, a combination drug that was found to be no more effective than a simple statin in reducing arterial plaque, many people are asking a more fundamental question about statins in general: Do they prolong your life?

And for many users, the surprising answer appears to be no.

Some patients do receive significant benefits from statins, like Lipitor (from Pfizer), Crestor (AstraZeneca) and Pravachol (Bristol-Myers Squibb). In studies of middle-aged men with cardiovascular disease, statin users were less likely to die than those who were given a placebo.

But many statin users don't have established heart disease; they simply have high cholesterol. For healthy men, for women with or without heart disease and for people over 70, there is little evidence, if any, that taking a statin will make a meaningful difference in how long they live.

"High-risk groups have a lot to gain," said Dr. Mark H. Ebell, a professor at the University of Georgia who is deputy editor of the journal American Family Physician. "But patients at low risk benefit very little if at all. We end up overtreating a lot of patients." (Like the other doctors quoted in this column, Dr. Ebell has no ties to drug makers.)

How is this possible, if statins lower the risk of heart attack? Because preventing a heart attack is not the same thing as saving a life. In many statin studies that show lower heart attack risk, the same number of patients end up dying, whether they are taking statins or not.

"You may have helped the heart, but you haven't helped the patient," said Dr. Beatrice Golomb, an associate professor of medicine at the University of California, San Diego, and a co-author of a 2004 editorial in *The Journal of the American College of Cardiology* questioning the data on statins. "You still have to look at the impact on the patient over all."

A 2006 study in *The Archives of Internal Medicine* looked at seven trials of statin use in nearly 43,000 patients, mostly middle-aged men without heart disease. In that review, statins didn't lower mortality.

Nor did they in a study called Prosper, published in *The Lancet* in 2002, which studied statin use in people 70 and older. Nor did they in a 2004 review in The Journal of the American Medical Association, which looked at 13 studies of nearly 20,000 women, both healthy and with established heart disease.

Indications are that statins aren't all they're cracked up to be.

A Pfizer spokeswoman notes that a decline in heart disease death rates reported recently by the American Heart Association suggests that medications like statins are having an impact. But to consistently show a mortality benefit from statins in a research setting would take years of study. "We've concentrated on whether Lipitor reduces risk of heart attacks and strokes," says Halit Bander, medical team leader for Lipitor. "We've proven that again and again."

This month, *The Journal of the American College of Cardiology* published a report combining data from several studies of people 65 and older who had a prior heart attack or established heart disease. This "meta-analysis" showed that 18.7 percent of the placebo users died during the studies, compared with 15.6 percent of the statin users.

This translates into a 22 percent lower mortality risk for high-risk patients over 65. A co-author of the study, Dr. Jonathan Afilalo, a cardiology fellow at McGill University in Montreal, says that for every 28 patients over 65 with heart disease who take statins, one life will be saved.

"If a patient has had a heart attack," Dr. Afilalo said, "they generally should be on a statin."

Of course, prolonging life is not the only measure that matters. If preventing a heart attack improved the quality of life, that would be an argument for taking statins even if it didn't reduce mortality. But critics say there's no evidence that statin users have a better quality of life than other people.

"If you can show me one study that people who have a disability from their heart are worse off than people who have a disability from other causes, I would find that a compelling argument," Dr. Golomb said. "There's not a shred of evidence that you've mitigated suffering in the groups where there is not a mortality benefit."

One big concern is that the side effects of statins haven't been well studied. Reported side effects include muscle pain, cognitive problems and impotence.

"Statins have side effects that are underrated," said Dr. Uffe Ravnskov, a retired Swedish physician and a vocal critic of statins. "It's much more frequent and serious than has been reported."

Dr. Ebell acknowledges that there are probably patients with heart disease who could benefit from a statin but who aren't taking it.

But he added, "There are probably more of the opposite—patients who are taking a statin when they probably don't need one."

Critical Thinking

1. What are the risks versus benefits of using statin drugs?
2. How do statin drugs reduce the risk of heart disease?

Caffeinated Alcohol in a Can, Four Loko Does the Job, Students Agree

Don Troop

It's friday night in this steep-hilled college town, and if anyone needs an excuse to party, here are two: In 30-minutes the Mountaineers football team will kick off against the UConn Huskies in East Hartford, Conn., and tonight begins the three-day Halloween weekend.

A few blocks from the West Virginia University campus, young people crowd the aisles of Asherbrooke Liquor Outlet, an airy shop that is popular among students. One rack in the chilled-beverage cooler is nearly empty—the one that is usually filled with 23.5-ounce cans of Four Loko, a fruity malt beverage that combines the caffeine of two cups of coffee with the buzz factor of four to six beers.

"That's what everyone's buying these days," says an employee. "Loko and Burnett's vodka," a line of distilled spirits that are commonly mixed with nonalcoholic energy drinks like Red Bull and Monster to create fruity cocktails with a stimulating kick.

Four Loko's name comes from its four primary ingredients—alcohol (12 percent by volume), caffeine, taurine, and guarana. Although it is among dozens of caffeinated alcoholic drinks on the market, Four Loko has come to symbolize the dangers of such beverages because of its role in binge-drinking incidents this fall involving students at New Jersey's Ramapo College and at Central Washington University. Ramapo and Central Washington have banned Four Loko from their campuses, and several other colleges have sent urgent e-mail messages advising students not to drink it. But whether Four Loko is really "blackout in a can" or just the highest-profile social lubricant of the moment is unclear.

Just uphill from Asherbrooke Liquor Outlet, four young men stand on a porch sipping cans of Four Loko—fruit punch and cranberry-lemonade. All are upperclassmen except for one, Philip Donnachie, who graduated in May. He says most Four Loko drinkers he knows like to guzzle a can at home before meeting up with friends, a custom that researchers in the field call "predrinking."

"Everyone that's going to go out for the night, they're going to start with a Four Loko first," Mr. Donnachie says, adding that he generally switches to beer.

A student named Tony says he paid $5.28 at Ashebrooke for two Lokos—a bargain whether the goal is to get tipsy or flat-out drunk.

Before the drink became infamous, he says, he would see students bring cans of it into classrooms. "The teachers didn't know what it was," Tony says, and if they asked, the student would casually reply, "It's an energy drink."

Farther uphill, on the sidewalk along Grant Avenue, the Tin Man from *The Wizard of Oz* carries a Loko—watermelon flavor, judging by its color. Down the block a keg party spills onto the front porch, where guests sprawl on a sofa and flick cigarette ashes over the railing. No one here is drinking Four Loko, but most are eager to talk about the product because they've heard that it could be banned by the federal government as a result of the student illnesses.

It's among dozens of caffeinated alcoholic drinks on the market, but Four Loko has come to symbolize the dangers of them all because of its role in binge-drinking incidents on colleges campuses this fall.

Research Gap

That's not likely to happen anytime soon, according to the Food and Drug Administration.

"The FDA's decision regarding the regulatory status of caffeine added to various alcoholic beverages will be a high priority for the agency," Michael L. Herndon, an FDA spokesman, wrote in an e-mail message. "However, a decision regarding the use of caffeine in alcoholic beverages could take some time." The FDA does not consider such drinks to be "generally recognized as safe." A year ago the agency gave 27 manufacturers 30 days to provide evidence to the contrary, if it existed. Only 19 of the companies have responded.

Dennis L. Thombs is chairman of the department of social and behavioral sciences at the University of North Texas Health Science Center, in Fort Worth. He knows a great deal about the drinking habits of young people.

Last year he was the lead author of a paper submitted to the journal *Addictive Behaviors* that described his team's study of bar patrons' consumption of energy drinks and alcohol in the college town of Gainesville, Fla.

After interviewing 802 patrons and testing their blood-alcohol content, Mr. Thombs and his fellow researchers concluded that energy drinks' labels should clearly describe the ingredients, their amounts, and the potential risks involved in using the products.

But Mr. Thombs says the government should have more data before it decides what to do about alcoholic energy drinks.

"There's still a big gap in this research," he says. "We need to get better pharmacological measures in natural drinking environments," like bars.

He says he has submitted a grant application to the National Institutes of Health in hopes of doing just that.

"Liquid Crack"

Back at the keg party in Morgantown, a student wearing Freddy Krueger's brown fedora and razorblade glove calls Four Loko "liquid crack" and says he prefers not to buy it for his underage friends. "I'll buy them something else," he says, "but not Four Loko."

Dipsy from the *Teletubbies* says the people abusing Four Loko are younger students, mostly 17- and 18-year-olds.

He calls the students who became ill at Ramapo and Central Washington "a bunch of kids that don't know how to drink."

Two freshmen at the party, Gabrielle and Meredith, appear to confirm that assertion.

"I like Four Loko because it's cheap and it gets me drunk," says Gabrielle, 19, who seems well on her way to getting drunk tonight, Four Loko or not. "Especially for concerts. I drink two Four Lokos before going, and then I don't have to spend $14 on a couple drinks at the stadium."

Meredith, 18 and equally intoxicated, says that although she drinks Four Loko, she favors a ban. "They're 600 calories, and they're gross."

An interview with Alex, a 19-year-old student at a religiously affiliated college in the Pacific Northwest, suggests one reason that the drink might be popular among a younger crowd. In his state and many others, the laws that govern the sale of Four Loko and beer are less stringent than those for hard liquor.

That eases the hassle for older friends who buy for Alex. These days that's not a concern, though. He stopped drinking Four Loko because of how it made him feel the next day.

"Every time I drank it I got, like, a blackout," says Alex. "Now I usually just drink beer."

Critical Thinking

1. What are the risks associated with the use of caffeinated alcoholic beverages?

The New Quitter

Falling off the wagon—whether by bakery binge or drug bender—doesn't mean total defeat. In fact, relapse is the best teacher on the road to recovery.

KATHLEEN MCGOWAN

Diane Potvin has been sober for 23 years, but is still acutely aware that she could fall off the wagon.

Mike Di Ioia lost more than 100 pounds by sticking to a rigid diet, but is haunted by memories of being sick, overweight, and afraid of dying. Diane Webber-Thrush tries to stop a modest wine-drinking habit, but a rough day at the office sends her back to the liquor store.

The dirty little secret about addictions is that relapsing is the rule, not the exception. Up to 80 percent of alcoholics treated for a drinking problem will hit the bottle again at least once. Between 60 and 90 percent of smokers light up within a year of stopping, and more than 90 percent of the gamblers who quit on their own will eventually place another bet. Even minor bad habits are hard to break: People make the same New Year's resolution for an average of five years running before they maintain the change for even six months.

When it comes to major behavioral changes—anything from losing weight to quitting hard drugs—few people do it perfectly the first time. For most, it's a long and winding road.

Yet many people do eventually overcome their bad habits. There are more ex-smokers (48 million) than current smokers (46 million) in the United States. In the biggest American survey of alcohol use, only one-quarter of the people dependent on alcohol were still drinking heavily the following year. Another long-term study revealed that for cocaine addicts who had gone through treatment, more than half were clean five years later.

Such statistics have inspired a new psychology of addiction that puts the problem of relapse front and center. It recognizes that relapse is distressingly common—but also that it can be just a stumble on the road to recovery. In fact, if handled the right way, a relapse can actually open the door to lasting success.

If handled the right way, a relapse can actually open the door to lasting success.

The abstinence-only doctrines that once dominated the thinking about addiction have given way to a more flexible—and more forgiving—approach. Overcoming a habit is understood to be a slow and halting process that is often plagued with slip-ups and setbacks. This understanding is motivated in part by evidence from neuroscience that addictions change the brain in ways that can take a long time to undo. "The last 10 years have given us a picture from a lot of different areas of science that once addiction sets in, it takes on the character of a chronic illness," says Jon Morgenstern, director of substance abuse services at Columbia University Medical Center in New York City. "It's very difficult for people to maintain behavioral change. Relapse is considered a part of the condition."

By the same token, relapse is no longer seen as a catastrophe. A fall off the wagon may feel like a failure that cancels out all the hard work of quitting, but that all-or-nothing perspective doesn't square with the facts, says G. Alan Marlatt, a professor of psychology and director of the Addictive Behaviors Research Center at the University of Washington. "It's like learning to ride a bicycle. Almost everybody falls at least once." A relapse can provide useful information. The trick is to view an episode of backsliding as a chance to learn, an opportunity to develop better techniques for anticipating and avoiding or overcoming urges. This insight applies to a range of problems, from life-threatening drug addictions to compulsions like overeating.

Out with Black-and-White Thinking

When Marlatt started working in an alcoholism ward in the 1960s, roughly 70 percent of the clients he saw bounced in and out of hospital-based treatment programs. But addiction counselors weren't supposed to acknowledge the high rate of relapse: The thinking then was talking about that would "just give people permission to do it," Marlatt recalls. Frustrated, he began studying how successful quitters maintained their sobriety over time. "We found that many had slips or lapses, and were able to get back on the wagon again," says Marlatt. "They were learning from their mistakes, and figuring out what to do next time."

He developed a recovery model that addressed the reality of relapse, identifying common triggers and concrete psychological skills that helped people get back on the straight and narrow.

One of his early insights was that black-and-white thinking can turn a minor lapse into a major one. After a small slip, many people throw in the towel. A new ex-smoker has a couple of drags of a friend's cigarette, bums another, and then buys a pack, figuring she's already negated all her progress. This "abstinence-violation effect," as Marlatt named it, is the belief that anything less than perfection is total failure. It leads the quitter to conclude he just doesn't have the willpower to succeed.

But having just one slipup does not inevitably lead to a full-blown relapse. The slide back into addiction can be reversed. Addiction psychologist Stanton Peele describes it as multiple stations of a journey. The first "stop" for a drinker might be seeing an old drinking buddy at a bar. The drinker could "get off" at that point by leaving. If he stays, he could order ginger ale. If he does have a beer, he can "get off" at the next stop by going home rather than drinking more. The idea is that there are many opportunities to avert a total relapse.

Listening to Professor Relapse

Marlatt encourages the backslider to see lapses as errors rather than defeats. Instead of stewing in guilt, the quitter should think analytically about how it occurred, dissecting the circumstances. What was he feeling? What happened earlier that day? Who was around? "We try to make it a learning process," says Marlatt. "We say: 'Hey, you fell off the wagon. How would you handle it differently next time?'" With this mentality, a recovering addict can learn to identify the situations that are likely to push him into a relapse. He can embrace the possibility of failure and see the broader horizon of change beyond it.

This mentality can help prevent the lapse from spiraling into a full-blown crisis, says Joshua P. Smith, assistant professor and program coordinator for the outpatient substance abuse clinic at the Medical University of South Carolina. "It's important to minimize the time spent in that slip, and the consequences of it," he says. Reframing relapses as learning experiences can enhance a quitter's confidence and resolve, giving him or her the mental energy to stick with it.

One of the reasons relapses are so common is that temptations seem to emerge out of nowhere. In fact, many invisible pressures, psychological and circumstantial, may build gradually, then suddenly combine to push you over the edge. For Diane Webber-Thrush, the moment came after a rough episode at her job at an educational nonprofit in Washington, D.C. Five months before, she had quit a long-standing habit, which was drinking a couple of glasses of wine every night after work. In the annals of vices, it was pretty mild: She stopped at two, so she didn't get drunk or have a hangover. But she didn't like the fact that she depended on the wine each night to relax. "It wasn't optional, and I saw that as a danger signal," she says.

So she quit. Every night, she walked right past the wine store and relaxed by listening to music instead. But then the pressure ramped up at work just as her boisterous 6-year-old twins went through an especially energetic phase. One day last fall, she got chewed out for missing a minor deadline. Walking out the door, she told herself, "I deserve a glass of wine at the end of this day." She bought a bottle on the way home, intending to have just one glass, and quickly slid back into her old two-drinks-a-night habit. "I reopened the door to the wine store, literally," she sighs. "And I haven't closed it yet."

Two types of factors play into such relapses. To learn from her slipup, Webber-Thrush could analyze them: *proximal* or short-term situational factors, and *distal* or underlying causes. Proximal factors often include personal conflicts, bad moods, and unpredictable events. For her, those would be the missed deadline and the reprimand. The biggest distal factor in her case might just be the fact that being a working mother demands a lot of energy and patience. "My life is wonderful, but it's stressful," she says. "I come home to little boys who are bouncing off the walls." Other common distal factors include having poor social support—your friends and family might be unavailable or even undermining. Not knowing how to recognize your feelings can be another underlying problem; if you don't realize what you are feeling, anger or frustration may overwhelm you.

By identifying proximal and distal factors, it's easier to anticipate and respond to an urge. Relapses often follow a similar pattern, psychologist Saul Shiffman has found in his studies of smokers. He uses a technique called "ecological momentary assessment" to scrutinize the exact moment of relapse. Smokers who are trying to quit get electronic diaries that regularly prompt them to record their mood and surroundings. If they do yield to temptation and light up, they are asked to fill out a more detailed record, including location, activity, and consumption of food or drink.

Being around other smokers and drinking alcohol are powerful triggers. No surprise there. But Shiffman found that the number-one predictor of lapses was emotional: the level of "negative affect" during the four to five hours leading up to the lapse. Anger, anxiety, depression, and upset are the most powerful potentiators, especially a bad mood that ramps up over a period of hours. "It's not a matter of how you feel these days, but a matter of hours and minutes," Shiffman told a national smoking cessation conference in the UK. "Life can come at you rather fast sometimes." Studies of alcohol, cocaine, and heroin relapses suggest that the same dynamic may be at work in these addictions.

The number one predictor of lapses is emotional: the level of "negative affect" during the four to five hours leading up to the lapse.

Plans, Tactics, and Grand Pursuits

Identifying the factors behind a relapse is only the start; the crucial step is to make an explicit plan to counteract or avoid them. If an addiction is not debilitating or severe, it is possible

Don't Be Trigger Happy

How to Navigate Potential Relapse Scenarios

1. **Your former drinking buddy is in town and wants to take you out.**

   The warmer the relationship, the more likely you'll remember the bonding and not the bad consequences of getting smashed together.

   The Plan: Tell him you're not drinking and you'd like to go to a cafe. If the place doesn't serve, he can't nudge you to join him. Arrange for a supportive tee-totaling friend to pick you up later in the evening, in case you feel tempted to move to a bar for old time's sake.

2. **You had a fight with your sweetheart, and now you're brooding.**

   The biggest predictor of relapses among smokers in one study was a negative mood that gets worse over a period of hours. Anxiety, anger, and tension can fester and build.

   The Plan: Know that you risk relapsing for the rest of the day, not just in the moments after the blow-out. Suggest the two of you go to a movie, where you can't smoke and you're bound to get distracted into a better frame of mind.

3. **Everyone is feting Becky in the conference room at 4 PM.**

   You'll look like a non-team player if you skip a workplace celebration, but if you go, you're bound to leave with a belly full of powdered sugar.

   The Plan: Walk in armed with your own healthy snack and bottle of water. Your hands will be too full to hold a slice of cake but you can still sing "Happy Birthday."

to engage in that exercise yourself, says James McKay, a professor of psychology in psychiatry at the University of Pennsylvania. "Some people are better at that than others, and you need some time to think about it," he says. The plan should be concrete: Webber-Thrush could change her route so that she doesn't walk past the wine store, for example.

People who are in the thrall of a life-threatening or mind-altering addiction may need professional help to analyze triggers and come up with a coping plan, says Morgenstern. In his work with alcoholics undergoing treatment, he asks them to think through potential scenarios that might emerge in the coming months, and helps each of them develop a plan to avoid the hazards. Each is unique: One person might be vulnerable to boredom, another to stress. "We ask, 'What are the situations that can potentially get you into trouble?' " says Morgenstern. "It's like disaster preparedness—you want to have a disaster kit at home."

Dieter Mike Di Ioia, a New Jersey-based graphic designer, has made a "disaster kit" out of a meticulous plan that itemizes every bite of food he puts in his mouth. Each day, he gets up at 5, has a cup of yogurt and hits the gym. At 10 AM he has exactly 28 pieces of cereal, and at 11 AM an apple. The rest of the day is mapped out just as precisely, to ensure he will never be blindsided by hunger and cravings. "I've always been goal-oriented," Di Ioia says. He writes down everything he eats, scripts detailed shopping lists, and has healthy low-calorie foods like carrots or fruit on hand at all times. (Quite a change for somebody who used to down two Big Mac meals at one sitting.)

He has thought through potential pitfalls and has plans for each of them. If someone brings pizzas into the office, he goes for a walk. If his train gets delayed on the way to the office, he has an alternate gym workout that takes less time. Di Ioia has shed 137 pounds since last summer, and is still losing weight. By preparing rigorously, he relapsed only once: pasta and stuffing at Thanksgiving, after which he got right back on his program.

Cognitive tricks are another way to prevent relapse. Marlatt teaches what he calls "urge surfing"—learning to mentally detach yourself from the craving by monitoring the way your desire builds and then recedes. In one study, he tantalized smokers by giving them cigarettes to hold and light, but did not allow them to actually inhale. They were asked to visualize their craving as an actual wave that rose and fell, and to imagine riding along with the wave rather than struggling against it. A week later, the participants who had been taught this and other techniques smoked an average of one-and-a-half cigarettes a day less than a control group.

Another trick is cultivating a vivid memory of the past you are trying to leave behind. Morgenstern found that people with a stronger "past-harm appraisal"—an enduring painful memory of the damage done by their addiction—were less likely to relapse. Di Ioia, for example, flashes back to the week and a half he spent in the hospital with a heart arrhythmia brought on in part by his bad habits. "Now, if I start overeating, I think about the way I was a year ago, and what it was like to be in that place"—seriously overweight and worried about his health. That mental image is a "kick in the ass," he says. The testimonials that are a part of every 12-step meeting serve the same effect.

A wide range of coping techniques can be effective, Shiffman found in his studies of smokers: Eating or drinking as a diversion, distracting yourself, escaping the situation, or focusing on the consequences of giving in. But doing *something* is essential: People who use some kind of coping technique in response to an urge are 25 times more likely to resist the temptation than those who try to just gut it out.

Cognitive techniques are just half of the equation. Morgenstern and other addiction psychologists also encourage recovering addicts to develop meaningful life goals, which may have been forgotten or cast aside in the obsession of addiction. Quitters need to reconnect with parts of life that provide pleasure, enjoyment and meaning—so-called "emotional future goals," as Morgenstern puts it. Renewing ties with friends and family and becoming involved in naturally rewarding activities weaken the pull of the addiction. New goals that are incompatible with the old habit—bicycling 50 miles instead of smoking, or looking good in a tight dress instead of eating donuts—also help. "It's not enough to have the threat of punishment," says Morgenstern. "People need to be embedded in a life that is rewarding."

> **Quitters need to reconnect with parts of life that provide pleasure, enjoyment, and meaning.**

A Long and Worthy Cause

THE FLIP SIDE of accepting relapse is recognizing that the work of kicking an addiction may never be fully complete. The way many researchers describe addiction today is a "chronic disease" that may be in remission but is rarely fully cured. It has been 23 years since Connecticut resident Diane Potvin has had a drink, but she says she is still "petrified" of relapse. She fell hard into alcoholism, and it controlled her life for a long time. "I never drew a sober breath for twenty-some-odd years," she says. All her friends drank; she had no career, no place to live, and no idea how to put her life back on track. At age 42, she went into a treatment plan, and slowly put the pieces into place. Now, in her work as director of recovery community centers for Connecticut Community for Addiction Recovery, she's seen people spiral back into addiction after many years of sobriety. For her, personally, the memories of her old bad life haunt her.

"I know if I pick up a drink, I am unemployed, I am homeless. Sooner or later, that's what's going to happen."

Even long after vanquishing an old bad habit, it's not entirely erased from the brain—on a biological level, the connections are still there. Continued "booster shots" of treatment or reevaluation may be necessary months or even years after stopping. "People can't just turn the light switch on and off," says Smith. "If somebody who smoked crack but has been sober for years comes across a crack pipe, they'll react."

So the real milestone to celebrate isn't the day you quit, or even your 20-year anniversary. It's every day you get back on track after a relapse. It's those nights that you decide to go home before you backslide because you know you want to get up early for a run. Eventually, moment by moment, the little successes add up. The result: one big triumph.

Critical Thinking

1. Why do so many people relapse when trying to change a harmful health behavior?
2. Does a relapse mean failure? Explain your answer.

KATHLEEN MCGOWAN is a science writer living in New York City.

From *Psychology Today,* July/August 2010, pp. 78–84. Copyright © 2010 by Sussex Publishers, LLC. Reprinted by permission.

UNIT 6

Sexuality and Relationships

Unit Selections

Learning Outcomes

After reading this unit, you should be able to:

- Understand how to end a relationship with dignity.
- Explain why conservatives might value and support same-sex marriage.
- Explain what role pornography may play in relationships.
- Describe why pornography may be considered adultery.

Student Website

www.mhhe.com/cls

Internet References

Planned Parenthood
www.plannedparenthood.org
Sexuality Information and Education Council of the United States (SIECUS)
www.siecus.org

Sexuality is an important part of both self-awareness and intimate relationships. But, how important is physical attraction in establishing and maintaining intimate relationships? Researchers in the area of evolutionary psychology have proposed numerous theories that attempt to explain the mutual attraction that occurs between the sexes. The most controversial of these theories postulates that our perception of beauty or physical attractiveness is not subjective but rather a biological component hardwired into our brains. It is generally assumed that perceptions of beauty vary from era to era and culture to culture, but evidence is mounting that suggests that people all over share a common sense of beauty that is based on physical symmetry. In addition to a sense of physical beauty, researchers believe that scent is an important component of who we end up with. Physical attraction may be based on smell, which may be a significant component of what we think of as "chemistry" between partners.

While physical attraction is clearly an important issue when it comes to dating, how important is it in long-term loving relationships? For many Americans the answer may be very important, because we tend to be a "Love Culture," a culture that places a premium on passion in the selection of our mates. Is passion an essential ingredient in love, and can passion serve to sustain a long-term meaningful relationship? Since most people can't imagine marrying someone that they don't love, we must assume that most marriages are based on this feeling we call love. That being the case, why is it that so few marriages survive the rigors of day-to-day living? Perhaps the answer has more to do with our limited definition of love rather than love itself.

The idea that pornography is related to marital infidelity has been a topic of discussion in recent years. Ross Douthat discusses this problem in "Is Pornography Adultery?" With the increase in online options to view pornography, there appears to be a connection to divorce.

The breakup of a relationship can be painful. Elizabeth Svoboda delves into how to end a relationship with dignity and without devaluing oneself or the other person in "The Thoroughly Modern Guide to Breakups." She also maintains that relationships can be ended with minimal distress and offers advice on how this can be accomplished.

"The Conservative Case for Gay Marriage" covers the controversial issue of same-sex marriage. While there are many individuals who oppose marriage for same sex couples, Theodore B. Olson believes that marriage for gay couples promotes the values that are supported by conservatives such as the creation of a loving household. Although many conservatives do not support same-sex marriage, Olson argues that the legalization of same sex marriage is a basic recognition of American principles and equal rights

Another important topic of interest and controversy in the area of human sexuality is sex education. While most states mandate some type of school-based sex education, many parents believe that they should be the source of their children's sex education and not the schools. Although the concept of "safe sex" is nothing new, the degree of open and public discussion regarding sexual behaviors is. With the emergence of AIDS as a disease of epidemic proportions and the rapid spreading of other sexually transmitted diseases (STDs), the surgeon general

© Royalty-Free/Corbis

of the United States initiated an aggressive educational campaign, based on the assumption that knowledge would change behavior. If STD rates among teens are any indication of the effectiveness of this approach, then we must conclude that our educational efforts are failing. Conservatives believe that while education may play a role in curbing the spread of STDs, the root of the problem is promiscuity, and that promiscuity rises when a society is undergoing a moral decline. The solution, according to conservatives, is a joint effort between parents and educators to teach students the importance of values such as respect, responsibility, and integrity. Liberals, on the other hand, think that preventing promiscuity is unrealistic, and instead the focus should be on establishing open and frank discussions between the sexes. Their premise is that we are all sexual beings, and the best way to combat STDs is to establish open discussions between sexual partners, so that condoms will be used correctly when couples engage in intercourse.

While education undoubtedly has had a positive impact on slowing the spread of STDs, perhaps it was unrealistic to think that education alone was the solution, given the magnitude and the nature of the problem. Most experts agree that for education to succeed in changing personal behaviors, the following conditions must be met: (1) The recipients of the information must first perceive themselves as vulnerable and, thus, be motivated to explore replacement behaviors and (2) the replacement behaviors must satisfy the needs that were the basis of the problem behaviors. To date most education programs have failed to meet these criteria. Given all the information that we now have on the dangers associated with AIDS and STDs, why is it that people do not perceive themselves at risk? It is not so much the denial of risks as it is the notion of most people that they use good judgment when it comes to choosing sex partners. Unfortunately, most decisions regarding sexual behavior are based on subjective criteria that bear little or no relationship to one's actual risk. Even when individuals do view themselves as vulnerable to AIDS and STDs, there are currently only two viable options for reducing the risk of contracting these diseases. The first is the use of a condom and the second is sexual abstinence, neither of which is an ideal solution to the problem.

The Thoroughly Modern Guide to Breakups

Yes, breaking up is hard to do, and we're primed to avoid delivering or digesting such deeply threatening news. Still, It's possible to end affairs with dignity and minimal distress.

ELIZABETH SVOBODA

Julie Spira isn't just any writer. She bills herself as an expert on Internet dating, and wrote a book called *The Perils of Cyber-Dating*. When, in 2005, she met The Doctor on an online dating site, Spira was positive she'd finally found The One. "He seemed very solid and close to his family," Spira recalls. He made it clear on their first date that, after the end of a lengthy marriage and a year of serial dating, he was looking for an enduring relationship. "That was very appealing to me."

She took it as a sign of his integrity. It didn't hurt that he was handsome, too. Eight months of exclusive dating later, The Doctor asked her to marry him.

They planned a simple wedding. But first, they put their individual homes up for sale so they could buy a place together. They went house-hunting together nearly every weekend. When her father got sick, The Doctor saved his life.

Fourteen months into their engagement, Spira received an email from her fiancé titled, simply, "Please Read This." She put the message aside to savor after work and other commitments. When she finally clicked on it, she wished she hadn't. "The email had an attached document. It said I was not the woman for him, that the relationship was over, and to please send back the ring. It said my belongings would be delivered tomorrow," Spira says. "I sat there and my whole body started to shake."

Spira had to plaster on a happy face for a few days—her parents were renewing their marriage vows at a family party on the other side of the country and she wasn't yet ready to tell anyone about the broken engagement. "I wore my ring. I pretended my fiancé had an emergency and couldn't make it. Then I went to my room and sobbed in secret." Once home, she cried every day for a month. Then another electronic communiqué arrived from The Doctor. It said, in its entirety, "Are you OK?"

That was all she ever heard from him.

The breakup left her socially paralyzed. She didn't, couldn't, date, even after many months. She remains single today, three years later. Disappointment ignites anger when she thinks about what happened. "It was cowardly and cruel. Where's the human side of it? Where's the respect from someone who was devoted to you for two years?" It's scant comfort when people tell her that Berger dumped Carrie by Post-it note on *Sex and the City*. "With email, you don't even have a guarantee that the person got your message."

Saying good-bye is heartbreaking, and most of us are total jerks about it. Bad dumping behavior is booming, especially among the young. In one recent survey, 24 percent of respondents aged 13 to 17 said it was completely OK to break up with someone by texting, and 26 percent of them admitted to doing so. "It's always been hard to break up with someone face to face," says Stanford University sociologist Clifford Nass, author of *The Man Who Lied to His Laptop*, "but lack of social skills makes it harder. And we're learning fewer and fewer social skills."

As a result, remote shortcuts like electronic endings look deceptively appealing—although, at the very least, they chip away at the self-respect of the dumpers and deprive dumpees of a needed shot at closure. Little wonder that hypersensitivity to rejection is on the rise, and it's contributing to large increases in stalking behavior, especially on college campuses. More than 3 million people report being stalking victims each year, the ultimate measure of collective cluelessness about ending love affairs well.

Hypersensitivity to rejection is on the rise, and it's contributing to large increases in stalking behavior.

As drive-by breakups like Spira's become more common, mastering the art of the ending is more necessary than ever. The average age of first marriage now hovers around 27, five years later than in 1970. Most people are having more and more serious relationships before they find the one that works. The emerging social reality demands some preparation for romantic rejection, given its potential to shatter one's sense of self.

The Clean Dozen: 12 Rules of Better Breakups

No question, breaking up is incredibly difficult because it involves giving, or receiving, bad news that engages our deepest vulnerability—the fear that we are unlovable. Most of us are designed not only to minimize discomfort but to dislike rupturing attachments, priming us for sleights of avoidance in delivering or digesting such deeply threatening information. It takes courage to recognize we have a moral obligation to put aside personal discomfort in approaching someone we cared for and who loved us—especially when means of ducking that responsibility are so readily available. But courage pays dividends in self-respect and accelerated recovery.

Not only do our biology, psychology, and morality influence how we weather breakups, but so do the circumstances of the act. There may be little anyone can do to alter biological responsiveness, but everyone can control the way breaking up is conducted. Here, say the experts, is how to do it so that both parties remain emotionally intact, capable of weathering the inevitable pain and sadness.

1. **Take full responsibility for initiating the breakup.**
   If your feelings or needs have changed, your dreams diverged, or your lives are going in opposite directions, don't provoke your partner into doing the breakup. Shifting responsibility is not only a weasel tactic that diminishes the doer, says Paul Falzone, CEO of the online dating service eLove, it's confusing. Adds Russell Friedman, executive director of the California-based Grief Recovery Institute and author of *Moving On,* "Trying to manipulate your partner into breaking up, like suddenly giving one-word answers in an attempt to make them say, 'The heck with it,' creates a sense of real distortion." The partner may not initially get the message that you want to break up, but "will start to question themselves: 'Am I not a valuable human being? Am I unattractive?'" The target may also question their own instincts and intuition. "You're setting up the sense that the other person is to blame. You have bypassed their intuition—they can't trust what they felt, saw, heard in the relationship." That kind of uncertainty can cripple them in future relationships; they may not be willing to trust a new partner's devotion or suitability.

2. **Do it only face to face.** Humans evolved to communicate face to face, which provides some built-in consolations. We may experience many nonverbal cues that reassure us of our essential lovability—the quick touch on the arm that says you're still valued even as the relationship ends. Anything less than face-to-face sends a distressing message: "You don't matter."

   Some dumpers might think that delivering the news by email, text, or even a Facebook statement is less cruel than directly speaking the truth. But remote modes of delivery actually inflict psychic scars on the dumpee that can impede future partnerships. "When you don't get any explanation, you spend a huge amount of time trying to figure out what's wrong with you," says eLove's Paul Falzone. "And you'll be hesitant about entering another relationship."

Being on the receiving end of remote dumping can leave us stuck in emotional limbo, says University of Chicago neuroscientist John Cacioppo. "The pain of losing a meaningful relationship can be especially searing in the absence of direct social contact." With no definitive closure, we're left wondering what the heck happened, which can lead to the kind of endless rumination that often leads to depression.

"Situations where you have an incomplete picture of what's going on are perfect ground for the development of rumination," says Yale University psychologist Susan Nolen-Hoeksema. "It can send people into a tailspin." Many dumpees emerge from the tailspin distrustful of others, making it difficult for them to establish closeness with future partners. "When you begin to distrust others, you make less of an investment in them," adds Bernardo Carducci, professor of psychology at Indiana University Southeast. "So the person you meet next is going to suffer for the sins of a stranger."

Dumpers themselves may come to regret surrogate sayonaras once they realize how badly their vanishing act hurt their former partners—and how little concern they showed. "Five years on, you don't want to be ashamed of how you handled this," says John Portmann, a moral philosopher at the University of Virginia. Guilt and shame encumber future interactions.

3. **Act with dignity.** Since a breakup is a potentially explosive scenario, resolve in advance to bite back any insults that are poised to fly out of your mouth. Preserving your partner's self-respect has the compound effect of salvaging your own.

4. **Be honest.** "I'm not in love with you anymore" is actually OK. But honesty need not be a bludgeon, nor does it demand total disclosure. If you secretly think your partner is a complete snooze in bed, you're probably better off keeping that opinion to yourself. "You have an obligation to watch out for the other person's self-esteem," Virginia's Portmann says. "Do not cut them down in such a way that it's impossible for them to have another successful relationship. Why rub salt in their wounds? That's torture."

   "The message to get across is, 'You're not what I'm looking for,'" adds Florida State University psychologist Roy Baumeister. "That doesn't imply that there's something wrong or deficient about your partner." It's simply straightforward.

5. **Avoid big, bad clichés like "It's not you, it's me."** Such generic explanations ring false and communicate a lack of respect. You owe your partner a genuine explanation, however brief, of why things aren't working. One big caveat: If you suspect that your partner might react violently to your decision to end the relationship, don't stick around to justify your reasoning; safety comes first.

6. **Avoid a point-by-point dissection of where things fell apart.** "It's not a good idea because there's never going to be agreement," says Russell Friedman. "I'll say, 'This is what happened,' and you'll say, 'No, no.'"

Prolonged back-and-forth often degenerates into a fight—or worse: If your partner gains the upper hand, he or she may succeed in luring you back into a dysfunctional relationship you've decided you want to end.

7. **Make it a clean break.** Do not try to cushion the blow by suggesting future friendly meetups. "Saying 'Let's be friends' might be a way for the rejecter to try to handle their own guilt, but it's not always good for the person being rejected," Baumeister observes. Such a misguided attempt to spare a partner pain can leave him or her hopeful there might be a chance at future reconciliation, which can hinder the efforts of both parties to move on.

8. **Communicate ongoing appreciation of the good times you shared.** In exchanging good-byes, it's even desirable, says Friedman. It's equally fine to confide disappointment that the hopes you shared for a future together won't be realized. Such statements convey a continued belief in your partner's inherent value.

9. **Don't protest a partner's decision.** And don't beg him or her to reconsider later on. The best thing a dumpee can do to speed emotional healing is to accept that the relationship has come to an unequivocal end. In her neuroimaging studies, Helen Fisher found that the withdrawal-like reaction afflicting romantic rejectees diminished with time, indicating that they were well on their way to healing. But the recovery process is fragile, says Fisher, and last-ditch attempts to make contact or win back an ex can scuttle it. "If you suddenly get an email from the person, you can get right into the craving for them again." To expedite moving on, she recommends abstaining from any kind of contact with the rejecter: "Throw out the cards and letters. Don't call. And don't try to be friends."

10. **Don't demonize your ex-partner.** It's a waste of your energy. And avoid plotting revenge; it will backfire by making him or her loom ever larger in your thoughts and postpone your recovery.

11. **Don't try to blot out the pain you're feeling, either.** Short of the death of a loved one, the end of a long-term relationship is one of the most severe emotional blows you'll ever experience. It's perfectly normal—in fact, necessary—to spend time grieving the loss. "Love makes you terribly vulnerable," Portmann says. "If you allow yourself to fall in love, you can get hurt really badly." The sooner you face the pain, the sooner it passes.

12. **Resist thinking you've lost your one true soul mate.** Don't tell yourself you've lost the one person you were destined to be with forever, says Baumeister. "There's something about love that makes you think there's only one person for you, and there's a mythology surrounding that. But there's nothing magical about one person." In reality, there are plenty of people with whom each of us is potentially compatible. It might be difficult to fathom in the aftermath of a breakup, but chances are you'll find someone else.

For both parties, the experience influences how—or even whether—one moves on with life and love.

The best breakups, if there is such a thing, enable acceptance and minimize psychic wreckage, so that the pain of the ending doesn't overwhelm the positive trace of the relationship. For the partnership will take up permanent residence in memory, likely to be revisited many times over the years. The challenge of breaking up is to close the relationship definitively and honorably, without devaluing oneself or the person who previously met one's deepest needs. Yes, Virginia, people can fall out of love with grace and dignity—if only they learn how to give breakups a chance.

Initially, everyone reacts to rejection like a drug user going through withdrawal.

Battered by Biology

Because our brains are wired from the beginning for bonding, breakups batter us biologically. Initially, says Rutgers University anthropologist Helen Fisher, everyone reacts to rejection like a drug user going through withdrawal. In the early days and weeks after a breakup, she has found, just thinking about the lover who dumped us activates several key areas of the brain—the ventral tegmental area of the midbrain, which controls motivation and reward and is known to be involved in romantic love; the nucleus accumbens and the orbitofrontal/ prefrontal cortex, part of the dopamine reward system and associated with craving and addiction; and the insular cortex and anterior cingulate, associated with physical pain and distress.

As reported in a recent issue of the *Journal of Neurophysiology*, Fisher rounded up 15 people who had just experienced romantic rejection, put them in an fMRI machine, and had them look at two large photographs: an image of the person who had just dumped them and an image of a neutral person to whom they had no attachment. When the participants looked at the images of their rejecters, their brains shimmered like those of addicts deprived of their substance of choice. "We found activity in regions of the brain associated with cocaine and nicotine addiction," Fisher says. "We also found activity in a region associated with feelings of deep attachment, and activity in a region that's associated with pain."

Fisher's work corroborates the findings of UCLA psychologist Naomi Eisenberger, who discovered that social rejection activates the same brain area—the anterior cingulate—that generates an adverse reaction to physical pain. Breakups likely stimulate pain to notify us how important social ties are to human survival and to warn us not to sever them lightly.

Although Eisenberger didn't study romantic rejection, she expects that it actually feels much worse than the social rejection she did document. "If you're getting pain-related activity from someone you don't care about, it would presumably be a lot more painful from someone you share memories with," she points out.

The intensity of the pain may be what compels some spurned lovers to stalk their ex-partners; they're willing to do just about anything to make the hurt go away. Fisher believes that activation of addictive centers in response to breakups also fuels stalking behavior, explaining "why the beloved is so difficult to give up."

A Time of Broken Dreams

Biology is nowhere near the whole story. Attachment styles that emerge early in life also influence how people handle breakups later on—and how they react to them. Those with a secure attachment style—whose caregivers, by being generally responsive, instilled a sense of trust that they would always be around when needed—are most likely to approach breakups with psychological integrity. Typically, they clue their partners in about any changes in their feelings while taking care not to be hurtful.

On the receiving end of a breakup, "the secure person acknowledges that the loss hurts, but is sensible about it," says Phillip Shaver, a University of California, Davis psychologist who has long studied attachment behavior. "They're going to have an undeniable period of broken dreams, but they express that to a reasonable degree and then heal and move on."

By contrast, people who develop an anxious or insecure attachment style—typically due to inconsistent parental attention during the first years of life—are apt to try to keep a defunct relationship going rather than suffer the pain of dissolving it. "The anxious person is less often the one who takes the initiative in breaking up," Shaver says. "More commonly, they hang on and get more angry and intrusive."

On the receiving end of a breakup, the insecurely attached react poorly. "They don't let go," says Shaver. "They're more likely to be stalkers, and they're more likely to end up sleeping with the old partner." Their defense against pain—refusing to acknowledge that the relationship is over—precludes healing. They pine on for the lost love with little hope of relief.

Whether we bounce back from a breakup or wallow in unhappiness also depends on our general self-regard. In a University of California, Santa Barbara study where participants experienced rejection in an online dating exchange, people with low self-esteem took rejection the worst: They were most likely to blame themselves for what had happened and to rail against the rejecter. Their levels of the stress hormone cortisol ran particularly high. Such reactivity to romantic rejection often creates unhealthy coping strategies—staying home alone night after night, for example, or remaining emotionally closed off from new partners.

People with high self-esteem were not immune to distress in the face of romantic rejection, whether they were rejecter or rejectee, but they were less inclined to assume a lion's share of the blame for the split. Best of all, they continued to see themselves in a positive light despite a brush-off.

Critical Thinking

1. How can couples end their relationship with dignity and without devaluing each other?

Elizabeth Svoboda is a freelance writer in San Jose, California.

The Conservative Case for Gay Marriage

Why Same-Sex Marriage Is an American Value

THEODORE B. OLSON

Together with my good friend and occasional courtroom adversary David Boies, I am attempting to persuade a federal court to invalidate California's Proposition 8—the voter-approved measure that overturned California's constitutional right to marry a person of the same sex.

My involvement in this case has generated a certain degree of consternation among conservatives. How could a politically active, lifelong Republican, a veteran of the Ronald Reagan and George W. Bush administrations, challenge the "traditional" definition of marriage and press for an "activist" interpretation of the Constitution to create another "new" constitutional right?

My answer to this seeming conundrum rests on a lifetime of exposure to persons of different backgrounds, histories, viewpoints, and intrinsic characteristics, and on my rejection of what I see as superficially appealing but ultimately false perceptions about our Constitution and its protection of equality and fundamental rights.

Many of my fellow conservatives have an almost knee-jerk hostility toward gay marriage. This does not make sense, because same-sex unions promote the values conservatives prize. Marriage is one of the basic building blocks of our neighborhoods and our nation. At its best, it is a stable bond between two individuals who work to create a loving household and a social and economic partnership. We encourage couples to marry because the commitments they make to one another provide benefits not only to themselves but also to their families and communities. Marriage requires thinking beyond one's own needs. It transforms two individuals into a union based on shared aspirations, and in doing so establishes a formal investment in the well-being of society. The fact that individuals who happen to be gay want to share in this vital social institution is evidence that conservative ideals enjoy widespread acceptance. Conservatives should celebrate this, rather than lament it.

Legalizing same-sex marriage would also be a recognition of basic American principles, and would represent the culmination of our nation's commitment to equal rights. It is, some have said, the last major civil-rights milestone yet to be surpassed in our two-century struggle to attain the goals we set for this nation at its formation.

Ted Olson would seem the unlikeliest champion of gay marriage. Now 69 years old, he is one of the more prominent Republicans in Washington and among the most formidable conservative lawyers in the country. As head of the Office of Legal Counsel under Ronald Reagan, he argued for ending racial preferences in schools and hiring, which he saw—and still sees—as a violation of the Constitution's guarantee of equal protection under the law. Years later, he advised Republicans in their efforts to impeach President Clinton. In 2000 he took the "Bush" side in *Bush v. Gore,* out-arguing his adversary (and friend) David Boies before the Supreme Court and ushering George W. Bush into the White House. As solicitor general under Bush, he defended the president's claims of expanded wartime powers. (Olson's wife at the time, Barbara, died on American Airlines Flight 77, which was crashed into the Pentagon on September 11, 2001.) Olson has won three quarters of the 56 cases he has argued before the high court. Feather quills commemorating each case, and signed thank-you photos from presidents, cover the walls of his Washington office.

Now once again in private practice, Olson has the time to take on causes that matter most to him. One of them has surprised, dismayed, and outraged many of his conservative friends and colleagues. This week, after months of preparation, he will argue on behalf of two gay couples in *Perry v. Schwarzenegger,* a federal case challenging Proposition 8, the California ballot initiative that outlawed same-sex marriage in the state.

Olson's brief against Prop 8 is straightforward: laws banning gay marriage not only make no sense, but are also unconstitutional. As a conservative, he says he believes in individual liberty and freedom from government interference in the private lives of citizens. Discriminating against people because of sexual orientation is a violation of both. "This case could change the way people think about one another," says Olson. "We are forever putting people into this box or that box, instead of just seeing each other as human beings."

He took on the case last fall, after he received a call from Chad Griffin, a Bay activist in California who was part of a team looking for a lawyer to challenge Prop 8. A former in-law of Olson's suggested they reach out to Olson. Griffin was skeptical. "He was the conservative enemy," he recalls thinking. Griffin was surprised to find that Olson was anything but hostile. The two men talked for hours. Olson spent the next several weeks consulting with friends, fellow lawyers, and family, starting with his wife and political sparring partner, Lady Booth Olson, herself an attorney and a Democrat. He put the same question to all of them: why shouldn't gay people have the right to marry? "I asked them to give me their best argument. They had all sorts of intangible instincts and feelings about what's 'right,'" he says. "But I didn't hear any persuasive response."

Still, Olson knew he would need help in preparing a sturdy case. Even if he prevails, the state will almost certainly appeal; ultimately the case may wind up before the Supreme Court—a possibility Olson clearly relishes. He had no doubt whom he wanted beside him at the plaintiff's table: Boies, his old liberal courtroom adversary and biking buddy. A fearsome litigator, Boies didn't hesitate to take on such a high-profile case. "The current administration has been decidedly halfway on this issue," he says, "and I think the specter of having George Bush's lawyer out in front of a Democratic president is something that, shall we say, might stimulate people to rethink their positions."

It has done that already, not all of it favorable to Olson. Some conservatives have accused him of apostasy, and of trying to bend the Constitution to fit clandestine liberal views. Ed Whelan, a lawyer who worked with Olson in the Bush administration, says his first reaction was "surprise, followed by disgust that Ted would abandon the legal principles he's purported to stand for, like originalism and judicial restraint." But Whelan also knows that Olson—who arrives at work each morning by 6:30 and reads centuries-old law texts in his spare time—is a formidable adversary. "There's a definite chance he'll win. That's what makes it all the more outrageous that he's pushing this."

"There's a definite chance he'll win. That's what makes it all the more outrageous that he's pushing this," says one conservative colleague.

Many gay activists weren't any happier at first, believing an incremental approach was safer than betting everything on one big case. They feared a loss would be a massive setback. "Racial segregation, for example, didn't take just one case; there were a series of strategic steps," says Molly McKay of Marriage Equality USA. Others sensed conspiracy, speculating that Olson took the case only to throw it. He has since convinced them he is genuine in his conviction that gay marriage is a civil-rights issue.

In fact, Olson is surprisingly emotional about the case, and his eyes mist up repeatedly when he talks about the hundreds of letters—positive and negative—that he's received. "We should be welcoming our gay colleagues and friends as equals," he says. Kristin Perry, one of the plaintiffs in the case, says that whenever Ted sees her and her partner, Sandy Stier, "he tells us, 'I think about you two every day. This is the reason I've taken this case.'" Some conservatives, still trying to figure out what happened to their old friend, have asked him when he decided he was for gay marriage. Olson seems puzzled by the question. "I don't know that I was ever against it."

This bedrock American principle of equality is central to the political and legal convictions of Republicans, Democrats, liberals, and conservatives alike. The dream that became America began with the revolutionary concept expressed in the Declaration of Independence in words that are among the most noble and elegant ever written: "We hold these truths to be self-evident, that all men are created equal, that they are endowed by their Creator with certain unalienable Rights, that among these are Life, Liberty and the pursuit of Happiness."

Sadly, our nation has taken a long time to live up to the promise of equality. In 1857, the Supreme Court held that an African-American could not be a citizen. During the ensuing Civil War, Abraham Lincoln eloquently reminded the nation of its founding principle: "our fathers brought forth on this continent, a new nation, conceived in liberty and dedicated to the proposition that all men are created equal."

At the end of the Civil War, to make the elusive promise of equality a reality, the 14th Amendment to the Constitution added the command that "no State . . . shall deprive any person of life, liberty or property, without due process of law; nor deny to any person . . . the equal protection of the laws."

Subsequent laws and court decisions have made clear that equality under the law extends to persons of all races, religions, and places of origin. What better way to make this national aspiration complete than applying the same protection to men and women who differ from others only on the basis of their sexual orientation? I cannot think of a single reason—and have not heard one since I undertook this venture—for continued discrimination against decent, hardworking members of our society on that basis.

Various federal and state laws have accorded certain rights and privileges to gay and lesbian couples, but these protections vary dramatically at the state level, and nearly universally deny true equality to gays and lesbians who wish to marry. The very idea of marriage is basic to recognition as equals in our society; any status short of that is inferior, unjust, and unconstitutional.

The United States Supreme Court has repeatedly held that marriage is one of the most fundamental rights that we have as Americans under our Constitution. It is an expression of our desire to create a social partnership, to live and share life's joys and burdens with the person we love, and to form a lasting bond and a social identity. The Supreme Court has said that marriage is a part of the Constitution's protections of liberty, privacy, freedom of association, and spiritual identification. In short, the right to marry helps us to define ourselves and our place in a community. Without it, there can be no true equality under the law.

It is true that marriage in this nation traditionally has been regarded as a relationship exclusively between a man and a woman, and many of our nation's multiple religions define marriage in precisely those terms. But while the Supreme Court has always previously considered marriage in that context, the underlying rights and liberties that marriage embodies are not in any way confined to heterosexuals.

Marriage is a civil bond in this country as well as, in some (but hardly all) cases, a religious sacrament. It is a relationship recognized by governments as providing a privileged and respected status, entitled to the state's support and benefits. The California Supreme Court described marriage as a "union unreservedly approved and favored by the community." Where the state has accorded official sanction to a relationship and provided special benefits to those who enter into that relationship, our courts have insisted that withholding that status requires powerful justifications and may not be arbitrarily denied.

What, then, are the justifications for California's decision in Proposition 8 to withdraw access to the institution of marriage for some of its citizens on the basis of their sexual orientation? The reasons I have heard are not very persuasive.

The explanation mentioned most often is tradition. But simply because something has always been done a certain way does not mean that it must always remain that way. Otherwise we would still have segregated schools and debtors' prisons. Gays and lesbians have always been among us, forming a part of our society, and they have lived as couples in our neighborhoods and communities. For a long time, they have experienced discrimination and even persecution; but we, as a society, are starting to become more tolerant, accepting, and understanding. California and many other states have allowed gays and lesbians to form domestic partnerships (or civil unions) with most of the rights of married heterosexuals. Thus, gay and lesbian individuals are now permitted to live together in state-sanctioned relationships. It therefore seems anomalous to cite "tradition" as a justification for withholding the status of marriage and thus to continue to label those relationships as less worthy, less sanctioned, or less legitimate.

Simply because something has always been done a certain way does not mean that it must always remain that way. Otherwise we would still have segregated schools and debtors' prisons.

The second argument I often hear is that traditional marriage furthers the state's interest in procreation—and that opening marriage to same-sex couples would dilute, diminish, and devalue this goal. But that is plainly not the case. Preventing lesbians and gays from marrying does not cause more heterosexuals to marry and conceive more children. Likewise, allowing gays and lesbians to marry someone of the same sex will not discourage heterosexuals from marrying a person of the opposite sex. How, then, would allowing same-sex marriages reduce the number of children that heterosexual couples conceive?

This procreation argument cannot be taken seriously. We do not inquire whether heterosexual couples intend to bear children, or have the capacity to have children, before we allow them to marry. We permit marriage by the elderly, by prison inmates, and by persons who have no intention of having children. What's more, it is pernicious to think marriage should be limited to heterosexuals because of the state's desire to promote procreation. We would surely not accept as constitutional a ban on marriage if a state were to decide, as China has done, to discourage procreation.

Another argument, vaguer and even less persuasive, is that gay marriage somehow does harm to heterosexual marriage. I have yet to meet anyone who can explain to me what this means. In what way would allowing same-sex partners to marry diminish the marriages of heterosexual couples? Tellingly, when the judge in our case asked our opponent to identify the ways in which same-sex marriage would harm heterosexual marriage, to his credit he answered honestly: he could not think of any.

The simple fact is that there is no good reason why we should deny marriage to same-sex partners. On the other hand, there are many reasons why we should formally recognize these relationships and embrace the rights of gays and lesbians to marry and become full and equal members of our society.

No matter what you think of homosexuality, it is a fact that gays and lesbians are members of our families, clubs, and workplaces. They are our doctors, our teachers, our soldiers (whether we admit it or not), and our friends. They yearn for acceptance, stable relationships, and success in their lives, just like the rest of us.

Conservatives and liberals alike need to come together on principles that surely unite us. Certainly, we can agree on the value of strong families, lasting domestic relationships, and communities populated by persons with recognized and sanctioned bonds to one another. Confining some of our neighbors and friends who share these same values to an outlaw or second-class status undermines their sense of belonging and weakens their ties with the rest of us and what should be our common aspirations. Even those whose religious convictions preclude endorsement of what they may perceive as an unacceptable "lifestyle" should recognize that disapproval should not warrant stigmatization and unequal treatment.

When we refuse to accord this status to gays and lesbians, we discourage them from forming the same relationships we encourage for others. And we are also telling them, those who love them, and society as a whole that their relationships are less worthy, less legitimate, less permanent, and less valued. We demean their relationships and we demean them as individuals. I cannot imagine how we benefit as a society by doing so.

I understand, but reject, certain religious teachings that denounce homosexuality as morally wrong, illegitimate, or unnatural; and I take strong exception to those who argue that same-sex relationships should be discouraged by society and law. Science has taught us, even if history has not, that gays and lesbians do not choose to be homosexual any more than the rest of us choose to be heterosexual. To a very large extent, these characteristics are immutable, like being left-handed. And, while our Constitution guarantees the freedom to exercise our individual religious convictions, it equally prohibits us from forcing our beliefs on others. I do not believe that our society can ever live up to the promise of equality, and the fundamental rights to life, liberty, and the pursuit of happiness, until we stop invidious discrimination on the basis of sexual orientation.

I do not believe that our society can ever live up to the promise of life, liberty, and the pursuit of happiness until we stop this invidious discrimination.

If we are born heterosexual, it is not unusual for us to perceive those who are born homosexual as aberrational and threatening. Many religions and much of our social culture have reinforced those impulses. Too often, that has led to prejudice, hostility, and discrimination. The antidote is understanding, and reason. We once tolerated laws throughout this nation that prohibited marriage between persons of different races. California's Supreme Court was the first to find that discrimination unconstitutional. The U.S. Supreme Court unanimously agreed 20 years later, in 1967, in a case called *Loving v. Virginia*. It seems inconceivable today that only 40 years ago there were places in this country where a black woman could not legally marry a white man. And it was only 50 years ago that 17 states mandated segregated public education—until the Supreme Court unanimously struck down that practice in *Brown v. Board of Education*. Most Americans are proud of these decisions and the fact that the discriminatory state laws that spawned them have been discredited. I am convinced that Americans will be equally proud when we no longer discriminate against gays and lesbians and welcome them into our society.

It is inconceivable that only 40 years ago there were places in this country where a black woman could not legally marry a white man.

Reactions to our lawsuit have reinforced for me these essential truths. I have certainly heard anger, resentment, and hostility, and words like "betrayal" and other pointedly graphic criticism. But mostly I have been overwhelmed by expressions of gratitude and good will from persons in all walks of life, including, I might add, from many conservatives and libertarians whose names might surprise. I have been particularly moved by many personal renditions of how lonely and personally destructive it is to be treated as an outcast and how meaningful it will be to be respected by our laws and civil institutions as an American, entitled to equality and dignity. I have no doubt

that we are on the right side of this battle, the right side of the law, and the right side of history.

Some have suggested that we have brought this case too soon, and that neither the country nor the courts are "ready" to tackle this issue and remove this stigma. We disagree. We represent real clients—two wonderful couples in California who have longtime relationships. Our lesbian clients are raising four fine children who could not ask for better parents. Our clients wish to be married. They believe that they have that constitutional right. They wish to be represented in court to seek vindication of that right by mounting a challenge under the United States Constitution to the validity of Proposition 8 under the equal-protection and due-process clauses of the 14th

---

Same-Sex Marriage Is Legal In:

Connecticut, District of Columbia*, Iowa, Massachusetts, New Hampshire, Vermont

*Pending Congressional Approval

Civil Union or Domestic Partnership Is Legal In:

California, Colorado, Hawaii, Maine, Maryland, Nevada, New Jersey, Oregon, Washington, Wisconsin

No State Laws Regarding Civil Unions, Domestic Partnerships, or Same-Sex Marriage In:

New Mexico, New York, Rhode Island

Same-Sex Marriage Is Illegal In:

Alabama, Alaska, Arizona, Arkansas, California, Colorado, Delaware, Florida, Georgia, Hawaii, Idaho, Illinois, Indiana, Kansas, Kentucky, Louisiana, Maine, Maryland, Michigan, Minnesota, Mississippi, Missouri, Montana, Nebraska, Nevada, North Carolina, North Dakota, Ohio, Oklahoma, Oregon, Pennsylvania, South Carolina, South Dakota, Tennessee, Texas, Utah, Virginia, Washington, West Virginia, Wisconsin, Wyoming

Amendment. In fact, the California attorney general has conceded the unconstitutionality of Proposition 8, and the city of San Francisco has joined our case to defend the rights of gays and lesbians to be married. We do not tell persons who have a legitimate claim to wait until the time is "right" and the populace is "ready" to recognize their equality and equal dignity under the law.

Citizens who have been denied equality are invariably told to "wait their turn" and to "be patient." Yet veterans of past civil-rights battles found that it was the act of insisting on equal rights that ultimately sped acceptance of those rights. As to whether the courts are "ready" for this case, just a few years ago, in *Romer v. Evans,* the United States Supreme Court struck down a popularly adopted Colorado constitutional amendment that withdrew the rights of gays and lesbians in that state to the protection of anti-discrimination laws. And seven years ago, in *Lawrence v. Texas,* the Supreme Court struck down, as lacking any rational basis, Texas laws prohibiting private, intimate sexual practices between persons of the same sex, overruling a contrary decision just 20 years earlier.

These decisions have generated controversy, of course, but they are decisions of the nation's highest court on which our clients are entitled to rely. If all citizens have a constitutional right to marry, if state laws that withdraw legal protections of gays and lesbians as a class are unconstitutional, and if private, intimate sexual conduct between persons of the same sex is protected by the Constitution, there is very little left on which opponents of same-sex marriage can rely. As Justice Antonin Scalia, who dissented in the *Lawrence* case, pointed out, "[W]hat [remaining] justification could there possibly be for denying the benefits of marriage to homosexual couples exercising '[t]he liberty protected by the Constitution'?" He is right, of course. One might agree or not with these decisions, but even Justice Scalia has acknowledged that they lead in only one direction.

California's Proposition 8 is particularly vulnerable to constitutional challenge, because that state has now enacted a crazy-quilt of marriage regulation that makes no sense to anyone.

California recognizes marriage between men and women, including persons on death row, child abusers, and wife beaters. At the same time, California prohibits marriage by loving, caring, stable partners of the same sex, but tries to make up for it by giving them the alternative of "domestic partnerships" with virtually all of the rights of married persons except the official, state-approved status of marriage. Finally, California recognizes 18,000 same-sex marriages that took place in the months between the state Supreme Court's ruling that upheld gay-marriage rights and the decision of California's citizens to withdraw those rights by enacting Proposition 8.

> **California recognizes marriages involving persons on death row, child abusers, and wife beaters, but not loving, stable partners of the same sex.**

So there are now three classes of Californians: heterosexual couples who can get married, divorced, and remarried, if they wish; same-sex couples who cannot get married but can live together in domestic partnerships; and same-sex couples who are now married but who, if they divorce, cannot remarry. This is an irrational system, it is discriminatory, and it cannot stand.

Americans who believe in the words of the Declaration of Independence, in Lincoln's Gettysburg Address, in the 14th Amendment, and in the Constitution's guarantees of equal protection and equal dignity before the law cannot sit by while this wrong continues. This is not a conservative or liberal issue; it is an American one, and it is time we, as Americans, embraced it.

Critical Thinking

1. Why might conservatives support legalization of same sex marriages?
2. What values are supported by same sex marriages?

Is Pornography Adultery?

Ross Douthat

The marriage of Christie Brinkley and Peter Cook collapsed the old-fashioned way in 2006, when she discovered that he was sleeping with his 18-year-old assistant. But their divorce trial this summer was a distinctly Internet-age affair. Having insisted on keeping the proceedings open to the media, Brinkley and her lawyers served up a long list of juicy allegations about Cook's taste in online porn: the $3,000 a month he dropped on adult Web sites, the nude photos he posted online, the user names he favored ("happyladdie2002," for instance, and "wannasee-all") while surfing swinger sites, even the videos he supposedly made of himself masturbating.

Perhaps the most interesting thing about the porn-related revelations, though, was the ambiguity about what line, precisely, Cook was accused of having crossed. Was the porn habit a betrayal in and of itself? Was it the financial irresponsibility that mattered most, or the addictive behavior it suggested? Was it the way his habit had segued into other online activities? Or was it about Cook's fitness as a parent, and the possibility that their son had stumbled upon his porn cache? Clearly, the court and the public were supposed to think that Cook was an even lousier husband than his affair with a teenager might have indicated. But it was considerably less clear whether the porn habit itself was supposed to prove this, or whether it was the particulars—the monthly bill, the swinger sites, the webcam, the danger to the kids—that made the difference.

The notion that pornography, and especially hard-core pornography, has *something* to do with marital infidelity has been floating around the edges of the American conversation for a while now, even as the porn industry, by some estimates, has swollen to rival professional sports and the major broadcast networks as a revenue-generating source of entertainment. A 2002 survey of the American Academy of Matrimonial Lawyers suggests that Internet porn plays a part in an increasing number of divorce cases, and the Brinkley-Cook divorce wasn't the first celebrity split to feature porn-related revelations. In 2005, at the start of their messy divorce, Denise Richards accused Charlie Sheen of posting shots of his genitalia online and cultivating a taste for "barely legal" porn sites. Two years later, Anne Heche,

Ellen DeGeneres's ex, accused her non-celeb husband of surfing porn sites when he was supposed to be taking care of their 5-year-old son. The country singer Sara Evans's 2006 divorce involved similar allegations, including the claim that her husband had collected 100 nude photographs of himself and solicited sex online.

But the attention paid to the connection between porn and infidelity doesn't translate into anything like a consensus on what that connection is. Polls show that Americans are almost evenly divided on questions like whether porn is bad for relationships, whether it's an inevitable feature of male existence, and whether it's demeaning to women. This divide tends to cut along gender lines, inevitably: women are more likely to look at pornography than in the past, but they remain considerably more hostile to porn than men are, and considerably less likely to make use of it. (Even among the Internet generation, the split between the sexes remains stark. A survey of American college students last year found that 70 percent of the women in the sample never looked at pornography, compared with just 14 percent of their male peers; almost half of the men surveyed looked at porn at least once a week, versus just 3 percent of the women.)

One perspective, broadly construed, treats porn as a harmless habit, near-universal among men, and at worst a little silly. This is the viewpoint that's transformed adult-industry icons like Jenna Jameson and Ron Jeremy from targets of opprobrium into C-list celebrities. It's what inspires fledgling stars to gin up sex tapes in the hope of boosting their careers. And it's made smut a staple of gross-out comedy: rising star funnyman Seth Rogen has gone from headlining Judd Apatow's *Knocked Up*, in which his character's aspiration to run a pornographic website was somewhat incidental to the plot, to starring in Kevin Smith's forthcoming *Zack and Miri Make a Porno*, in which the porn business promises to be rather more central.

A second perspective treats porn as a kind of gateway drug—a vice that paves the way for more-serious betrayals. A 2004 study found that married individuals who cheated on their spouses were three times as likely to have used Internet pornography as married people who hadn't committed adultery. In Tom Perrotta's bestselling *Little Children,* the female protagonist's husband—who is himself being cuckolded—progresses from obsessing over an online porn star named "Slurry Kay" to sending away for her panties to joining a club of fans who pay to vacation with her in person. Brinkley's husband may have followed a similar trajectory, along with many of the other porn-happy celebrity spouses who've featured in the gossip pages and divorce courts lately.

Maybe it's worth sharpening the debate. Over the past three decades, the VCR, on-demand cable service, and the Internet have completely overhauled the ways in which people interact with porn. Innovation has piled on innovation, making modern pornography a more immediate, visceral, and personalized experience. Nothing in the long history of erotica compares with the way millions of Americans experience porn today, and our moral intuitions are struggling to catch up. As we try to make sense of the brave new world that VHS and streaming video have built, we might start by asking a radical question: Is pornography use a form of adultery?

Nothing in the history of erotica compares with the way Americans experience porn today, and our moral intuitions are struggling to catch up.

The most stringent take on this matter comes, of course, from Jesus of Nazareth: "I tell you that anyone who looks at a woman lustfully has already committed adultery with her in his heart." But even among Christians, this teaching tends to be grouped with the Gospel injunctions about turning the other cheek and giving would-be robbers your possessions—as a guideline for saintliness, useful to Francis of Assisi and the Desert Fathers but less helpful to ordinary sinners trying to figure out what counts as a breach of marital trust. Jimmy Carter's confession to *Playboy* that he had "lusted in [his] heart" still inspires giggles three decades later. Most Americans, devout or secular, are inclined to distinguish lustful thoughts from lustful actions, and hew to the *Merriam-Webster* definition of adultery as "voluntary sexual intercourse between a married man and someone other than his wife or between a married woman and someone other than her husband."

On the face of things, this definition would seem to let porn users off the hook. Intercourse, after all, involves physicality, a flesh-and-blood encounter that Internet Explorer and the DVD player can't provide, no matter what sort of adultery the user happens to be committing in his heart.

But there's another way to look at it. During the long, late winter week that transformed the governor of New York, Eliot Spitzer, into an alleged john, a late-night punch line, and finally an ex-governor, there was a lively debate on blogs and radio shows and op-ed pages about whether prostitution ought to be illegal at all. Yet amid all the chatter about whether the FBI should have cared about Spitzer's habit of paying for extramarital sex, next to nobody suggested, publicly at least, that *his wife* ought not to care—that Silda Spitzer ought to have been grateful he was seeking only sexual gratification elsewhere, and that so long as he was loyal to her in his mind and heart, it shouldn't matter what he did with his penis.

Start with the near-universal assumption that what Spitzer did in his hotel room constituted adultery, and then ponder whether Silda Spitzer would have had cause to feel betrayed if the FBI probe had revealed that her husband had paid merely to *watch* a prostitute perform sexual acts while he folded himself into a hotel armchair to masturbate. My suspicion is that an awful lot of people would say yes—not because there isn't some distinction between the two acts, but because the distinction isn't morally significant enough to prevent both from belonging to the zone, broadly defined, of cheating on your wife.

You can see where I'm going with this. If it's cheating on your wife to watch while another woman performs sexually in front of you, then why isn't it cheating to watch while the same sort of spectacle unfolds on your laptop or TV? Isn't the man who uses hard-core pornography already betraying his wife, whether or not the habit leads to anything worse? (The same goes, of course, for a wife betraying her husband—the arguments in this essay should be assumed to apply as well to the small minority of women who use porn.)

Fine, you might respond, but there are betrayals and then there are betrayals. The man who lets his eyes stray across the photo of Gisele Bündchen, bare-assed and beguiling on the cover of *GQ,* has betrayed his wife in some sense, but only a 21st-century Savonarola would describe that sort of thing as adultery. The line that matters is the one between fantasy and reality—between the call girl who's really there having sex with you, and the porn star who's selling the *image* of herself having sex to a host of men she'll never even meet. In this reading, porn is "a fictional, fantastical, even allegorical realm," as the cultural critic Laura Kipnis described it in the mid-1990s—"mythological and hyperbolic" rather than realistic, and experienced not as a form of intercourse but as a "popular-culture genre" like true crime or science fiction.

This seems like a potentially reasonable distinction to draw. But the fantasy-versus-reality, pixels-versus-flesh binary feels more appropriate to the pre-Internet landscape than to one where people spend hours every day in entirely virtual worlds, whether they're accumulating "friends" on Facebook, acting out Tolkienesque fantasies in World of Warcraft, or flirting with a sexy avatar in Second Life. And it feels much more appropriate to the tamer sorts of pornography, from the increasingly archaic (dirty playing cards and pinups, smutty books and the *Penthouse* letters section) to the of-the-moment (the topless photos and sex-scene stills in the more restrained precincts of the online pornosphere), than it does to the harder-core material at the heart of the porn economy. Masturbating to a *Sports Illustrated* swimsuit model (like Christie Brinkley, once upon a time) or a *Playboy* centerfold is a one-way street: the images are intended to provoke fantasies, not to embody reality, since the women pictured aren't having sex for the viewer's gratification. Even strippers, for all their flesh-and-blood appeal, are essentially fantasy objects—depending on how you respond to a lap dance, of course. But hard-core pornography is real sex by definition, and the two sexual acts involved—the on-camera copulation, and the masturbation it enables—are interdependent: neither would happen without the other. The whole point of a centerfold is her unattainability, but with hard-core porn, it's precisely the reverse: the star isn't just attainable, she's already being attained, and the user gets to be in on the action.

Moreover, the way the porn industry is evolving reflects the extent to which the Internet subverts the fantasy-reality dichotomy. After years of booming profits, the "mainstream" porn studios are increasingly losing ground to start-ups and freelancers—people making sex videos on their beds and sofas and shag carpeting and uploading them on the cheap. It turns out that, increasingly, Americans don't want porn as a "kind of science fiction," as Kipnis put it—they want realistic porn, porn that resembles the sex they might be having, and porn that at every moment holds out the promise that they can join in, like Peter Cook masturbating in front of his webcam.

So yes, there's an obvious line between leafing through a *Playboy* and pulling a Spitzer on your wife. But the line between Spitzer and the suburban husband who pays $29.95 a month to stream hard-core sex onto his laptop is considerably blurrier. The suburbanite with the hard-core porn hookup is masturbating to real sex, albeit at a DSL-enabled remove. He's experiencing it in an intimate setting, rather than in a grind house alongside other huddled masturbators in raincoats, and in a form that's customized to his tastes in a way that mass-market porn like *Deep Throat and Debbie Does Dallas* never was. There's no emotional connection, true—but there presumably wasn't one on Spitzer's part, either.

This isn't to say the distinction between hiring a prostitute and shelling out for online porn doesn't matter; in moral issues, every distinction matters. But if you approach infidelity as a continuum of betrayal rather than an either/or

proposition, then the Internet era has ratcheted the experience of pornography much closer to adultery than I suspect most porn users would like to admit.

It's possible, of course, to consider hard-core porn use a kind of infidelity and shrug it off even so. After all, human societies have frequently made sweeping accommodations for extramarital dalliances, usually on the assumption that the male libido simply can't be expected to submit to monogamy. When apologists for pornography aren't making Kipnis-style appeals to cultural transgression and sexual imagination, they tend to fall back on the defense that it's pointless to moralize about porn, because men are going to use it anyway.

Here's Dan Savage, the popular Seattle-based sex columnist, responding to a reader who fretted about her boyfriend's porn habit—"not because I'm jealous," she wrote, "but because I'm insecure. I'm sure many of those girls are more attractive than me":

> All men look at porn . . . The handful of men who claim they don't look at porn are liars or castrates. Tearful discussions about your insecurities or your feminist principles will not stop a man from looking at porn. That's why the best advice for straight women is this: GET OVER IT. If you don't want to be with someone who looks at porn . . . get a woman, get a dog, or get a blind guy . . . While men shouldn't rub their female partners' noses in the fact that they look at porn—that's just inconsiderate—telling women that the porn "problem" can be resolved through good communication, couples counseling, or a chat with your pastor is neither helpful nor realistic.

Savage's perspective is hardly unique, and is found among women as well as men. In 2003, three psychology professors at Illinois State University surveyed a broad population of women who were, or had been, in a relationship with a man who they knew used pornography. About a third of the women described the porn habit as a form of betrayal and infidelity. But the majority were neutral or even positively disposed to their lover's taste for smut, responding slightly more favorably than not to prompts like "I do not mind my partner's pornography use" or "My partner's pornography use is perfectly normal."

This point of view—that looking at pornography is a "perfectly normal" activity, one that the more-judgmental third of women need to just stop whining about—has been strengthened by the erosion of the second-order arguments against the use of porn, especially the argument that it feeds misogyny and encourages rape. In the great porn debates of the 1980s, arguments linking porn to violence against women were advanced across the ideological spectrum.

Feminist crusaders like Andrea Dworkin and Catharine MacKinnon denounced smut as a weapon of the patriarchy; the Christian radio psychologist (and future religious-right fixture) James Dobson induced the serial killer Ted Bundy to confess on death row to a pornography addiction; the Meese Commission on Pornography declared, "In both clinical and experimental settings, exposure to sexually violent materials has indicated an increase in the likelihood of aggression." It all sounded plausible—but between 1980 and 2004, an era in which porn became more available, and in more varieties, the rate of reported sexual violence *dropped,* and by 85 percent. Correlation isn't necessarily causation, but the sharpness of the decline at least suggests that porn may reduce sexual violence by providing an outlet for some potential sex offenders. (Indeed, the best way to deter a rapist might be to hook him up with a high-speed Internet connection: in a 2006 study, the Clemson economist Todd Kendall found that a 10 percent increase in Internet access is associated with a 7 percent decline in reported rapes.)

And what's true of rapists could be true of ordinary married men, a porn apologist might argue. For every Peter Cook, using porn *and* sleeping around, there might be countless men who use porn as a substitute for extramarital dalliances, satisfying their need for sexual variety without hiring a prostitute or kicking off a workplace romance.

Like Philip Weiss's friends, for instance. In the wake of the Spitzer affair, Weiss, a New York-based investigative journalist, came closer than any mainstream writer to endorsing not only the legalization of prostitution but the destigmatization of infidelity in a rambling essay for *New York* magazine on the agonies that monogamy imposes on his buddies. Amid nostalgia for the days of courtesans and concubines and the usual plaints about how much more sophisticated things are in Europe, Weiss depicted porn as the modern man's "common answer" to the marital-sex deficit. Here's one of his pals dilating on his online outlets:

> "Porn captures these women [its performers] before they get smart," he said in a hot whisper as we sat in Schiller's Liquor Bar on the Lower East Side. Porn exploited the sexual desires, and naiveté, of women in their early twenties, he went on . . . He spoke of acts he observed online that his wife wouldn't do. "It's painful to say, but that's your boys' night out, and it takes an enlightened woman to say that."

The use of the term *enlightened* is telling, since the strongest argument for the acceptance of pornography—and the hard-core variety in particular—is precisely that it represents a form of sexual progress, a more civilized approach to the problem of the male libido than either the toleration of mass prostitution or the attempt, from the Victorian era onward, to simultaneously legislate prostitution away and hold married couples to an unreasonably high standard of fidelity. Porn may be an evil, this argument goes, but it's the least of several evils. The man who uses porn is cheating sexually, but he isn't involving himself in an emotional relationship. He's cheating in a way that carries none of the risks of intercourse, from pregnancy to venereal disease. And he's cheating with women who may be trading sex for money, but are doing so in vastly safer situations than streetwalkers or even high-end escorts.

Indeed, in a significant sense, the porn industry looks like what advocates of legalized prostitution hope to achieve for "sex workers." There are no bullying pimps and no police officers demanding sex in return for not putting the prostitutes in jail. There are regular tests for STDs, at least in the higher-end sectors of the industry. The performers are safely separated from their johns. And freelancers aren't wandering downtown intersections on their own; they're filming from the friendly confines of their homes.

If we would just accept Dan Savage's advice, then, and *get over it,* everyone would gain something. Weiss and his pals could have their "boys' night out" online and enjoy sexual experiences that their marriages deny them. The majority of wives could rest secure in the knowledge that worse forms of infidelity are being averted; some women could get into the act themselves, either solo or with their spouse, experiencing the thrill of a threesome or a '70s key party with fewer of the consequences. The porn industry's sex workers could earn a steady paycheck without worrying about pimps, police, or HIV. Every society lives with infidelity in one form or another, whether openly or hypocritically. Why shouldn't we learn to live with porn?

Live with it we almost, certainly will. But it's worth being clear about what were accepting. Yes, adultery is inevitable, but it's never been universal in the way that pornography has the potential to become—at least if we approach the use of hard-core porn as a normal outlet from the rigors of monogamy, and invest ourselves in a cultural paradigm that understands this as something all men do and all women need to live with. In the name of providing a low-risk alternative for males who would otherwise be tempted by "real" prostitutes and "real" affairs, we're ultimately universalizing, in a milder but not all that much milder form, the sort of degradation and betrayal that only a minority of men have traditionally been involved in.

Go back to Philip Weiss's pal and listen to him talk: *Porn captures these women before they get smart . . . It's painful to say, but that's your boys' night out.* This is the language of a man who has accepted, not as a temporary lapse but as a permanent and necessary aspect of his married life, a paid sexual relationship with women other than his wife. And it's the language of a man who has internalized a view of marriage as a sexual prison, rendered bearable only by frequent online furloughs with women more easily exploited than his spouse.

Calling porn a form of adultery isn't about pretending that we can make it disappear. The temptation will always be there, and of course people will give in to it. I've looked at porn; if you're male and breathing, chances are so have you. Rather, it's about what sort of people we aspire to be: how we define our ideals, how we draw the lines in our relationships, and how we feel about ourselves if we cross them. And it's about providing a way for everyone involved, men and women alike—whether they're using porn or merely tolerating it—to think about what, precisely, they're involving themselves in, and whether they should reconsider.

The extremes of anti-porn hysteria are unhelpful in this debate. If the turn toward an "everybody does it" approach to pornography and marriage is wrong, it's because that approach is wrong in and of itself, not because porn is going to wreck society, destroy the institution of marriage, and turn thousands of rapists loose to prey on unsuspecting women. Smut isn't going to bring down Western Civilization any more than Nero's orgies actually led to the fall of Rome, and a society that expects near-universal online infidelity may run just as smoothly as a society that doesn't.

Which is precisely why it's so easy to say that the spread of pornography means that we're just taking a turn, where sex and fidelity are concerned, toward realism, toward adulthood, toward sophistication. All we have to give up to get there is our sense of decency.

Critical Thinking

1. What role does pornography play in relationships?
2. Why is pornography considered adultery among some couples?

Ross Douthat, an *Atlantic* senior editor, blogs at rossdouthat .theatlantic.com.

UNIT 7

Preventing and Fighting Disease

Unit Selections

Learning Outcomes

After reading this unit, you should be able to:

- Describe how the prison environment fosters the spread of HIV.

- Explain how prison inmates are able to engage in drug use while incarcerated.

- Contrast the new versus the previous mammogram guidelines.

- Describe why mammogram guidelines were changed.

- Explain why people are still dying from AIDS despite the many anti-viral drugs.

- Identify the lifestyle changes that you can make to reduce your risk of developing cardiovascular disease, cancer, diabetes, and AIDS.

- Describe why or why not all young girls should be vaccinated against HPV.

- Distinguish the risks vs. the benefits of the HPV vaccination.

Student Website

www.mhhe.com/cls

Internet References

American Cancer Society
www.cancer.org
American Diabetes Association Home Page
www.diabetes.org
American Heart Association
www.amhrt.org
National Institute of Allergy and Infectious Diseases (NIAID)
www.niaid.nih.gov

Cardiovascular disease and cancer are the leading killers in this country. This is not altogether surprising given that the American population is growing increasingly older, and one's risk of developing both of these diseases is directly proportional to one's age. Another major risk factor, which has received considerable attention over the past 30 years, is one's genetic predisposition or family history. Historically, the significance of this risk factor has been emphasized as a basis for encouraging at-risk individuals to make prudent lifestyle choices, but this may be about to change as recent advances in genetic research, including mapping the human genome, may significantly improve the efficacy of both diagnostic and therapeutic procedures.

Just as cutting-edge genetic research is transforming the practice of medicine, startling new research findings in the health profession are transforming our views concerning adult health. This new research suggests that the primary determinants of our health as adults are the environmental conditions we experienced during our life in the womb. According to Dr. Peter Nathanielsz of Cornell University, conditions during gestation, ranging from hormones that flow from the mother to how well the placenta delivers nutrients to the tiny limbs and organs, program how our liver, heart, kidneys, and especially our brains function as adults. While it is too early to draw any firm conclusions regarding the significance of the "life in the womb factor," it appears that this avenue of research may yield important clues as to how we may best prevent or forestall chronic illness.

Of all the diseases in America, coronary heart disease is this nation's number one killer. Frequently, the first and only symptom of this disease is a sudden heart attack. Epidemiological studies have revealed a number of risk factors that increase one's likelihood of developing this disease. These include hypertension, a high serum cholesterol level, diabetes, cigarette smoking, obesity, a sedentary lifestyle, a family history of heart disease, age, sex, race, and stress. In addition to these well-established risk factors, scientists think they may have discovered several additional risk factors. These include the following: low birth weight, cytomegalovirus, *Chlamydia pneumoniae,* porphyromonasgingivalis, and c-reactive protein (CRP). CRP is a measure of inflammation somewhere in the body. In theory, a high CRP reading may be a good indicator of an impending heart attack.

One of the most startling and ominous health stories was the recent announcement by the Centers for Disease Control and Prevention (CDC) that the incidence of Type 2 adult onset diabetes increased significantly over the past 15 years. This sudden rise appears to cross all races and age groups, with the sharpest increase occurring among people aged 30 to 39 (about 70 percent). Health experts at the CDC believe that this startling rise in diabetes among 30- to 39-year-olds is linked to the rise in obesity observed among young adults (obesity rates rose from 12 to 20 percent nationally during this same time period). Experts at the CDC believe that there is a time lag of about 10–15 years between the deposition of body fat and the manife station of Type 2 diabetes. This time lag could explain why individuals in their 30s are experiencing the greatest increase in developing Type 2 diabetes today. Current estimates suggest that 16 million Americans have diabetes; it kills approximately 180,000 Americans each year. Many experts now believe that our couch potato culture is fueling the rising rates of both obesity and diabetes. Given what we know about the relationship between obesity and Type 2 diabetes, the only practical solution is for Americans to watch their total calorie intake and exercise regularly.

Cardiovascular disease is America's number one killer, but cancer takes top billing in terms of the "fear factor." This fear of cancer stems from an awareness of the degenerative and disfiguring nature

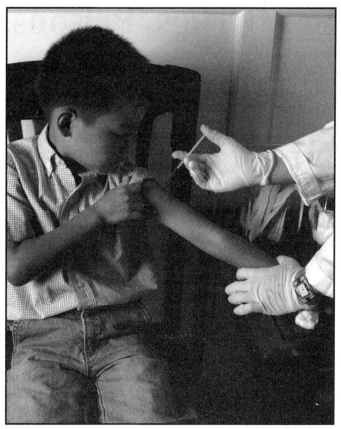

© The McGraw-Hill Companies, Inc./Jill Braaten, photographer

of the disease. Today, cancer specialists are employing a variety of complex agents and technologies, such as monoclonal antibodies, interferon, and immunotherapy, in their attempt to fight the disease. Progress has been slow, however, and the results, while promising, suggest that a cure may be several years away. A very disturbing aspect of this country's battle against cancer is the fact that millions of dollars are spent each year trying to advance the treatment of cancer, while the funding for the technologies used to detect cancer in its early stages is quite limited. A reallocation of funds would seem appropriate, given the medical community posits that early detection and issue related to early detection has arisen. A government task force recently announced that women in their 40s do not need annual mammograms, a long held belief. This task force recommendation is addressed in "New Mammogram Guidelines Raise Questions." Until we have more effective methods for detecting cancer in the early stages, our best hope for managing cancer is to prevent it through our lifestyle choices. The same lifestyle choices that may help prevent cancer can also help reduce the incidence of heart disease and diabetes.

The four articles in this unit address topics such as fighting disease and preventing cancer. In the first, Susan Okie discusses the risky health behaviors that occur among inmates. These behaviors increase the risk of transmitting HIV. New mammogram guidelines are described in the second article, while Gary Taubes discusses why the AIDS virus can still trump modern medicine and kill its victims in the third. Last, Kate O'Beirne addresses the issue of the HPV vaccine and the questions that remain over who should be immunized.

Sex, Drugs, Prisons, and HIV

SUSAN OKIE, MD

One recent morning at a medium-security compound at Rhode Island's state prison, Mr. M, a middle-aged black inmate, described some of the high-risk behavior he has witnessed while serving time. "I've seen it all," he said, smiling and rolling his eyes. "We have a lot of risky sexual activities. . . . Almost every second or minute, somebody's sneaking and doing something." Some participants are homosexual, he added; others are "curious, bisexual, bored, lonely, and . . . experimenting." As in all U.S. prisons, sex is illegal at the facility; as in nearly all, condoms are prohibited. Some inmates try to take precautions, fashioning makeshift condoms from latex gloves or sandwich bags. Most, however, "are so frustrated that they are not thinking of the consequences except for later," said Mr. M.

Drugs, and sometimes needles and syringes, find their way inside the walls. "I've seen the lifers that just don't care," Mr. M said. "They share needles and don't take a minute to rinse them." In the 1990s, he said, "needles were coming in by the handful," but prison officials have since stopped that traffic, and inmates who take illicit drugs usually snort or swallow them. Tattooing, although also prohibited, has been popular at times. "A lot of people I've known caught hepatitis from tattooing," Mr. M said. "They use staples, a nail . . . anything with a point."

Mr. M had just undergone a checkup performed by Dr. Josiah D. Rich, a professor of medicine at Brown University Medical School, who provides him with medical care as part of a long-standing arrangement between Brown and the Adult Correctional Institute in Cranston. Two years ago, Mr. M was hospitalized with pneumonia and meningitis. "I was scared and in denial," he said. Now, thanks to treatment with antiretroviral drugs, "I'm doing great, and I feel good," he reported. "I am HIV-positive and still healthy and still look fabulous."

U.S. public health experts consider the Rhode Island prison's human immunodeficiency virus (HIV) counseling and testing practices, medical care, and prerelease services to be among the best in the country. Yet according to international guidelines for reducing the risk of HIV transmission inside prisons, all U.S. prison systems fall short. Recognizing that sex occurs in prison despite prohibitions, the World Health Organization (WHO) and the Joint United Nations Program on HIV/AIDS (UNAIDS) have recommended for more than a decade that condoms be made available to prisoners. They also recommend that prisoners have access to bleach for cleaning injecting equipment,

that drug-dependence treatment and methadone maintenance programs be offered in prisons if they are provided in the community, and that needle-exchange programs be considered.

Prisons in several Western European countries and in Australia, Canada, Kyrgyzstan, Belarus, Moldova, Indonesia, and Iran have adopted some or all of these approaches to "harm reduction," with largely favorable results. For example, programs providing sterile needles and syringes have been established in some 50 prisons in eight countries; evaluations of such programs in Switzerland, Spain, and Germany found no increase in drug use, a dramatic decrease in needle sharing, no new cases of infection with HIV or hepatitis B or C, and no reported instances of needles being used as weapons.[1] Nevertheless, in the United States, condoms are currently provided on a limited basis in only two state prison systems (Vermont and Mississippi) and five county jail systems (New York, Philadelphia, San Francisco, Los Angeles, and Washington, DC). Methadone maintenance programs are rarer still, and no U.S. prison has piloted a needle-exchange program.

The U.S. prison population has reached record numbers—at the end of 2005, more than 2.2 million American adults were incarcerated, according to the Justice Department. And drug-related offenses are a major reason for the population growth, accounting for 49% of the increase between 1995 and 2003. Moreover, in 2005, more than half of all inmates had a mental health problem, and doctors who treat prisoners say that many have used illicit drugs as self-medication for untreated mental disorders.

In the United States in 2004 (see table), 1.8% of prison inmates were HIV-positive, more than four times the estimated rate in the general population; the rate of confirmed AIDS cases is also substantially higher (see graph).[2] Some behaviors that increase the risk of contracting HIV and other bloodborne or sexually transmitted infections can also lead to incarceration, and the burden of infectious diseases in prisons is high. It has been estimated that each year, about 25% of all HIV-infected persons in the United States spend time in a correctional facility, as do 33% of persons with hepatitis C virus (HCV) infection and 40% of those with active tuberculosis.[3]

Critics in the public health community have been urging U.S. prison officials to do more to prevent HIV transmission, to improve diagnosis and treatment in prisons, and to expand programs for reducing high-risk behavior after release. The

HIV–AIDS among Prison Inmates at the End of 2004*

Jurisdictions with the Most Prisoners Living with HIV–AIDS	No. of Inmates Living with HIV–AIDS	Prevalence of HIV–AIDS %
New York	4500	7.0
Florida	3250	3.9
Texas	2405	1.7
Federal system	1680	1.1
California	1212	0.7
Georgia	1109	2.2

*Data are from Maruschak.[2]

debate over such preventive strategies as providing condoms and needles reflects philosophical differences, as well as uncertainty about the frequency of HIV transmission inside prisons. The UNAIDS and WHO recommendations assume that sexual activity and injection of drugs by inmates cannot be entirely eliminated and aim to protect both prisoners and the public from HIV, HCV, and other diseases.

But many U.S. prison officials contend that providing needles or condoms would send a mixed message. By distributing condoms, "you're saying sex, whether consensual or not, is OK," said Lieutenant Gerald Ducharme, a guard at the Rhode Island prison. "It's a detriment to what we're trying to enforce." U.S. prison populations have higher rates of mental illness and violence than their European counterparts, which, some researchers argue, might make providing needles more dangerous. And some believe that whereas European prison officials tend to be pragmatic, many U.S. officials adopt a "just deserts" philosophy, viewing infections as the consequences of breaking prison rules.

Studies involving state-prison inmates suggest that the frequency of HIV transmission is low but not negligible. For example, between 1988—when the Georgia Department of Corrections began mandatory HIV testing of all inmates on entry to prison and voluntary testing thereafter—and 2005, HIV seroconversion occurred in 88 male inmates in Georgia state prisons. HIV transmission in prison was associated with men having sex with other men or receiving a tattoo.[4] In another study in a southeastern state, Christopher Krebs of RTI International documented that 33 of 5265 male prison inmates (0.63%) contracted HIV while in prison.[5] But Krebs points out that "when you have a large prison population, as our country does . . . you do start thinking about large numbers of people contracting HIV."

Studies of high-risk behavior in prisons yield widely varying frequency estimates: for example, estimates of the proportion of male inmates who have sex with other men range from 2 to 65%, and estimates of the proportion who are sexually assaulted range from 0 to 40%.[5] Such variations may reflect differences in research methods, inmate populations, and prison conditions that affect privacy and opportunity. Researchers emphasize that classifying prison sex as either consensual or forced is often overly simplistic: an inmate may provide sexual favors to another in

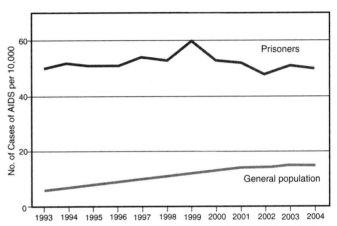

Rates of Confirmed AIDS Cases in the General Population and among State and Federal Prisoners, 1993–2004.

Data are from Maruschak.[2]

return for protection or for other reasons. Better information on sexual transmission of HIV in prisons may eventually become available as a result of the Prison Rape Elimination Act of 2003, which requires the Justice Department to collect statistics on prison rape and to provide funds for educating prison staff and inmates about the subject.

Theodore M. Hammett of the Domestic Health, Health Policy, and Clinical Research Division of Abt Associates, a Massachusetts-based policy research and consulting firm, acknowledged that for political reasons U.S. prisons are unlikely to accept needle-exchange programs, but he said adoption of other HIV-prevention measures is long overdue. "Condoms ought to be widely available in prisons," he said. "From a public health standpoint, I think there's little question that that should be done. Methadone, also—all kinds of drug [abuse] treatment should be much more widely available in correctional settings." Methadone maintenance programs for inmates have been established in a few jails and prisons, including those in New York City, Albuquerque, and San Juan, Puerto Rico. Brown University's Rich is currently conducting a randomized, controlled trial at the Rhode Island facility, sponsored by the National Institutes of Health, to determine whether starting methadone maintenance in heroin-addicted inmates a month before their release will lead to better health outcomes and reduced recidivism, as compared with providing either usual care or referral to community methadone programs at the time of release.

At the Rhode Island prison, the medical program focuses on identifying HIV-infected inmates, treating them, teaching them how to avoid transmitting the virus, addressing drug dependence, and when they're released, referring them to a program that arranges for HIV care and other assistance, including methadone maintenance treatment if needed. The prison offers routine HIV testing, and 90% of inmates accept it. One third of the state's HIV cases have been diagnosed at the prison. "These people are a target population and a captive one," noted Rich. "We should use this time" for health care and prevention. Nationally, 73% of state inmates and 77% of federal inmates surveyed in 2004 said they had been tested for HIV in prison. State policies vary, with 20 states reportedly testing all inmates and the rest offering tests for high-risk groups, at inmates' request, or in specific situations. Researchers said inmate acceptance rates also vary widely, depending on how the test is presented. Drugs for treating HIV-infected prisoners are not covered by federal programs, and prison budgets often contain inadequate funding for health services. "You can see how, in some cases, there could be a disincentive for really pushing testing," Hammett said.

Critics of U.S. penal policies contend that incarceration has exacerbated the HIV epidemic among blacks, who are disproportionately represented in the prison population, accounting for 40% of inmates. A new report by the National Minority AIDS Council calls for routine, voluntary HIV testing in prisons and on release, making condoms available, and expanding reentry programs that address HIV prevention, substance abuse, mental health, and housing needs as prisoners return to the community. "Any reservoir of infection that is as large as a prison would warrant, by simple public health logic, that we do our best . . . to reduce the risk of transmission" both inside and outside the walls, said Robert E. Fullilove of Columbia University's Mailman School of Public Health, who wrote the report. "The issue has never been, Do we understand what has to happen to reduce the risks? . . . It's always been, Do we have the political will necessary to put what we know is effective into operation?"

Notes

1. Dolan K, Rutter S, Wodak AD. Prison-based syringe exchange programmes: a review of international research and development. Addiction 2003;98:153–158.
2. Maruschak LM. HIV in prisons, 2004. Washington, DC: Bureau of Justice Statistics, November 2006.
3. Hammett TM, Harmon MP, Rhodes W. The burden of infectious disease among inmates of and releasees from US correctional facilities, 1997. Am J Public Health 2002;92:1789–1794.
4. HIV transmission among male inmates in a state prison system—Georgia, 1992–2005. MMWR Morb Mortal Wkly Rep 2006;55:421–6.
5. Krebs CP. Inmate factors associated with HIV transmission in prison. Criminology Public Policy 2006;5:113–36.

Critical Thinking

1. Why are inmates able to abuse drugs while incarcerated?
2. How does the environment in prison foster the spread of HIV?

DR. OKIE is a contributing editor of the *Journal*.

From *The New England Journal of Medicine*, January 11, 2007, pp. 105–108. Copyright © 2007 by Massachusetts Medical Society. All rights reserved. Reprinted by permission.

New Mammogram Guidelines Raise Questions

Benefits of screening before age 50 don't outweigh risks, task force says.

JOCELYN NOVECK

For many women, getting a mammogram is already one of life's more stressful experiences.

Now, women in their 40s have the added anxiety of trying to figure out if they should even be getting one at all.

A government task force said Monday that most women don't need mammograms in their 40s and should get one every two years starting at 50—a stunning reversal and a break with the American Cancer Society's long-standing position. What's more, the panel said breast self-exams do no good, and women shouldn't be taught to do them.

The news seemed destined to leave many deeply confused about whose advice to follow.

"I've never had a scare, but isn't it better to be safe than sorry?" asked Beth Rosenthal, 41, sitting in a San Francisco cafe on Monday afternoon with her friend and their small children. "I've heard of a lot of women in their 40s, and even 30s, who've gotten breast cancer. It just doesn't seem right to wait until 50."

Her friend agreed. "I don't think I'll wait," said Leslie David-Jones, also 41, shaking her head.

For most of the past two decades, the American Cancer Society has been recommending annual mammograms beginning at 40, and it reiterated that position on Monday. "This is one screening test I recommend unequivocally, and would recommend to any woman 40 and over," the society's chief medical officer, Dr. Otis Brawley, said in a statement.

But the government panel of doctors and scientists concluded that getting screened for breast cancer so early and so often is harmful, causing too many false alarms and unneeded biopsies without substantially improving women's odds of surviving the disease.

"The benefits are less and the harms are greater when screening starts in the 40s," said Dr. Diana Petitti, vice chair of the panel.

The new guidelines were issued by the U.S. Preventive Services Task Force, whose stance influences coverage of screening tests by Medicare and many insurance companies. But Susan Pisano, a spokeswoman for America's Health Insurance Plans, an industry group, said insurance coverage isn't likely to change because of the new guidelines.

Experts expect the revisions to be hotly debated, and to cause confusion for women and their doctors.

"Our concern is that as a result of that confusion, women may elect not to get screened at all. And that, to me, would be a serious problem," said Dr. Len Lichtenfeld, the cancer society's deputy chief medical officer.

The guidelines are for the general population, not those at high risk of breast cancer because of family history or gene mutations that would justify having mammograms sooner or more often.

The new advice says:

Most women in their 40s should not routinely get mammograms.

Women 50 to 74 should get a mammogram every other year until they turn 75, after which the risks and benefits are unknown. (The task force's previous guidelines had no upper limit and called for exams every year or two.)

The value of breast exams by doctors is unknown. And breast self-exams are of no value.

Medical groups such as the cancer society have been backing off promoting breast self-exams in recent years because of scant evidence of their effectiveness. Decades ago, the practice was so heavily promoted that organizations distributed cards that could be hung in the shower demonstrating the circular motion women should use to feel for lumps in their breasts.

The guidelines and research supporting them were released Monday and are being published in Tuesday's issue of the Annals of Internal Medicine.

Sharp Criticism from Cancer Society

The new advice was sharply challenged by the cancer society.

"This is one screening test I recommend unequivocally, and would recommend to any woman 40 and over," the society's chief medical officer, Dr. Otis Brawley, said in a statement.

The task force advice is based on its conclusion that screening 1,300 women in their 50s to save one life is worth it, but that screening 1,900 women in their 40s to save a life is not, Brawley wrote.

That stance "is essentially telling women that mammography at age 40 to 49 saves lives, just not enough of them," he said. The cancer society feels the benefits outweigh the harms for women in both groups.

International guidelines also call for screening to start at age 50; the World Health Organization recommends the test every two years, Britain says every three years.

Breast cancer is the most common cancer and the second leading cause of cancer deaths in American women. More than 192,000 new cases and 40,000 deaths from the disease are expected in the U.S. this year.

Mammograms can find cancer early, and two-thirds of women over 40 report having had the test in the previous two years. But how much they cut the risk of dying of the disease, and at what cost in terms of unneeded biopsies, expense and worry, have been debated.

In most women, tumors are slow-growing, and that likelihood increases with age. So there is little risk by extending the time between mammograms, some researchers say. Even for the minority of women with aggressive, fast-growing tumors, annual screening will make little difference in survival odds.

The new guidelines balance these risks and benefits, scientists say.

The probability of dying of breast cancer after age 40 is 3 percent, they calculate. Getting a mammogram every other year from ages 50 to 69 lowers that risk by about 16 percent.

"It's an average of five lives saved per thousand women screened," said Georgetown University researcher Dr. Jeanne Mandelblatt.

False Alarms

Starting at age 40 would prevent one additional death but also lead to 470 false alarms for every 1,000 women screened. Continuing mammograms through age 79 prevents three additional deaths but raises the number of women treated for breast cancers that would not threaten their lives.

"You save more lives because breast cancer is more common, but you diagnose tumors in women who were destined to die of something else. The overdiagnosis increases in older women," Mandelblatt said.

She led six teams around the world who used federal data on cancer and mammography to develop mathematical models of what would happen if women were screened at different ages and time intervals. Their conclusions helped shape the new guidelines.

Several medical groups say they are sticking to their guidelines that call for routine screening starting at 40.

"Screening isn't perfect. But it's the best thing we have. And it works," said Dr. Carol Lee, a spokeswoman for the American College of Radiology. She suggested that cutting health care costs may have played a role in the decision, but Petitti said the task force does not consider cost or insurance in its review.

The American College of Obstetricians and Gynecologists also has qualms. The organization's Dr. Hal Lawrence said there is still significant benefit to women in their 40s, adding: "We think that women deserve that benefit."

But Dr. Amy Abernethy of the Duke Comprehensive Cancer Center agreed with the task force's changes.

"Overall, I think it really took courage for them to do this," she said. "It does ask us as doctors to change what we do and how we communicate with patients. That's no small undertaking."

Abernethy, who is 41, said she got her first mammogram the day after her 40th birthday, even though she wasn't convinced it was needed. Now she doesn't plan to have another mammogram until she is 50.

Barbara Brenner, executive director of the San Francisco-based Breast Cancer Action, said the group was "thrilled" with the revisions. The advocacy group doesn't support screening before menopause, and will be changing its suggested interval from yearly to every two years, she said.

Mammograms, like all medical interventions, have risks and benefits, she said.

"Women are entitled to know what they are and to make their best decisions," she said. "These guidelines will help that conversation."

Critical Thinking

1. Why did the panel publish changes in mammogram requirements?
2. What are some of the benefits and risks associated with early screening?

Who Still Dies of AIDS, and Why

In the age of HAART, the virus can still outwit modern medicine.

GARY TAUBES

In the video, filmed last November, Mel Cheren appears understandably dismayed. He's being interviewed by a reporter for CBS News on *Logo,* a gay-themed news program; he's sitting in a wheelchair, and he's talking about the indignity and the irony of dying from AIDS at a time when AIDS should be a chronic disease, not a fatal one. Cheren, a music producer and founder of West End Records, had been an AIDS activist since the earliest days of the epidemic. It was Cheren, in 1982, who gave the Gay Men's Health Crisis its first home, providing a floor of his brownstone on West 22nd Street. In the interview, Cheren talks about what it's like to lose more than 300 friends to the AIDS epidemic, outlive them all, and then get diagnosed yourself at age 74.

Indeed, the fact that Cheren had plenty of sex through the height of the epidemic, had been tested regularly, and had apparently emerged uninfected had led him to believe that testing was no longer necessary, or at least so one doctor had told him half a dozen years earlier. He's only learned the truth after he began losing weight, had trouble walking, and was finally referred to a specialist who didn't consider AIDS an unreasonable diagnosis for a man of Cheren's experience and advanced years and so ordered up the requisite blood test. "There was one guy," Cheren says in the interview, explaining how he might have been infected. A male escort. "We really hit it off, sexually . . ."

By the time Cheren learned he had AIDS, he was already suffering from a rare, drug-resistant pneumonia, what infectious-disease specialists refer to as an opportunistic infection, and he had lymphoma, an AIDS-related cancer that had spread to his bones.

Within a month of his diagnosis, Cheren was dead. The official cause was pneumonia, although, as his cousin Mark Cheren points out, cause of death in these cases is a moot point. "Infection from pneumonia was probably the culprit," he says, "but only because that acts quickest when you don't stop it."

Dying from AIDS, or dying with an HIV infection, which may not be the same thing, is a significantly less common event than it was a decade ago, but it's not nearly as uncommon as anyone would like. Bob Hattoy, for instance, died last year as well. Hattoy, 56, was "the first gay man with AIDS many Americans had knowingly laid eyes on," as the *New York Times* described him after Hattoy announced his condition to the world in a speech at the 1992 Democratic National Convention. Hattoy went on the work in the Clinton White House as an advocate for gay and lesbian issues. In the summer of 1993, he told the *New York Times,* "I don't make real long-term plans." But the advent of an anti-retroviral drug known as a protease inhibitor, in 1995, and then, a year later multidrug cocktails called HAART—for highly active anti-retroviral therapy—gave Hattoy and a few hundred thousand HIV-infected Americans like him the opportunity to do just that.

If the pharmaceutical industry ever needed an icon for evidence of its good works, HAART would be it. Between 1995 and 1997, annual AIDS deaths in New York City dropped from 8,309 to 3,426, and that number has continued to decline ever since. The success of HAART has been so remarkable that it now tends to take us by surprise when anybody does succumb, although 2,076 New Yorkers died in 2006 (2007 figures are not yet available). Though many of the most prominent deaths, like Cheren's and Hattoy's, tend to be of gay men, the percentage of the dead who contracted the disease through gay sex is now reportedly as low as 15 percent (with a large proportion still reported as unknown). Intravenous-drug users make up the biggest group, 38.5 percent, and women account for almost one in three of total AIDS deaths.

One of the ironies of the success of HAART is that it has fostered the myth that the AIDS epidemic has come to an end, and that living with HIV is only marginally more problematic than living with herpes or genital warts. This is one obvious explanation for why HIV infection is once again on the rise among young men—specifically, MSMs, as they're now known in the public-health jargon, for men who have sex with men—increasing by a third between 2001 and 2006. Among those 30 and over, the infection rate is still decreasing, notes Thomas Frieden, commissioner of the city's Department of Health and Mental Hygiene, suggesting that the increased rate of infection among men under 30 is due in part to decreased awareness of the disease or the toll it can take.

"If you do the mathematics," Frieden says, "HAART became available in 1996. If you were of age before then, sexually active, and you saw a lot of people dying or sick or disfigured from AIDS, maybe you're more careful than if you came of age after 1996 and didn't see that. When we've done focus groups, what young men have told us is that the only thing they hear about HIV these days is that if you get it, you can climb mountains, like Magic Johnson. Certainly it's true that the treatment for HIV is very effective and it's possible to live a long and productive life with an HIV infection It's also true that it remains an incurable infection. That the treatment is very arduous and sometimes unsuccessful. It remains a disease often fatal, and frequently disabling."

At the moment some 100,000 New Yorkers are infected with the HIV virus, and AIDS remains the third leading cause of death in men under 65, exceeded only by heart disease and cancer. The question of who will die from AIDS in the HAART era—or who dies with an HIV infection but not technically from AIDS—and what kills them is worth asking now that such deaths have become relatively infrequent.

Frieden's department of Health and Mental Hygiene tried to answer this question with a study it published in the summer of 2006. The newsworthy conclusions were that deaths among New Yorkers with AIDS were still dropping, thanks to HAART, and that one in four of these individuals was now living long enough to die of the same chronic diseases that are likely to kill the uninfected—particularly cancer or heart disease—although most of these non-HIV-related deaths were from the side effects of drug abuse. HIV-related illnesses were still responsible for the remaining three out of four deaths. Or at least "HIV disease," in these cases, was recorded as a cause of death on the death certificates.

What the Health Department study couldn't do is say precisely what these HIV-related deaths were. For the answer to this question, you have to go to physicians who specialize in treating HIV-infected patients. Michael Mullen, clinical director of infectious diseases at Mount Sinai School of Medicine, for instance, says the best way to think about AIDS deaths is to divide HIV-infected individuals into three groups.

The bulk of these deaths occur within the first group, those who either never started HAART to begin with or didn't stay on it once they did. For these patients, "it might as well still be the eighties," says Mullen, and they die from the same AIDS-defining illnesses that were the common causes of death twenty years ago—pneumocystis pneumonia, central-nervous system opportunistic infections (such as toxoplasmosis), lymphoma, Kaposi's sarcoma, etc.

A large proportion of these victims are indigent; many are intravenous-drug users—IVDUs, as they're known in the official jargon, accounted for 21 percent of HIV-positive New Yorkers in 2006, but, as noted above, 38.5 percent of the city's AIDS deaths. The virus is not more aggressive or virulent in these cases. Rather, these are the people who either don't or can't do what it takes to fight it. "These individuals are repeatedly admitted to the hospital," says Mullen, "sometimes for opportunistic infections, sometimes for drug-related issues, often for HIV-related lymphomas and malignancies. They will not take the medication, nine times out of ten, because of drug use." Often these individuals are co-infected with hepatitis, which increases the risk that the more toxic side effects of the anti-retroviral drugs will lead to permanent liver or kidney damage.

By far the highest death rates in this group are in what the authorities now refer to as concurrent HIV/AIDS diagnoses. These patients never get diagnosed with HIV infection until they already have active AIDS. (Cheren, because of his age and his AIDS awareness, is an extreme case.) These constituted more than a quarter of the 3,745 new cases of HIV infections diagnosed in New York in 2006. "Those people have never been tested before," says Mullen. "Believe it or not, people like this still exist." Typically, they've had the infection for ten years—the average time between HIV infection and the emergence of AIDS—but won't know it or acknowledge it until admitted to the emergency room with pneumonia or some other opportunistic infection. These individuals are twice as likely to die in the three to four years after their diagnosis as someone who was just diagnosed with HIV alone. Half of these deaths will occur in the first four months after diagnosis, often from whatever AIDS-related ailment led them to the emergency room in the first place.

It's because of these concurrent HIV/AIDS diagnoses that the Centers for Disease Control and Prevention and the city's Department of Health and Mental Hygiene have been lobbying for HIV tests to be given routinely to anyone who visits an emergency room for any reason. In one recent study from South Carolina, almost three out of four of those people with concurrent HIV/AIDS diagnoses had visited a medical facility after their infection and prior to getting their blood tested for the virus—averaging six visits each before they were finally tested and diagnosed. "By remaining untested during their routine contacts with the health-care system," said Frieden, in testimony to the New York State Assembly Committee on Health, "they have missed the high-quality treatment that could improve their health and extend their lives. Many may have unknowingly infected their partners—and these partners may not learn that they are infected until they too are sick with AIDS. And so this cycle of death continues."

The second group of HIV-infected patients consists of those at the other extreme, the ones who are least likely to die from AIDS or its complications. These individuals were diagnosed with HIV after the advent of HAART and have taken their medications religiously ever since. In these cases, HAART is likely to suppress their virus for decades, and they're now significantly more likely to die of heart disease or cancer than of anything related to AIDS. To get an idea of the mortality rate among these patients, consider Alexander McMeeking's practice, on East 40th Street. McMeeking ran the HIV clinic at Bellevue from 1987 to 1989 and then left to start a private practice. To the best of his knowledge, only three of his 300-odd Bellevue patients survived long enough to get on HAART. They are still alive today. "Fortunately, thank God, all three are doing great," says McMeeking. "I tell them they will essentially die of old age."

McMeeking's practice now includes 600 HIV-infected patients, and last year he lost only two of those—one to lung cancer, another to liver cancer.

Now the question is whether these patients doing well with HAART are actually more susceptible to the kind of chronic diseases that kill the uninfected. Are they more likely to die from heart disease, cancers, liver and kidney failure, and other chronic diseases either because of the HIV itself or the anti-retroviral regimen keeping it under control? One observation made repeatedly in studies—including the 2006 report from the Department of Health and Mental Hygiene—is that these HIV-infected individuals appear to have higher rates of several different cancers, in particular lung cancer among smokers, non-Hodgkins lymphoma, and cancers of the rectal area. These cancers appear both more precocious and more aggressive in HIV-infected patients—they strike earlier and kill quicker. The reason is not yet clear, although a likely explanation is that the ability of the immune system to search out and destroy incipient malignancies is sufficiently compromised from either the anti-retroviral drugs, the virus, or the coexistence of several viruses—squamous-cell cancers of the rectal area are caused by the same human papilloma virus that causes cervical cancer in woman—that the cancers get a foothold they don't get in non-HIV-infected individuals.

One finding that's considered indisputable is that HAART, and particularly the protease inhibitors that are a critical part of the anti-retroviral cocktail, can play havoc with risk factors for heart disease. They raise cholesterol and triglyceride levels; they lower HDL, and they can cause increased resistance to the hormone insulin. These changes often accompany a condition known as HIV-related lipodystrophy, which afflicts maybe half of all individuals who go on HAART. Subcutaneous fat is lost on the face, arms, legs, and buttocks, while fat accumulates in the gut, upper back (a condition known as a buffalo hump), and breasts. The question is whether these metabolic disturbances actually increase the likelihood of having a heart attack. It's certainly reasonable to think they would, but it's remarkably difficult to demonstrate that the drugs or the virus itself is responsible: The fact that a relatively young man or woman with AIDS has a heart attack does not mean that the heart attack was caused by HIV or the disturbance in cholesterol and lipid levels induced by the therapy.

"If it's 1988, 1989," says one doctor, "and I have a patient with HIV disease and hypertension, he's not going to live long enough to die of hypertension. I want to treat the disease."

Any difference in disease incidence between HIV-infected and uninfected individuals, explains John Brooks, leader of the clinical-epidemiology team within the CDC's Division of HIV/AIDS Prevention, can be due to the infection itself, to the therapy—HAART—or to "the host, the person who has HIV infection, both physiologically and socioculturally." It's the last factor—the host—that complicates the science. Until recently, for instance, physicians saw little reason to worry about heart-disease risk factors in their HIV-infected patients and so didn't bother to aggressively treat risk factors in those patients, as they did the HIV-negative. "Think about it," says Brooks, "if it's 1988, 1989, and I have a patient with HIV disease and hypertension, he's not going to live long enough to die of hypertension. I want to treat the disease."

The rate of cigarette smoking among HIV-infected individuals is also twice as high as the national average. The rate of intravenous drug use is far higher, as is the rate of infection with hepatitis B or C, because intravenous drug use is a common route to getting both HIV and hepatitis. So the fact that an HIV-infected patient may seem to be suffering premature heart disease, diabetes, or liver or kidney disease earlier than seems normal for the population as a whole—or the fact that a study reports such a finding about a population of HIV-infected individuals—only raises the issue of whether the population as a whole is the relevant comparison group. "Since one of the major risk factors for HIV is intravenous drug use," says Brooks, "you have to ask, what's the contribution of heroin to somebody's kidney disease versus the HIV versus untreated high blood pressure versus smoking?"

"I still expect most of my patients to live a normal life expectancy," says an AIDS doctor, "but they may do so with a bit more nips and scrapes."

From his own clinical experience, McMeeking agrees that heart disease, certain cancers, and liver and kidney disease do seem to pose a greater threat to his HIV-infected patients than might otherwise be expected in a comparable uninfected population. "I still expect most of my patients to live a normal life expectancy," he says, "but they may do so with a bit more nips and scrapes."

The third group of HIV-infected individuals consists of those in the middle of the two extremes. HAART, in these cases, has literally been a life saver, but has not guaranteed a normal life expectancy. These are the patients, like Bob Hattoy, who were diagnosed with AIDS in the late eighties or early nineties, before the advent of HAART. They began on one drug (AZT, for instance) and then stayed alive long enough to get on protease inhibitors and the HAART cocktails. These patients were on the cusp of the HIV transformation from a deadly to a chronic-disease epidemic; they were infected late enough to survive but too early to derive all the benefits from HAART.

The anti-retroviral drugs of HAART work by attacking the life cycle of the virus. The earliest generation of HAART drugs attacked the enzymes that the virus virus uses to reproduce in the cells. (Protease inhibitors, for instance, go after an enzyme called HIV-1 protease, which the virus uses to assemble itself during reproduction.) The latest drugs go after the methods that the virus uses to enter cells in which it will replicate. The key to the effectiveness of HAART, as researchers discovered in the mid-nineties, was to include at least three drugs in the cocktail to which the patient's specific virus had no resistance. This would suppress viral replication sufficiently so that the virus wouldn't be able to mutate fast enough to evolve resistance to any of the drugs. But patients who began on one or two anti-AIDS drugs and only then moved to HAART already had time to evolve resistance to a few of the drugs in the cocktail. This made the entire package less effective and increased the likelihood that they would evolve resistance to the other drugs as well.

"We call it 'sins of the past,'" says Mullen. "We gave these patients sequential monotherapy; it was state-of-the-art at the time, and a lot of those people are alive today because of that. It got them through until HAART came along, but their HAART is not highly active, only fairly active. Their virus has baseline mutations that interfere with the response." This group of patients also includes those who were infected initially with a strain of HIV already resistant to one or several of the components of HAART, or those patients who were less than 99 percent faithful in taking the regimen of pills that constitute HAART. Anything less than that and the virus has the opportunity to evolve resistance.

Perhaps a quarter of all new cases, says Mullen, are infected with a strain of the virus resistant to one or more drugs in the HAART cocktail. "You can't use the frontline regimen, because the virus has already seen those drugs," he says. "You have to go to more complicated regimens. This is why we do resistance testing before we start a person on medication. We see what drugs the virus has seen or is resistant to and can take that into account."

Sins-of-the-past patients have to have faith that the pharmaceutical industry can stay one step ahead of their disease. The prognosis, at the moment, is promising. There are several entirely new classes of AIDS drugs, including one by Merck, called an integrase inhibitor, that was just approved by the FDA last October. A recent report of the discovery of 270 new human proteins employed by the AIDS virus to hijack cells and start replicating—the definition of a successful infection—means the pharmaceutical industry will not run out of new targets to block the infection in the near future.

Still, some sins-of-the-past patients simply do worse than others, and the occasional patient will lose the battle before new drugs come along or simply give up. "I had a friend who died last week," one sins-of-the-past patient told me recently. "He just lost faith. He would get sick a lot, would get better, then sick again. Finally he decided to try Eastern medicine, and stopped taking his [HAART] medications entirely. It killed him. It's not a good example, other than to show that people can reach their breaking point."

Critical Thinking

1. What are the lifestyle changes that you can make to reduce your risk of developing cardiovascular disease, cancer, diabetes, and AIDS?

2. Why are people still dying from AIDS?

3. What population groups are most likely to die from AIDS and why?

A Mandate in Texas

The Story of a Compulsory Vaccination and What It Means

KATE O'BEIRNE

On February 2, Texas became the first state to require that young girls be vaccinated against some sexually transmitted viruses. This happened when Gov. Rick Perry issued an executive order requiring that students receive a new vaccine before entering the sixth grade. Perry's order has met with criticism from state legislators who object to his unilateral action, medical groups that welcome the breakthrough vaccine but oppose a mandate, and parents who believe that such coercion usurps their authority. The vaccine's manufacturer is aggressively lobbying other state legislatures to back mandates, and legislation to require the new vaccine is pending in over a dozen states.

Last June, the Food and Drug Administration approved Merck & Co.'s Gardasil vaccine for females aged 9 to 26. When administered to girls before they become sexually active, the vaccine can protect against two of the strains of the human papillomavirus (HPV) that cause about 70 percent of cervical cancers. Within a few weeks of the approval, the vaccine was added to the federal list of recommended routine immunizations for eleven- and twelve-year-old girls. The duration of immunity for the three-dose vaccine series, at a cost of about $360, is not yet known. The federal, means-tested Vaccines for Children program will now include the HPV vaccine, and insurance companies are expected to begin covering its costs.

There is little controversy over the recommendation that the vaccine be broadly used. HPV is the most common sexually transmitted infection, with about half of those who are sexually active carrying it at some point in their lives and about 6.2 million infected annually. The number of sexual partners is the most important risk factor for genital HPV infection. There are no treatments to cure HPV infections, but most are cleared by the immune system, with 90 percent disappearing within two years. Some infections do persist, causing genital warts, cancers of the cervix, and other types of cancer. Each year, over 9,000 new cases of cervical cancer are diagnosed, and the disease kills 3,700 women. Routine Pap tests have dramatically reduced the incidence of cervical cancers over the past 50 years, and it is recommended that even those immunized with the new vaccine continue to be tested, as the vaccine doesn't guard against eleven other high-risk strains of HPV that cause cancer.

Governor Perry recognized that "the newly approved HPV vaccine is a great advance in the protection of women's health" in a "whereas" clause on the way to his "therefore" order that rules be adopted to "mandate the age appropriate vaccination of all female children for HPV prior to admission to the sixth grade." In turning a federal recommendation into a state mandate, Perry has thrilled the vaccine manufacturer, while acting against the balance of medical opinion. And critics object to an opt-out provision that puts the onus on parents to file an affidavit seeking approval of their objection.

The American College of Pediatricians opposes requiring the vaccination for school attendance, saying that such a mandate would represent a "serious, precedent-setting action that trespasses on the rights of parents to make medical decisions for their children as well as on the rights of the children to attend school." The chairman of the American Academy of Pediatrics Committee on Infectious Diseases, Dr. Joseph A. Bocchini, believes a vaccine mandate is premature. "I think it's too early," he said. "This is a new vaccine. It would be wise to wait until we have additional information about the safety of the vaccine." The Texas Medical Association also opposes the mandate, expressing concerns over liability and costs.

Mandatory-education laws create a responsibility to make sure that children are vaccinated against contagious diseases they might be exposed to at school. Now states are considering compelling vaccination in the name of a broad public good, even though the disease in question would not be spread at schools.

Dr. Jon Abramson, the chairman of the Advisory Committee on Immunization Practices of the Centers for Disease Control, explains that protecting children against a virus that is spread by sexual activity is different from preventing the spread of measles. Abramson believes that mandating the HPV vaccine "is a much harder case to make, because you're not going to spread it in a school unless you're doing something you're not supposed to be doing in school." Non-vaccinated students would pose no risk to others while at school.

Texas state senator Glenn Hegar has introduced legislation to reverse Governor Perry's order on the grounds that research trials are still underway and "such mandates take away parents' rights to make medical decisions for their children and usurp parental authority." Twenty-six of 31 state senators believe the governor has usurped legislative authority too, and are calling on him to rescind the executive order. Perry stands by the order, but the rising controversy has discouraged other supporters of mandates.

The *Washington Post* recently reported that Virginia and 17 other states are considering the vaccine requirement "at the urging of New Jersey–based pharmaceutical giant Merck & Co. . . . [which] stands to earn hundreds of millions of dollars annually on Gardasil, according to Wall Street estimates." Public-health organizations have joined Merck in urging that the vaccine be made available in public clinics and encouraging its coverage by private insurers, but they don't support Merck's push for a school requirement.

There were 210 cases of cervical cancer in Maryland last year. Democratic state senator Delores Kelley introduced a bill to require the HPV vaccine for sixth-grade girls. Following complaints from parents and recent non-compliance problems with current mandated vaccinations, Kelley has withdrawn her bill (though she has spoken openly of reintroducing it next session). She explains that she was unaware of Merck & Co.'s lobbying efforts, and that she learned about the new HPV vaccine through a nonpartisan group of female legislators called Women in Government. More than half of its listed supporters are pharmaceutical manufacturers or other health-related companies. Women in Government is spearheading the campaign to mandate the HPV vaccine through school requirements, and some watchdog groups question the support it receives from Merck & Co. "It's not the vaccine community pushing for this," explains the director of the National Network for Immunization Information. Governor Perry's critics point to his own connection with Gardasil's manufacturer: His former chief of staff is a lobbyist for Merck & Co. in Texas.

The profit motive of a company can coincide with public-health interests, but the case for an HPV-vaccine mandate has not been made. The new vaccine does not prevent cervical cancer, but is a welcome protection against some strains of HPV. It is already available to parents who can decide whether it is appropriate for their young daughters. In substituting his judgment for theirs, Governor Perry has attempted to intrude upon their prerogatives and responsibilities. He has also substituted his own judgment for expert medical opinion. State officials who follow his lead won't enjoy immunity from the firestorm of criticism they will rightly earn.

Critical Thinking

1. Should all young girls be vaccinated against HPV?
2. What are the risks versus the benefits of the HPV vaccination?

UNIT 8

Health Care and the Health Care System

Unit Selections

Learning Outcomes

After reading this unit, you should be able to:

- Explain why or why not pharmacists should be permitted to refuse to fill certain prescriptions.

- Explain why some pharmacists refuse to dispense birth control pills.

- Discuss why women's health is threatened when pharmacists refuse to dispense certain medications.

- Describe what can be done to help reduce health care costs.

- Discuss whether individuals without health insurance die earlier than those who are insured.

- Distinguish whether quality health care is a right or a privilege.

- Explain why patients may be treated independently of their wishes.

- Discuss whether there should be limits on health care provided to the terminally ill.

- Explain whether health care is just another commodity.

- Explain who should be involved in making health care decisions for the terminally ill.

Student Website

www.mhhe.com/cls

Internet References

American Medical Association (AMA)
   www.ama-assn.org
MedScape: The Online Resource for Better Patient Care
   www.medscape.com

Americans are healthier today than they have been at any time in this nation's history. Americans suffer more illness today than they have at any time in this nation's history. Which statement is true? They both are, depending on the statistics you quote. According to longevity statistics, Americans are living longer today and, therefore, must be healthier. Still, other statistics indicate that Americans today report twice as many acute illnesses as did our ancestors 60 years ago. They also report that their pain lasts longer. Unfortunately, this combination of living longer and feeling sicker places additional demands on a health care system that, according to experts, is already in a state of crisis.

Despite the clamor about the problems with our health care system, if you can afford it, then the American health care system is one of the best in the world. However, being the best does not mean that it is without problems. Each year, more than half a million Americans are injured or die due to preventable mistakes made by medical care professionals. In addition, countless unnecessary tests are preformed that not only add to the expense of health care, but may actually place the patient at risk. Reports such as these fuel the fire of public skepticism toward the quality of health care that Americans receive. while these aspects of our health care system indicate a need for repair, they represent just the tip of the iceberg. Jonathan Gruber in "The Cost Implications of Health Care Reform" discusses the number of Americans who are uninsured and the problems they face. As the number continues to rise, Gruber calls for the government to address the cost concerns related to health care reform. He believes that universal coverage will not only insure all Americans, but it will also impact the cost of health care. Gruber also believes that costs continue to rise due to the blockage of price controls by the pharmaceutical industry. A related article, "The *Case for* Killing Granny," addresses the cost of treating the elderly at the end of their lives.

An issue related to access to health services is presented in "Pharmacist Refusals: A Threat to Women's Health." It relates to pharmacists who refuse to fill prescriptions for certain medications that violate their personal beliefs. These typically include oral contraceptives and morning after pills, which some pharmacists believe cause abortions.

While choices in health care providers are increasing, paying for services continues to be a challenge as medical costs continue to rise. Why have health care costs risen so much? The answer to this question is multifaceted and includes such factors as physicians' fees, hospital costs, insurance costs, pharmaceutical costs, and health fraud. It could be argued that while these factors operate within any health care system, the lack of a meaningful form of outcomes assessment has permitted and encouraged waste and inefficiency within our system. Ironically, one of the major factors for the rise in the cost of health care is our rapidly expanding aging population—tangible evidence of an improving health care delivery system. This is obviously one factor that we hope will continue to rise. Another significant factor that is often overlooked is the constantly expanding boundaries

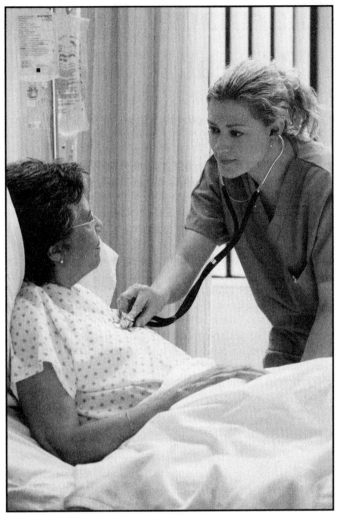

© Jose Luis Pelaez/Getty Images

of health care. It is somewhat ironic that as our success in treating various disorders has expanded, so has the domain of health care, and often into areas where previously health care had little or no involvement. "Incapacitated, Alone and Treated to Death" offers an interesting perspective of how the care and treatment of patients is often made independent of their wishes.

Traditionally, Americans have felt that the state of their health was largely determined by the quality of the health care available to them. This attitude has fostered an unhealthy dependence upon the health care system and contributed to the skyrocketing costs. It should be obvious by now that while there is no simple solution to our health care problems, we would all be a lot better off if we accepted more personal responsibility for our health. While this shift would help ease the financial burden of health care, it might necessitate a more responsible coverage of medical news in order to educate and enlighten the public on personal health issues.

Pharmacist Refusals: A Threat to Women's Health

MARCIA D. GREENBERGER AND RACHEL VOGELSTEIN

Pharmacist refusals to fill prescriptions for birth control based on personal beliefs have been increasingly reported around the world. In the United States, reports of pharmacist refusals have surfaced in over a dozen states. These refusals have occurred at major drugstore chains like CVS and Walgreens and have affected everyone from rape survivors in search of emergency contraception to married mothers needing birth control pills. Pharmacists who refuse to dispense also often have refused to transfer a woman's prescription to another pharmacist or to refer her to another pharmacy. Other pharmacists have confiscated prescriptions, misled women about availability of drugs, lectured women about morality, or delayed access to drugs until they are no longer effective.

Pharmacist refusal incidents have also been reported in other countries. For example, a pharmacist at a popular London pharmacy chain recently refused to fill a woman's prescription for emergency contraception (EC), or the "morning-after pill," due to religious beliefs; two pharmacists refused to fill contraceptive prescriptions for women at a pharmacy in Salleboeuf, France; and in the small country town of Merriwa, Australia, the local pharmacist refuses to stock EC altogether.[1–3] Pharmacists for Life International, a group refusing to fill prescriptions for contraception, currently claims to have over 1600 members worldwide and represents members in 23 countries.[4]

Pharmacist refusals can have devastating consequences for women's health. Access to contraception is critical to preventing unwanted pregnancies and to enabling women to control the timing and spacing of their pregnancies. Without contraception, the average woman would bear between 12 and 15 children in her lifetime. For some women, pregnancy can entail great health risks and even life-endangerment. Also, women rely on prescription contraceptives for a range of medical reasons in addition to birth control, such as amenorrhea, dysmenorrhea, and endometriosis. Refusals to fill prescriptions for EC (a form of contraception approved by the U.S. Food and Drug Administration and relied on worldwide) are particularly burdensome, as EC is an extremely time-sensitive drug. EC is most effective if used within the first 12 to 24 hours after contraceptive failure, unprotected sex, or sexual assault. If not secured in a timely manner, this drug is useless. Rural and low-income women, as well as survivors of sexual assault, are at particular risk of harm.

In the United States, most states have an implied duty to dispense. Personal beliefs are omitted from the enumerated instances where pharmacists are authorized to refuse; such as where the pharmacist has concerns about therapeutic duplications, drug-disease contraindications, drug interactions, incorrect dosage, or drug abuse. In New Hampshire, the pharmacy regulations' Code of Ethics states that a pharmacist shall "[h]old the health and safety of patients to be of first consideration and render to each patient the full measure of his/her ability as an essential health practitioner."[5] Pharmacists who refuse to fill valid prescriptions based on personal beliefs do not hold patient health and safety as their first consideration.

Illinois explicitly charges pharmacies with a duty to ensure that women's prescriptions for birth control are filled without delay or interference.[6] Massachusetts and North Carolina have interpreted their laws to ensure that women's access to medication is not impeded by pharmacists' personal beliefs.[7,8] However, Arkansas, Georgia, Mississippi, and South Dakota explicitly grant pharmacists the right to refuse to dispense prescriptions for birth control based on personal beliefs.[9]

In addition, a small number of administrative and judicial bodies have considered challenges to pharmacist refusals. In the United States, the Wisconsin pharmacy board found that a pharmacist's failure to transfer a birth control prescription fell below the expected standard of care and constituted a danger to the health and welfare of the patient. The board formally reprimanded the pharmacist for his actions, charged him with the $20,000 cost of adjudication, and conditioned his license on provision of proper notification to his employer about anticipated refusals and his assurances about steps he will take to protect patient access to medication.[10]

Outside of the United States, the European Court of Human Rights rejected an appeal of a conviction of pharmacists under the French consumer code for a refusal to sell contraceptive pills. The Court held that the right to freedom of religion does not allow pharmacists to impose their beliefs on others, so long as the sale of contraceptives is legal.[2]

Some have questioned how such rules comport with the treatment of other medical professionals. In general, medical professionals have a duty to treat patients, with only limited exceptions. The majority of refusal laws apply to doctors and nurses and are limited to abortion services. Allowing pharmacists to refuse to dispense prescriptions for contraception would dramatically expand the universe of permissible refusals. Moreover, unlike doctors and nurses, pharmacists do not select or administer treatments or perform procedures. Therefore, pharmacists' involvement is not as direct, nor would patients' safety be potentially compromised in the same way as would be the case if a doctor or nurse were forced to perform a procedure that they personally oppose.

Since 1997, 28 states have introduced legislation that would permit pharmacists to refuse to dispense, and sometimes to refer or transfer, drugs on the basis of moral or religious grounds. Fifteen states have introduced such bills in the 2005 legislative session alone; while some are specific to contraception, others apply to all medication. These bills have implications for future refusals to fill prescriptions, such as in HIV regimens or treatments derived from embryonic stem cell research. On the other hand, bills have been introduced in four state legislatures and the U.S. Congress that would require pharmacists or pharmacies either to fill prescriptions for contraception or ensure that women have timely access to prescription medication in their pharmacies.

Some professional and medical associations have issued guidelines that protect women against pharmacist refusals. Value VIII of the *Code of Ethics* of the College of Pharmacists of British Columbia requires pharmacists to ensure "continuity of care in the event of . . . conflict with moral beliefs."[11] It permits pharmacists to refuse to dispense prescriptions based on moral beliefs, but only if there is another pharmacist "within a reasonable distance or available within a reasonable time willing to provide the service."

In the United States, several associations have issued similar, although not legally binding, policies. The American Public Health Association states that "[h]ealth systems are urged to establish protocols to ensure that a patient is not denied timely access to EC based on moral or religious objections of a health care provider."[12] The American Medical Women's Association has stated that "pharmacies should guarantee seamless delivery, without delay (within the standard practice for ordering), judgment, or other interference, of all contraceptive drugs and devices lawfully prescribed by a physician."[13]

The American Pharmacists Association (APhA) articulates a standard of professionalism in its *Code of Ethics* that is not legally binding. It mandates that pharmacists place "concern for the well-being of the patient at the center of professional practice."[14] The code also emphasizes that pharmacists are "dedicated to protecting the dignity of the patient" and must "respect personal and cultural differences . . ."[14] This language precludes refusals, lectures, and other barriers erected by pharmacists who disagree with a woman's decision, made in consultation with her health-care provider, to use birth control. Some state pharmacy associations have similar codes.

However, the APhA has another policy that conflicts with these principles. It allows for refusals based on personal beliefs, as long as pharmacists refer prescriptions to another pharmacist or pharmacy.[15] The APhA has not formally explained how to square this policy with its ethical principles of patient-protective care, let alone with state laws and regulations.

Recommendations

Women must be provided timely access to prescription medication. One solution is to require pharmacists to dispense all drugs despite their personal beliefs, in line with their professional duties and ethical obligations. Another solution is to shift the duty to fill from pharmacists onto pharmacies. Under this approach, pharmacies would be charged with ensuring that prescriptions for all drugs are filled without delay or other interference. Such a requirement would allow pharmacies to make arrangements to accommodate the personal beliefs of individual pharmacists. However, active obstruction by pharmacists of women's access to prescription medication—such as withholding or delaying prescriptions or providing misinformation—should be deemed unethical or unprofessional conduct subject to legal sanction.

References and Notes

1. "I Won't Sell Pill, It's Against My Religion," *Sunday Mirror* (27 February 2005).
2. Pichon and Sajous v. France, App. No. 49853/99, Eur. Court H.R. (2001).
3. "U.S. Firm Ships Free Contraceptives to Condom-Deprived Australian Town," *Financial Times,* 31 March 2005 [source: Agence France-Presse].
4. See www.pfli.org/main.php?pfli=locations
5. N.H. Code Admin. R. Ph. 501.01(b)(1) (2005).
6. Illinois Pharmacy Practice Act, § 1330.91 (j)(1) (2005).
7. Massachusetts Board of Pharmacy, letter on file with the National Women's Law Center, 6 May 2004.
8. Conscience concerns in pharmacist decisions, *North Carolina Board Pharm. Newsl.* 26 (3), 1 (2005), 1; available as item 2061 at www.ncbop.org/Newsletters/NC012005.pdf
9. Ark. Code. Ann. § 20-16-304 (1973); Ga. Comp. R. & Regs. r. 480-5-.03(n) (2001); Miss. Code. Ann. § 41-107-1 (2004); S.D. Codified Laws § 36-11-70 (1998).
10. See www.naralwi.org/assets/files/noesendecision &finalorder.pdf
11. See www.bcpharmacists.org/standards/ethicslong/
12. American Public Health Association (APHA), Policy statement 2003-15 (APHA, Washington, DC, 2003).
13. American Medical Women's Association (AMWA), Statement of AMWA supporting pharmacies' obligation to dispense birth control (Alexandria, VA, 2005) (on file with the National Women's Law Center).
14. See www.aphanet.org/AM/Template.cfm ?Section=Pharmacy_ Practice&CONTENTID=2903&TEMPLATE=/CM /HTMLDisplay.cfm
15. S. C. Winckler, American Pharmacists Association (1 July 2004) (letter to the editor, unpublished); available at www.aphanet.org/AM/Template.cfm? Section=Public_ Relations&Template=/CM/HTML Display.cfm& ContentID=2689

Critical Thinking

1. Should pharmacists be permitted to refuse to fill certain prescriptions?

2. Why do some pharmacists refuse to fill prescriptions for birth control pills?

3. Why is women's health compromised when pharmacists refuse to dispense certain medications?

The authors are with the National Women's Law Center, Washington, DC 20036, USA. For correspondence, e-mail: rlaser@nwlc.org.

The Cost Implications of Health Care Reform

JONATHAN GRUBER, PH.D.

On March 23, 2010, President Barack Obama signed into law the most significant piece of U.S. social policy legislation in almost 50 years. There is little disagreement over the premise that the Patient Protection and Affordable Care Act (ACA) will dramatically expand health insurance coverage. But there is concern about its implications for health care costs. These concerns have been heightened by a recent report from the actuary at the Centers for Medicare and Medicaid Services (CMS), which shows that health care reform will cause an expansion of national health care expenditures.

The ACA includes a major investment in the affordability of health insurance for low-income families: under the law, all individuals with family incomes below 133% of the poverty line (i.e., below about $30,000 for a family of four) are eligible for free public insurance, and there are tax credits to help make health insurance affordable for families with incomes of up to 400% of the poverty level. At the same time, the ACA incorporates a number of fund-raising mechanisms, including a reduction in the overpayment to Medicare Advantage insurers, a reduction in the update factor for Medicare hospital reimbursement, an increase in the Medicare tax (and extension to unearned income) for high-income families, an assessment on employers whose employees use subsidies rather than employer-sponsored insurance, and the "Cadillac tax" (an assessment on the highest-cost insurance plans). The Congressional Budget Office estimates that these revenue increases will exceed the new spending, reducing the federal deficit by more than $100 billion in the first decade and more than $1 trillion in the second decade.[1]

Some have questioned the likelihood of this deficit reduction, claiming, for example, that the numbers are "front loaded" because some of the revenue-raising mechanisms begin before 2014, whereas the majority of spending doesn't start until after 2014. But the trend under the law will actually be toward larger deficit reduction over time; indeed, the reduction in the deficit is expected to increase in the last 2 years of the budget window. The cuts in spending and increases in taxes are actually "back-loaded," with the revenue increases rising faster over time than the spending increases, so that this legislation improves our nation's fiscal health more and more over time.[1]

Others have raised the possibility that the cuts that provide much of this financing will never take place, and they point to the physician-payment cuts required by the Balanced Budget Act of 1997, which have been repeatedly delayed by Congress. But as Van de Water and Horney have highlighted,[2] Congress has passed many Medicare cuts during the past 20 years, and the physician-payment cut is the only one that has not taken effect.

With U.S. health care spending already accounting for 17% of the gross domestic product (GDP) and growing, there is also concern about policies that increase this spending. And, as the CMS actuary points out, the ACA will increase national health care expenditures. At the peak of its effect on spending, in 2016, the law will increase health care expenditures by about 2%; by 2019, the ACA-related increase will be 1%, or 0.2% of the GDP.

However, these increases are quite small relative to the gains in coverage under the new law. There are currently 220 million insured Americans, and the CMS predicts that 34 million more will be insured by 2019. The agency also estimates that without this reform, health care costs would grow by 6.6% per year between 2010 and 2019. So we'll be increasing the ranks of the insured by more than 15% at a cost that is less than one sixth of 1 year's growth in national health care expenditures.

Alternatively, consider the fact that under this legislation, by 2019, the United States will be spending $46 billion more on medical care than we do today. In 2010 dollars, this amounts to only $800 per newly insured person—quite a low cost as compared (for example) with the $5,000 average single premium for employer-sponsored insurance.[3]

U.S. spending on health care is very high and a source of great concern, but it is the growth rate of medical spending, not the level of spending, that ultimately determines our country's financial well-being. If current trends persist, we will be spending an unsustainable 38% of our GDP on health care by 2075, as the growth rate of health care costs continues to outstrip the growth rate of the overall economy. In this environment, whether annual health care costs rise or fall by 1% or even 5% is irrelevant—all we do is move the day of reckoning less than 1 year closer or farther away. Clearly, the key to the long-term viability of our health care system is to lower the rate of cost growth, often referred to as "bending the cost curve."

On this count, the CMS actuary's news is good: although the ACA will boost medical spending somewhat, its incremental impact on spending will decrease over time (from 2% in 2016 to 1% in 2019). These declining estimates imply that by the second decade, the ACA will have reduced national health care spending. This effect is due to provisions such as the Cadillac tax, for which the definition of a high-cost plan is indexed to the growth in overall prices in the economy, not to the (higher) growth in health insurance premiums. As a result, an increasing proportion of plans will be taxed, and more people will shift into lower-cost insurance options in order to avoid paying the tax, thus reducing national health care expenditures.

Yet the real question concerns how far the ACA will go in slowing cost growth. There is great uncertainty, mostly because there is such uncertainty in general about how to control the rate of growth in health care costs. There is no shortage of good ideas for ways of doing so, ranging from reducing consumer demand for health care services, to reducing payments to health care providers, to reorganizing the payment for and delivery of care, to promoting cost-effectiveness standards in care delivery, to reducing pressure from the threat of medical malpractice claims. There is, however, a shortage of evidence regarding which approaches will actually work—and therefore no consensus on which path is best to follow.

Given this uncertainty, it is best to cautiously pursue many different approaches toward cost control and study them to see which ones work best. That is exactly the approach taken in the ACA, which includes provisions to reduce consumer demand through the Cadillac tax, to reduce provider payments by appointing a depoliticized board to make up-or-down recommendations to Congress on changes to Medicare's provider payments, to run dozens of pilots to test various approaches to revamping provider-payment incentives and organizational structure, to invest hundreds of millions of dollars in new comparative-effectiveness research, and to launch pilot programs to assess the impact of various reorganizations of the medical malpractice process. None of these is guaranteed to work, but together they represent a significant step toward fundamental cost control.

In summary, analysis by both the Congressional Budget Office and the CMS actuary show that the ACA will substantially reduce the federal deficit, only slightly increase national medical spending (despite an enormous expansion in insurance coverage), begin to reduce the growth rate of medical spending, and introduce various new initiatives that may lead to more fundamental reductions in the long-term rate of health care cost growth. The ACA will not solve our health care cost problems, but it is a historic and cost-effective step in the right direction.

Notes

1. Letter from Douglas W. Elmendorf to House Speaker Nancy Pelosi, March 18, 2010. (Accessed May 6, 2010, at http://www.cbo.gov/ftpdocs/113xx/doc11355/hr4872.pdf.)

2. Van de Water PN, Horney JR. Health reform will reduce the deficit: charges of budgetary gimmickry are unfounded. Washington, DC: Center on Budget and Policy Priorities, March 25, 2010. (Accessed May 6, 2010, at http://www.cbpp.org/cms/index.cfm?fa=view&id=3134.)

3. Employer health benefits: 2009 annual survey. Washington, DC: Henry J. Kaiser Family Foundation, 2009.

Critical Thinking

1. Is the expansion of health insurance coverage worth its cost? Explain your answer.

Myth Diagnosis

Everyone knows that people without health insurance are more likely to die. But are they?

MEGAN MCARDLE

Outside of the few states where it is illegal to deny coverage based on medical history, I am probably uninsurable. Though I'm in pretty good health, I have several latent conditions, including an autoimmune disease. If I lost the generous insurance that I have through *The Atlantic,* even the most charitable insurer might hesitate to take me on.

So I took a keen interest when, at the fervid climax of the health-care debate in mid-December, a *Washington Post* blogger, Ezra Klein, declared that Senator Joseph Lieberman, by refusing to vote for a bill with a public option, was apparently "willing to cause the deaths of hundreds of thousands" of uninsured people in order to punish the progressives who had opposed his reelection in 2006. In the ensuing blogstorm, conservatives condemned Klein's "venomous smear," while liberals solemnly debated the circumstances under which one may properly accuse one's opponents of mass murder.

But aside from an exchange between Matthew Yglesias of the Center for American Progress and Michael Cannon of the Cato Institute, few people addressed the question that mattered most to those of us who cannot buy an individual insurance policy at any price—the question that was arguably the health-care debate's most important: Was Klein (not to mention other like-minded editorialists who cited similar numbers) *right?* If we lost our insurance, would this gargantuan new entitlement really be the only thing standing between us and an early grave?

Perhaps few people were asking, because the question sounds so stupid. Health insurance buys you health care. Health care is supposed to save your life. So if you don't have someone buying you health care . . . well, you can complete the syllogism.

Last year's national debate on health-care legislation tended to dwell on either heart-wrenching anecdotes about costly, unattainable medical treatments, or arcane battles over how many people in the United States lacked insurance. Republicans rarely plumbed the connection between insurance and mortality, presumably because they would look foolish and heartless if they expressed any doubt about health insurance's benefits. It was politically safer to harp on the potential problems of government interventions—or, in extremis, to point out that more than half the uninsured were either affluent, lacking citizenship, or already eligible for government programs in which they hadn't bothered to enroll.

Even Democratic politicians made curiously little of the plight of the uninsured. Instead, they focused on cost control, so much so that you might have thought that covering the uninsured was a happy side effect of really throttling back the rate of growth in Medicare spending. When progressive politicians or journalists did address the disadvantages of being uninsured, they often fell back on the same data Klein had used: a 2008 report from the Urban Institute that estimated that about 20,000 people were dying every year for lack of health insurance.

But when you probe that claim, its accuracy is open to question. Even a rough approximation of how many people die because of lack of health insurance is hard to reach. Quite possibly, lack of health insurance has no more impact on your health than lack of flood insurance.

Part of the trouble with reports like the one from the Urban Institute is that they cannot do the kind of thing we do to test drugs or medical procedures: divide people randomly into groups that do and don't have health insurance, and see which group fares better. Experimental studies like this would be tremendously expensive, and it's hard to imagine that they'd attract sufficient volunteers. Moreover, they might well violate the ethical standards of doctors who believed they were condemning the uninsured patients to a life nasty, brutish, and short.

So instead, researchers usually do what are called "observational studies": they take data sets that include both insured and uninsured people, and compare their health outcomes—usually mortality rates, because these are unequivocal and easy to measure. For a long time, two of the best studies were Sorlie et al. (1994), which used a large sample of census data from 1982 to 1985; and Franks, Clancy, and Gold (1993), which examined a smaller but richer data set from the National Health and Nutrition Examination Survey, and its follow-up studies, between 1971 and 1987. The Institute of Medicine used the math behind these two studies to produce a 2002 report on an increase in illness and death from lack of insurance; the Urban Institute, in turn, updated those numbers to produce the figure that became the gold standard during the debate over healthcare reform.

The first thing one notices is that the original studies are a trifle elderly. Medicine has changed since 1987; presumably, so has the riskiness of going without health insurance.

Moreover, the question of who had insurance is particularly dodgy: the studies counted as "uninsured" anyone who lacked insurance in the initial interview. But of course, not all of those people would have stayed uninsured—a separate study suggests that only about a third of those who reported being uninsured over a two-year time frame lacked coverage for the entire period. Most of the "uninsured" people probably got insurance relatively quickly, while some of the "insured" probably lost theirs. The effect of this churn could bias your results either way; the inability to control for it makes the statistics less accurate.

The bigger problem is that the uninsured generally have more health risks than the rest of the population. They are poorer, more likely to smoke, less educated, more likely to be unemployed, more likely to be obese, and so forth. All these things are known to increase your risk of dying, independent of your insurance status.

There are also factors we can't analyze. It's widely believed that health improves with social status, a quality that's hard to measure. Risk-seekers are probably more likely to end up uninsured, and also to end up dying in a car crash—but their predilection for thrills will not end up in our statistics. People who are suspicious of doctors probably don't pursue either generous health insurance or early treatment. Those who score low on measures of conscientiousness often have trouble keeping jobs with good health insurance—or following complicated treatment protocols. And so on.

The studies relied upon by the Institute of Medicine and the Urban Institute tried to control for some of these factors. But Sorlie et al.—the larger study—lacked data on things like smoking habits and could control for only a few factors, while Franks, Clancy, and Gold, which had better controls but a smaller sample, could not, as an observational study, categorically exclude the possibility that lack of insurance has no effect on mortality at all.

The possibility that no one risks death by going without health insurance may be startling, but some research supports it. Richard Kronick of the University of California at San Diego's Department of Family and Preventive Medicine, an adviser to the Clinton administration, recently published the results of what may be the largest and most comprehensive analysis yet done of the effect of insurance on mortality. He used a sample of more than 600,000, and controlled not only for the standard factors, but for how long the subjects went without insurance, whether their disease was particularly amenable to early intervention, and even whether they lived in a mobile home. In test after test, he found no significantly elevated risk of death among the uninsured.

This result is not, perhaps, as shocking as it seems. Health care heals, but it also kills. Someone who lacked insurance over the past few decades might have missed taking their Lipitor, but also their Vioxx or Fen-Phen. According to one estimate, 80,000 people a year are killed just by "nosocomial infections"—infections that arise as a result of medical treatment. The only truly experimental study on health insurance, a randomized study of almost 4,000 subjects done by Rand and concluded in 1982, found that increasing the generosity of people's health insurance caused them to use more health care, but made almost no difference in their health status.

> **Health care heals, but it also kills. Someone who lacked insurance over the past decade might have missed taking Lipitor, but also Vioxx or Fen-Phen.**

If gaining insurance has a large effect on people's health, we should see outcomes improve dramatically between one's early and late 60s. Yet like the Kronick and Rand studies, analyses of the effect of Medicare, which becomes available to virtually everyone in America at the age of 65, show little benefit. In a recent review of the literature, Helen Levy of the University of Michigan and David Meltzer of the University of Chicago noted that the latest studies of this question "paint a surprisingly consistent picture: Medicare increases consumption of medical care and may modestly improve self-reported health but has no effect on mortality, at least in the short run."

Of course, that might be an indictment of programs like Medicare and Medicaid. Indeed, given the uncertainties about their impact on mortality rates—uncertainties that the results from Sorlie et al. don't resolve—it's possible that, by blocking the proposed expansion of health care through Medicare, Senator Lieberman, rather than committing the industrial-scale slaughter Klein fears, might not have harmed anyone at all. We cannot use one study to "prove" that having government insurance is riskier than having none. But we also cannot use a flawed and conflicting literature to "prove" that Lieberman was willing to risk the deaths of hundreds of thousands. Government insurance should have some effect, but if that effect is not large enough to be unequivocally evident in the data we have, it must be small.

Even if we did agree that insurance rarely confers significant health benefits, that would not necessarily undermine the case for a national health-care program. The academics who question the mass benefits of expanding coverage still think that doing so improves outcomes among certain vulnerable subgroups, like infants and patients with HIV. Besides, a national health program has nonmedical benefits. Leaving tens of millions of Americans without health insurance violates our sense of equity—and leaves those millions exposed to the risk of mind-boggling medical bills.

But we should have had a better handle on the case for expanded coverage—and, more important, the evidence behind it—before we embarked on a year-long debate that divided our house against itself. Certainly, we should have had it before Congress voted on the largest entitlement expansion in 40 years. Unfortunately, most of us forgot to ask a fundamental question, because we were certain we already knew the answer. By the time we got around to challenging our assumptions, it was too late to do anything except scream at each other from the sidelines.

Critical Thinking

1. Do individuals without health insurance die earlier than those who are insured? Why or why not?

2. Is quality health care a right or a privilege? Defend your answer.

MEGAN MCARDLE is *The Atlantic*'s business and economics editor, and the editor of the business channel at theatlantic.com.

The *Case for* Killing Granny

Evan Thomas et al.

Rethinking End-of-Life Care

My mother wanted to die, but the doctors wouldn't let her. At least that's the way it seemed to me as I stood by her bed in an intensive-care unit at a hospital in Hilton Head, S.C., five years ago. My mother was 79, a longtime smoker who was dying of emphysema. She knew that her quality of life was increasingly tethered to an oxygen tank, that she was losing her ability to get about, and that she was slowly drowning. The doctors at her bedside were recommending various tests and procedures to keep her alive, but my mother, with a certain firmness I recognized, said no. She seemed puzzled and a bit frustrated that she had to be so insistent on her own demise.

The hospital at my mother's assisted-living facility was sustained by Medicare, which pays by the procedure. I don't think the doctors were trying to be greedy by pushing more treatments on my mother. That's just the way the system works. The doctors were responding to the expectations of almost all patients. As a doctor friend of mine puts it, "Americans want the best, they want the latest, and they want it now." We expect doctors to make heroic efforts—especially to save our lives and the lives of our loved ones.

The idea that we might ration health care to seniors (or anyone else) is political anathema. Politicians do not dare breathe the R word, lest they be accused—however wrongly—of trying to pull the plug on Grandma. But the need to spend less money on the elderly at the end of life is the elephant in the room in the health-reform debate. Everyone sees it but no one wants to talk about it. At a more basic level, Americans are afraid not just of dying, but of talking and thinking about death. Until Americans learn to contemplate death as more than a scientific challenge to be overcome, our health-care system will remain unfixable.

Compared with other Western countries, the United States has more health care—but, generally speaking, not better health care. There is no way we can get control of costs, which have grown by nearly 50 percent in the past decade, without finding a way to stop overtreating patients. In his address to Congress, President Obama spoke airily about reducing inefficiency, but he slid past the hard choices that will have to be made to stop health care from devouring ever-larger slices of the economy and tax dollar. A significant portion of the savings will have to come from the money we spend on seniors at the end of life because, as Willie Sutton explained about why he robbed banks, that's where the money is.

As President Obama said, most of the uncontrolled growth in federal spending and the deficit comes from Medicare; nothing else comes close. Almost a third of the money spent by Medicare—about $66.8 billion a year—goes to chronically ill patients in the last two years of life. This might seem obvious—of course the costs come at the end, when patients are the sickest. But that can't explain what researchers at Dartmouth have discovered: Medicare spends twice as much on similar patients in some parts of the country as in others. The average cost of a Medicare patient in Miami is $16,351; the average in Honolulu is $5,311. In the Bronx, N.Y., it's $12,543. In Fargo, N.D., $5,738. The average Medicare patient undergoing end-of-life treatment spends 21.9 days in a Manhattan hospital. In Mason City, Iowa, he or she spends only 6.1 days.

Maybe it's unsurprising that treatment in rural towns costs less than in big cities, with all their high prices, varied populations, and urban woes. But there are also significant disparities in towns that are otherwise very similar. How do you explain the fact, for instance, that in Boulder, Colo., the average cost of Medicare treatment is $9,103, whereas an hour away in Fort Collins, Colo., the cost is $6,448?

The answer, the Dartmouth researchers found, is that in some places doctors are just more likely to order more tests and procedures. More specialists are involved. There is very little reason for them not to order more tests and treatments. By training and inclination, doctors want to do all they can to cure ailments. And since Medicare pays by procedure, test, and hospital stay—though less and less each year as the cost squeeze tightens—there is an incentive to do more and more. To make a good living, doctors must see more patients, and order more tests.

All this treatment does not necessarily buy better care. In fact, the Dartmouth studies have found worse outcomes in many states and cities where there is more health care. Why? Because just going into the hospital has risks—of infection, or error, or other unforeseen complications. Some studies estimate that Americans are overtreated by roughly 30 percent. "It's not about rationing care—that's always the bogeyman people use to block reform," says Dr. Elliott Fisher, a professor at Dartmouth Medical School. "The real problem is unnecessary and unwanted care."

But how do you decide which treatments to cut out? How do you choose between the necessary and the unnecessary? There has been talk among experts and lawmakers of giving more power to a panel of government experts to decide—Britain has one, called the National Institute for Health and Clinical Excellence (known by the somewhat ironic acronym NICE). But no one wants the horror stories of denied care and long waits that are said to plague state-run national health-care systems. (The criticism is unfair: patients wait longer to see primary-care physicians in the United States than in Britain.) After the summer of angry town halls, no politician is going to get anywhere near something that could be called a "death panel."

There's no question that reining in the lawyers would help cut costs. Fearing medical-malpractice suits, doctors engage in defensive medicine, ordering procedures that may not be strictly necessary—but why take the risk? According to various studies, defensive medicine adds perhaps 2 percent to the overall bill—a not-insignificant number when more than $2 trillion is at stake. A number of states have managed to institute some kind of so-called tort reform, limiting the size of damage awards by juries in medical-malpractice cases. But the trial lawyers—big donors to the Democratic Party—have stopped Congress from even considering reforms. That's why it was significant that President Obama even raised the subject in his speech last week, even if he was vague about just what he'd do. (Best idea: create medical courts run by experts to rule on malpractice claims, with no punitive damages.)

But the biggest cost booster is the way doctors are paid under most insurance systems, including Medicare. It's called fee-for-service, and it means just that. So why not just put doctors on salary? Some medical groups that do, like the Mayo Clinic, have reduced costs while producing better results. Unfortunately, putting doctors on salary requires that they work for someone, and most American physicians are self-employed or work in small group practices. The alternative—paying them a flat rate for each patient they care for—turned out to be at least a partial bust. HMOs that paid doctors a flat fee in the 1990s faced a backlash as patients bridled at long waits and denied service.

Ever-rising health-care spending now consumes about 17 percent of the economy (versus about 10 percent in Europe). At the current rate of increase, it will devour a fifth of GDP by 2018. We cannot afford to sustain a productive economy with so much money going to health care. Over time, economic reality may force us to adopt a national health-care system like Britain's or Canada's. But before that day arrives, there are steps we can take to reduce costs without totally turning the system inside out.

One place to start is to consider the psychological aspect of health care. Most people are at least minor hypochondriacs (I know I am). They use doctors to make themselves feel better, even if the doctor is not doing much to physically heal what ails them. (In ancient times, doctors often made people sicker with quack cures like bleeding.) The desire to see a physician is often pronounced in assisted-living facilities. Old people, far from their families in our mobile, atomized society, depend on their doctors for care and reassurance. I noticed that in my mother's retirement home, the talk in the dining room was often about illness; people built their day around doctor's visits, partly, it seemed to me, to combat loneliness.

Physicians at Massachusetts General Hospital are experimenting with innovative approaches to care for their most ill patients without necessarily sending them to the doctor. Three years ago, Massachusetts enacted universal care—just as Congress and the Obama administration are attempting to do now. The state quickly found it could not afford to meet everyone's health-care demands, so it's scrambling for solutions. The Mass General program assigned nurses to the hospital's 2,600 sickest—and costliest—Medicare patients. These nurses provide basic care, making sure the patients take their medications and so forth, and act as gatekeepers—they decide if a visit to the doctor is really necessary. It's not a perfect system—people will still demand to see their doctors when it's unnecessary—but the Mass General program cut costs by 5 percent while providing the elderly what they want and need most: caring human contact.

Other initiatives ensure that the elderly get counseling about end-of-life issues. Although demagogued as a "death panel," a program in Wisconsin to get patients to talk to their doctors about how they want to deal with death was actually a resounding success. A study by the Archives of Internal Medicine shows that such conversations between doctors and patients can decrease costs by about 35 percent—while improving the quality of life at the end. Patients should be encouraged to draft living wills to make their end-of-life desires known. Unfortunately, such paper can be useless if there is a family member at the bedside demanding heroic measures. "A lot of the time guilt is playing a role," says Dr. David Torchiana, a surgeon and CEO of the Massachusetts General Physicians Organization. Doctors can feel guilty, too—about overtreating patients. Torchiana recalls his unease over operating to treat a severe heart infection in a woman with two forms of metastatic cancer who was already comatose. The family insisted.

Studies show that about 70 percent of people want to die at home—but that about half die in hospitals. There has been an important increase in hospice or palliative care—keeping patients with incurable diseases as comfortable as possible while they live out the remainder of their lives. Hospice services are generally intended for the terminally ill in the last six months of life, but as a practical matter, many people receive hospice care for only a few weeks.

Our medical system does everything it can to encourage hope. And American health care has been near miraculous—the envy of the world—in its capacity to develop new lifesaving and life-enhancing treatments. But death can be delayed only so long, and sometimes the wait is grim and degrading. The hospice ideal recognized that for many people, quiet and dignity—and loving care and good painkillers—are really what's called for.

That's what my mother wanted. After convincing the doctors that she meant it—that she really was ready to die—she was transferred from the ICU to a hospice, where, five days later, she passed away. In the ICU, as they removed all the monitors and pulled out all the tubes and wires, she made a fluttery motion with her hands. She seemed to be signaling goodbye to all that—I'm free to go in peace.

Critical Thinking

1. Why are terminally ill patients treated independently of their wishes?
2. Describe some of the initiatives that are being developed for terminally ill and elderly patients. What do you think of these programs?

Evan Thomas with Pat Wingert, Suzanne Smalley, and Claudia Kalb.

Incapacitated, Alone and Treated to Death

JOSEPH SACCO, MD

Mr. Green lay in the bed next to the window, 15 floors above the Cross-Bronx Expressway. Fifty-nine years old and suffering from AIDS-related dementia, he was bedbound, permanently tethered to a ventilator and, though conscious, unaware of his medical condition. In medico-legal parlance, he was incapacitated: unable to understand the consequences of his decisions and unable to direct the doctors caring for him.

The view from his bedside was impressive—a thousand acres of worn, low-slung apartment buildings set off by the massed arc of Manhattan, rising from the distance like the Emerald City.

That no friend or family member would ever share this view was another of his mounting misfortunes. Referred to the hospital from a nursing home for fever and weight loss—he was so thin that the skin of his chest would not even hold EKG leads—he had no identified relatives or friends. His personal history had vanished into the maze of health care facilities that had been his home for more than a year. Other than name, Social Security number and date of birth, his life story had disappeared.

Mr. Green was one of thousands of New Yorkers—physically devastated, mentally depleted, without hope of recovery and without surrogates—for whom the prolongation of life at all costs was the only legally sanctioned course of treatment. Even if friends or relatives were found, New York prohibits the withholding or withdrawing of life-sustaining treatment without a signed health care proxy or "clear and convincing" evidence of a patient's wishes. A "do not resuscitate" order can be put in place by doctors, but only in the absence of identified surrogates and only if resuscitation is considered futile.

Other states, to varying extents, allow family members, friends or guardians to make the decision about life support, even without knowledge of a patient's prior wishes. A few states grant it to the doctor in the absence of such surrogates. A treatment that preserves a heartbeat but offers no hope of recovery—long-term ventilator support in a vegetative state, say—may be withdrawn. New York permits no such possibility. Physicians not wanting to find themselves at the center of precedent-setting test cases on patients' rights will treat, treat and treat, no matter the cost to the patient or their own souls.

Mention the idea of withholding or withdrawing medical care from patients who cannot express their wishes, and people get uncomfortable. Advocacy groups use the term "medical killing," and despite the hyperbole, their concerns are merited. Doctors have no right to judge the value of a life. Many patients want their lives prolonged, regardless of prognosis, quality or need for invasive treatment.

Yet a 2007 study found that doctors in intensive-care units across the country commonly withheld or withdrew life support in critically or terminally ill patients who lacked surrogates, without knowledge of their wishes. Most such decisions were made by a single physician, without regard to hospital policy, professional society recommendations or state law. In other words, doctors are withholding treatment from this vulnerable population, a practice that is neither regulated nor publicly recognized.

Many things influenced the patient's care. Just not his own wishes.

Mr. Green's monetary value cannot be underestimated as an influence on his care. He was a valuable commodity. A ventilator-dependent patient, especially one undergoing the surgical incision necessary for long-term vent support, is among the highest-paying under Medicare's prospective hospital reimbursement system; his need for skilled care outside the hospital made him a lucrative nursing home patient.

Prognosis is not a factor in this equation. Forever on life support without hope of recovery, Mr. Green would develop pneumonias, urinary infections and other complications, each requiring transfer from the nursing home to the hospital, stabilization and transfer back again. The providers would be reimbursed for each of these procedures.

Extraordinary advances have been made in the treatment of H.I.V. Still, Mr. Green's dementia worsened, as did his terrible wasting and bedsores. In July, despite a full volley of high-tech interventions, he died, without ever having done anything volitional, never mind eating, talking or making eye contact. His well-intentioned hospital and doctors, fully aware of his dismal prognosis, continued the excruciating process of inserting pencil-thick IV catheters and cleaning fist-size bed sores.

No one asked if Mr. Green wanted these interventions, assuming instead that to do otherwise was both unethical and illegal, and he was treated to death. Modern American medicine owed him a better way.

Critical Thinking

1. Should there be limits on health care provided to the terminally ill?

2. Who should be involved in making health care decisions for the mentally incapacitated, terminally ill patient?

JOSEPH SACCO is director of the palliative medicine consultation service at Bronx Lebanon Hospital Center.

UNIT 9

Consumer Health

Unit Selections

Learning Outcomes

After reading this unit, you should be able to:

- Distinguish whether vaccination is more dangerous than getting the disease prevented by the vaccine.

- Explain why some parents opt out of vaccinating their children.

- Describe medical tourism.

- Discuss the risks versus benefits of medical tourism.

- Discuss why the number of bed bug infestations has been increasing.

- Address the means of eradicating bed bugs.

- List the steps you should take to prevent food-borne illness while processing meat and produce at home.

- Discuss what consumers should look for when choosing health insurance.

- Distinguish between adequate and inadequate health care coverage.

- Describe why humans are getting less sleep these days.

- Explain the health implications of sleep deprivation.

- Discuss why obesity plays a role in getting adequate health care.

Student Website

www.mhhe.com/cls

Internet References

FDA Consumer Magazine
www.fda.gov/fdac

Global Vaccine Awareness League
www.gval.com

National Sleep Foundation
www.sleepfoundation.org

For many people the term *consumer health* conjures up images of selecting health care services and paying medical bills. While these two aspects of health care are indeed consumer health issues, the term *consumer health* encompasses all consumer products and services that influence the health and welfare of people. A definition this broad suggests that almost everything we see or do may be construed to be a consumer health issue. In many ways consumer health is an outward expression of our health-related behaviors and decision-making processes, and as such, is based on our desire to make healthy choices, be assertive, and be in possession of accurate information on which to base our decisions. In "Vaccine Refusal, Mandatory Immunization, and the Risks of Vaccine-Preventable Diseases," author Saad B. Omer et al. discusses the risk versus benefit of vaccination, while *Consumer Reports* covers the adequacy of many health insurance plans in "Hazardous Health Plans."

Another consumer health issue is addressed by Lorene Burkhart and Lorna Gentry in "Medical Tourism: What You Should Know." During the past few years, nearly a half million Americans went overseas for medical and dental treatment—a number that's expected to rise. These travelers find that the costs of many treatments are much lower than in the United States, and they can also seek those treatments that are not yet available back home.

These days, travelers within the United States may come home with more than they bargained for, as described by Rebecca Berg in "Bed Bugs: The Pesticide Dilemma." While pesticide-resistant bed bugs don't appear to cause disease with their bites, they invade beds, interfere with sleep, and can affect people emotionally. Pesticides used to control them however, may pose health risks.

Even though animal foods are more likely to be contaminated, there has been an increase of food-borne illness from fruit and vegetable consumption. Mark Fischetti discusses this issue in "Is Your Food Contaminated?"

Author Michael J. Breus provides an overview of the need for adequate sleep in "The Rough Road to Dreamland." Since the invention of electric lights, Americans have increasingly gotten by with less sleep. Unfortunately, sleep deprivation is linked to mortality, and overall health status, including obesity.

While being overweight may increase the risk for certain health problems, how much a person weighs may also affect the quality of health care that he or she receives. Ginny Graves addresses this issue in "The *Surprising Reason* Why Heavy Isn't Healthy."

The health-conscious consumer seeks to be as informed as possible when making dietary and medical decisions—but the

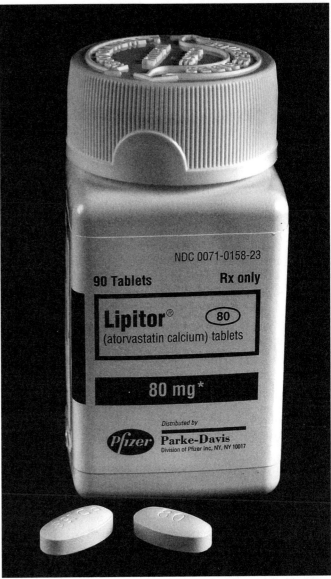

best intentions come to no avail when consumers base their decisions on inaccurate information, old beliefs, or media hype that lacks a scientific base. Knowledge (based on accurate information) and critical thinking are the key elements required to become proactive in managing your daily health concerns.

Vaccine Refusal, Mandatory Immunization, and the Risks of Vaccine-Preventable Diseases

SAAD B. OMER ET AL.

Vaccines are among the most effective tools available for preventing infectious diseases and their complications and sequelae. High immunization coverage has resulted in drastic declines in vaccine-preventable diseases, particularly in many high- and middle-income countries. A reduction in the incidence of a vaccine-preventable disease often leads to the public perception that the severity of the disease and susceptibility to it have decreased.[1] At the same time, public concern about real or perceived adverse events associated with vaccines has increased. This heightened level of concern often results in an increase in the number of people refusing vaccines.[1,2]

In the United States, policy interventions, such as immunization requirements for school entry, have contributed to high vaccine coverage and record or near-record lows in the levels of vaccine-preventable diseases. Herd immunity, induced by high vaccination rates, has played an important role in greatly reducing or eliminating continual endemic transmission of a number of diseases, thereby benefiting the community overall in addition to the individual vaccinated person.

Recent parental concerns about perceived vaccine safety issues, such as a purported association between vaccines and autism, though not supported by a credible body of scientific evidence,[3-8] have led increasing numbers of parents to refuse or delay vaccination for their children.[9,10] The primary measure of vaccine refusal in the United States is the proportion of children who are exempted from school immunization requirements for nonmedical reasons. There has been an increase in state-level rates of nonmedical exemptions from immunization requirements.[11] In this article, we review the evidentiary basis for school immunization requirements, explore the determinants of vaccine refusal, and discuss the individual and community risks of vaccine-preventable diseases associated with vaccine refusal.

Evolution of U.S. Immunization Requirements

Vaccination was introduced in the United States at the turn of the 19th century. The first U.S. law to require smallpox vaccination was passed soon afterward, in 1809 in Massachusetts, to prevent and control frequent smallpox outbreaks that had substantial health and economic consequences.[12–14] Subsequently, other states enacted similar legislation.[13] Despite the challenges inherent in establishing a reliable and safe vaccine delivery system, vaccination became widely accepted as an effective tool for preventing smallpox through the middle of the 19th century, and the incidence of smallpox declined between 1802 and 1840.[15] In the 1850s, "irregular physicians, the advocates of unorthodox medical theories,"[16] led challenges to vaccination. Vaccine use decreased, and smallpox made a major reappearance in the 1870s.[15] Many states passed new vaccination laws, whereas other states started enforcing existing laws. Increased enforcement of the laws often resulted in increased opposition to vaccination. Several states, including California, Illinois, Indiana, Minnesota, Utah, West Virginia, and Wisconsin, repealed compulsory vaccination laws.[15] Many other states retained them.

In a 1905 landmark case, *Jacobson v. Massachusetts,* which has since served as the foundation for public health laws, the U.S. Supreme Court endorsed the rights of states to pass and enforce compulsory vaccination laws.[17] In 1922, deciding a case filed by a girl excluded from a public school (and later a private school) in San Antonio, Texas, the Supreme Court found school immunization requirements to be constitutional.[18] Since then, courts have been generally supportive of the states' power to enact and implement immunization requirements.

Difficulties with efforts to control measles in the 1960s and 1970s ushered in the modern era of immunization laws in the United States.[12] In 1969, a total of 17 states had laws that required children to be vaccinated against measles before entering school, and 12 states had legally mandated requirements for vaccination against all six diseases for which routine immunization was carried out at the time.[13] During the 1970s, efforts were made to strengthen and strictly enforce immunization laws.[12,13] During measles outbreaks, some state and local health officials excluded from school those students who did not comply with immunization requirements, resulting in minimal backlash, quick improvement in local coverage, and control of outbreaks.[19-22] Efforts by the public health community and other immunization advocates to increase measles vaccine coverage among school-age children resulted in enforcement of immunization requirements for all vaccines and the introduction of such requirements in states that did not already have them. By the beginning of the 1980s, all 50 states had school immunization requirements.

Recent School Immunization Requirements

Because laws concerning immunization are state-based, there are substantial differences in requirements across the country. The requirements from state to state differ in terms of the school grades covered, the vaccines included, the processes and authority used to introduce new vaccines, reasons for exemptions (medical reasons, religious reasons, philosophical or personal beliefs), and the procedures for granting exemptions.[23]

State immunization laws contain provisions for certain exemptions. As of March 2008, all states permitted medical exemptions from school immunization requirements, 48 states allowed religious exemptions, and 21 states allowed exemptions based on philosophical or personal beliefs.[23] Several states (New York, Arkansas, and Texas) have recently expanded eligibility for exemptions.

Secular and Geographic Trends in Immunization Refusal

Between 1991 and 2004, the mean state-level rate of nonmedical exemptions increased from 0.98 to 1.48%. The increase in exemption rates was not uniform.[11] Exemption rates for states that allowed only religious exemptions remained at approximately 1% between 1991 and 2004; however, in states that allowed exemptions for philosophical or personal beliefs, the mean exemption rate increased from 0.99 to 2.54%.[11]

Like any average, the mean exemption rate presents only part of the picture, since geographic clustering of nonmedical exemptions can result in local accumulation of a critical mass of susceptible children that increases the risk of outbreaks. There is evidence of substantial geographic heterogeneity in nonmedical-exemption rates between and within states.[24] For example, in the period from 2006 through 2007, the state-level nonmedical-exemption rate in Washington was 6%; however, the county-level rate ranged from 1.2 to 26.9%.[25] In a spatial analysis of Michigan's exemption data according to census tracts, 23 statistically significant clusters of increased exemptions were identified.[26] Similar heterogeneity in exemption rates has been identified in Oregon[27] and California (unpublished data).

The reasons for the geographic clustering of exemptions from school vaccination requirements are not fully understood, but they may include characteristics of the local population (e.g., cultural issues, socioeconomic status, or educational level), the beliefs of local health care providers and opinion leaders (e.g., clergy and politicians), and local media coverage. The factors known to be associated with exemption rates are heterogeneity in school policies[28] and the beliefs of school personnel who are responsible for compliance with the immunization requirements.[29]

Instead of refusing vaccines, some parents delay vaccination of their children.[30-32] Many parents follow novel vaccine schedules proposed by individual physicians (rather than those developed by expert committees with members representing multiple disciplines).[32,33] Most novel schedules involve administering vaccines over a longer period than that recommended by the Advisory Committee on Immunization Practices and the American Academy of Pediatrics or skipping the administration of some vaccines.

Individual Risk and Vaccine Refusal

Children with nonmedical exemptions are at increased risk for acquiring and transmitting vaccine-preventable diseases.[34,35] In a retrospective cohort study based on nationwide surveillance data from 1985 through 1992, children with exemptions were 35 times as likely to contract measles as nonexempt children (relative risk, 35; 95% confidence interval [CI], 34 to 37).[34] In a retrospective cohort study in Colorado based on data for the years 1987 through 1998, children with exemptions, as compared with unvaccinated children, were 22 times as likely to have had measles (relative risk, 22.2; 95% CI, 15.9 to 31.1) and almost six times as likely to have had pertussis (relative risk, 5.9; 95% CI, 4.2 to 8.2).[35] Earlier data showed that lower incidences of measles and mumps were associated with the existence and enforcement of immunization requirements for school entry.[12,36-38]

The consequences of delayed vaccination, as compared with vaccine refusal, have not been studied in detail. However, it is known that the risk of vaccine-preventable diseases and the risk of sequelae from vaccine-preventable diseases are not constant throughout childhood. Young children are often at increased risk for illness and death related to infectious diseases, and vaccine delays may leave them vulnerable at ages with a high risk of contracting several vaccine-preventable diseases. Moreover, novel vaccine schedules that recommend administering vaccines over a longer period may exacerbate health inequities, since parents with high socioeconomic status are more likely to make the extra visits required under the alternative schedules than parents with low socioeconomic status.[39]

Clustering of Vaccine Refusals and Community Risk

Multiple studies have shown an increase in the local risk of vaccine-preventable diseases when there is a geographic aggregation of persons refusing vaccination. In Michigan, significant overlap between geographic clusters of nonmedical exemptions and pertussis clusters was documented.[26] The odds ratio for the likelihood that a census tract included in a pertussis cluster would also be included in an exemptions cluster was 2.7 (95% CI, 2.5 to 3.6) after adjustment for demographic factors.

In Colorado, the county-level incidence of measles and pertussis in vaccinated children from 1987 through 1998 was associated with the frequency of exemptions in that county.[35] At least 11% of the nonexempt children who acquired measles were infected through contact with an exempt child.[35] Moreover, school-based outbreaks in Colorado have been associated with increased exemption rates; the mean exemption rate among schools with outbreaks was 4.3%, as compared with 1.5% for the schools that did not have an outbreak (P = 0.001).[35]

High vaccine coverage, particularly at the community level, is extremely important for children who cannot be vaccinated, including children who have medical contraindications to vaccination and those who are too young to be vaccinated. These groups are often more susceptible to the complications of infectious diseases than the general population of children and depend on the protection provided by the vaccination of children in their environs.[40–42]

Vaccine Refusal and the Recent Increase in Measles Cases

Measles vaccination has been extremely successful in controlling a disease that previously contributed to considerable morbidity and mortality. In the United States, the reported number of cases dropped from an average of 500,000 annually in the era before vaccination (with reported cases considered to be a fraction of the estimated total, which was more than 2 million) to a mean of 62 cases per year from 2000 through 2007.[43–45] Between January 1, 2008, and April 25, 2008, there were five measles outbreaks and a total of 64 cases reported.[45] All but one of the persons with measles were either unvaccinated or did not have evidence of immunization. Of the 21 cases among children and adolescents in the vaccine-eligible age group (16 months to 19 years) with a known reason for nonvaccination, 14, or 67%, had obtained a nonmedical exemption and all of the 10 school-age children had obtained a nonmedical exemption.[45] Thirteen cases occurred in children too young to be vaccinated, and in more than a third of the cases (18 of 44) occurring in a known transmission setting the disease was acquired in a health care facility.[45]

Outbreaks of vaccine-preventable disease often start among persons who refused vaccination, spread rapidly within unvaccinated populations, and also spread to other subpopulations. For example, of the four outbreaks with discrete index cases (one outbreak occurred by means of multiple importations) reported January through April 2008, three out of four index cases occurred in people who had refused vaccination due to personal beliefs; vaccination status could not be verified for the remaining cases.[45,46] In Washington State, a recent outbreak of measles occurred between April 12, 2008, and May 30, 2008, involving 19 cases. All of the persons with measles were unimmunized with the exception of the last case, a person who had been vaccinated. Of the other 18 cases, 1 was an infant who was too young to be vaccinated, 2 were younger than 4 years of age, and the remaining 15 were of school age (unpublished data).

Who Refuses Vaccines and Why

Using data from the National Immunization Survey for the period from 1995 through 2001, Smith et al. compared the characteristics of children between the ages of 19 and 35 months who did not receive any vaccine (unvaccinated) with the characteristics of those who were partially vaccinated (undervaccinated).[47] As compared with the undervaccinated children, the unvaccinated children were more likely to be male, to be white, to belong to households with higher income, to have a married mother with a college education, and to live with four or more children.[47] Other studies have shown that children who are unvaccinated are likely to belong to families that intentionally refuse vaccines, whereas children who are undervaccinated are likely to have missed some vaccinations because of factors related to the health care system or sociodemographic characteristics.[48–51]

In a case–control study of the knowledge, attitudes, and beliefs of parents of exempt children as compared with parents of vaccinated children, respondents rated their views of their children's vulnerability to specific diseases, the severity of these diseases, and the efficacy and safety of the specific vaccines available for them. Composite scores were created on the basis of these vaccine-specific responses. As compared with parents of vaccinated children, significantly more parents of exempt children thought their children had a low susceptibility to the diseases (58% vs. 15%, P < 0.05), that the severity of the diseases was low (51% vs. 18%, P < 0.05), and that the efficacy and safety of the vaccines was low (54% vs. 17% for efficacy and 60% vs. 15% for safety, P < 0.05 for both comparisons).[52] Moreover, parents of exempt children were more likely than parents of vaccinated children both to have providers who offered complementary or alternative health care and to obtain information from the Internet and groups opposed to aspects of immunization.[52] The most frequent reason for nonvaccination, stated by 69% of the parents, was concern that the vaccine might cause harm.[52]

Other studies have also reported the importance of parents' concerns about vaccine safety when they decide against vaccination.[53–56] A national survey of parents from 2001 through 2002 showed that although only 1% of respondents thought vaccines were unsafe, the children of these parents were almost three times as likely to not be up to date on recommended vaccinations as the children of parents who thought that vaccines were safe.[54] In a separate case–control study with a national sample, underimmunization was associated with negative perceptions of vaccine safety (odds ratio, 2.0; 95% CI, 1.2 to 3.4).[55] And in another case–control study, Bardenheier et al. found that although concerns regarding general vaccine safety did not differ between the parents of vaccinated children and the parents of undervaccinated or unvaccinated children, more than half of the case and control parents did express concerns about vaccine safety to their child's health care provider.[57] Moreover, parents of undervaccinated or unvaccinated children were more likely to believe that children receive too many vaccines.[57]

The Role of Health Care Providers

Clinicians and other health care providers play a crucial role in parental decision making with regard to immunization. Health care providers are cited by parents, including parents of unvaccinated children, as the most frequent source of information about vaccination.[52]

In a study of the knowledge, attitudes, and practices of primary care providers, a high proportion of those providing care for children whose parents have refused vaccination and those providing care for appropriately vaccinated children were both found to have favorable opinions of vaccines.[58] However, those providing care for unvaccinated children were less likely to have confidence in vaccine safety (odds ratio, 0.37; 95% CI, 0.19 to 0.72) and less likely to perceive vaccines as benefitting individuals and communities.[58] Moreover, there was overlap between clinicians' unfavorable opinions of vaccines and the likelihood that they had unvaccinated children in their practice.[58]

There is evidence that health care providers have a positive overall effect on parents' decision making with regard to vaccination of their children. In a study by Smith et al., parents who reported that their immunization decisions were influenced by their child's health care provider were almost twice as likely to consider vaccines safe as parents who said their decisions were not influenced by the provider.[59]

In focus-group discussions, several parents who were not certain about vaccinating their child were willing to discuss their immunization concerns with a health care provider and wanted the provider to offer information relevant to their specific concerns.[56] These findings highlight the critical role that clinicians can play in explaining the benefits of immunization and addressing parental concerns about its risks.

Clinicians' Response to Vaccine Refusal

Some clinicians have discontinued or have considered discontinuing their provider relationship with families that refuse vaccines.[60,61] In a national survey of members of the American Academy of Pediatrics, almost 40% of respondents said they would not provide care to a family that refused all vaccines, and 28% said they would not provide care to a family that refused some vaccines.[61]

The academy's Committee on Bioethics advises against discontinuing care for families that decline vaccines and has recommended that pediatricians "share honestly what is and is not known about the risks and benefits of the vaccine in question."[62] The committee also recommends that clinicians address vaccine refusal by respectfully listening to parental concerns, explaining the risk of nonimmunization, and discussing the specific vaccines that are of most concern to parents.[62] The committee advises against more serious action in a majority of cases: "Continued refusal after adequate discussion should be respected unless the child is put at significant risk of serious

harm (e.g., as might be the case during an epidemic). Only then should state agencies be involved to override parental discretion on the basis of medical neglect."[62]

Policy-Level Determinants of Vaccine Refusal

Immunization requirements and the policies that ensure compliance with the requirements vary considerably among the states; these variations have been associated with state-level exemption rates.[11,63] For example, the complexity of procedures for obtaining exemption has been shown to be inversely associated with rates of exemption.[63] Moreover, between 1991 and 2004, the mean annual incidence of pertussis was almost twice as high in states with administrative procedures that made it easy to obtain exemptions as in states that made it difficult.[11]

One possible way to balance individual rights and the greater public good with respect to vaccination would be to institute and broaden administrative controls. For example, a model law proposed for Arkansas suggested that parents seeking nonmedical exemptions be provided with counseling on the hazards of refusing vaccination.[64]

States also differ in terms of meeting the recommendations for age-appropriate coverage for children younger than 2 years of age.[65] School immunization requirements ensure completion by the time of school entry, but they do not directly influence the timeliness of vaccination among preschoolers. However, there is some evidence that school immunization laws have an indirect effect on preschool vaccine coverage. For example, varicella vaccine was introduced in the United States in 1995 and has played an important role in reducing the incidence of chickenpox.[66] In 2000, states that had implemented mandatory immunization for varicella by the time of school entry had coverage among children 19 to 35 months old that was higher than the average for all states. Having an immunization requirement could be an indicator of the effectiveness of a state's immunization program, but the effect of school-based requirements on coverage among preschoolers cannot be completely discounted.

Conclusions

Vaccine refusal not only increases the individual risk of disease but also increases the risk for the whole community. As a result of substantial gains in reducing vaccine-preventable diseases, the memory of several infectious diseases has faded from the public consciousness and the risk–benefit calculus seems to have shifted in favor of the perceived risks of vaccination in some parents' minds. Major reasons for vaccine refusal in the United States are parental perceptions and concerns about vaccine safety and a low level of concern about the risk of many vaccine-preventable diseases. If the enormous benefits to society from vaccination are to be maintained, increased efforts will be needed to educate the public about those benefits and to increase public confidence in the systems we use to monitor and ensure vaccine safety. Since clinicians have an influence on parental decision making, it is important that they understand the benefits and risks of vaccines and anticipate questions that parents may have about safety. There are a number of sources of information on vaccines that should be useful to both clinicians and parents (e.g., Appendix 1 in the fifth edition of *Vaccines*, edited by Plotkin et al.; the list of Web sites on vaccine safety posted on the World Health Organization's Web site; and the Web site of the National Center for Immunization and Respiratory Diseases).[67–69]

References

1. Chen RT, Hibbs B. Vaccine safety: current and future challenges. *Pediatr Ann* 1998;27:445–55.

2. Chen RT, DeStefano F. Vaccine adverse events: causal or coincidental? *Lancet* 1998;351:611–2.

3. DeStefano F. Vaccines and autism: evidence does not support a causal association. *Clin Pharmacol Ther* 2007;82:756–9.

4. Doja A, Roberts W. Immunizations and autism: a review of the literature. *Can J Neurol Sci* 2006;33:341–6.

5. Fombonne E, Cook EH. MMR and autistic enterocolitis: consistent epidemiological failure to find an association. *Mol Psychiatry* 2003;8:133–4.

6. Fombonne E. Thimerosal disappears but autism remains. *Arch Gen Psychiatry* 2008;65:15–6.

7. Schechter R, Grether JK. Continuing increases in autism reported to California's developmental services system: mercury in retrograde. *Arch Gen Psychiatry* 2008;65:19–24.

8. Thompson WW, Price C, Goodson B, et al. Early thimerosal exposure and neuropsychological outcomes at 7 to 10 years. *N Engl J Med* 2007;357:1281–92.

9. Offit PA. Vaccines and autism revisited—the Hannah Poling case. *N Engl J Med* 2008;358:2089–91.

10. Smith MJ, Ellenberg SS, Bell LM, Rubin DM. Media coverage of the measles-mumps-rubella vaccine and autism controversy and its relationship to MMR immunization rates in the United States. *Pediatrics* 2008;121(4):e836–e843.

11. Omer SB, Pan WK, Halsey NA, et al. Nonmedical exemptions to school immunization requirements: secular trends and association of state policies with pertussis incidence. *JAMA* 2006;296:1757–63.

12. Orenstein WA, Hinman AR. The immunization system in the United States—the role of school immunization laws. *Vaccine* 1999;17:Suppl 3:S19–S24.

13. Jackson CL. State laws on compulsory immunization in the United States. *Public Health Rep* 1969;84:787–95.

14. Colgrove J, Bayer R. Could it happen here? Vaccine risk controversies and the specter of derailment. *Health Aff* (Millwood) 2005;24:729–39.

15. Kaufman M. The American anti-vaccinationists and their arguments. *Bull Hist Med* 1967;41:463–78.

16. Stern BJ. Should we be vaccinated? A survey of the controversy in its historical and scientific aspects. New York: Harper & Brothers, 1927:93–109.

17. Jacobson v. Massachusetts, 197 U.S. 11 (1905).

18. Zucht v. King, 260 U.S. 174 (Nov. 13, 1922).

19. Middaugh JP, Zyla LD. Enforcement of school immunization law in Alaska. *JAMA* 1978;239:2128–30.

20. Lovejoy GS, Giandelia JW, Hicks M. Successful enforcement of an immunization law. *Public Health Rep* 1974;89:456–8.

21. Fowinkle EW, Barid S, Bass CM. A compulsory school immunization program in Tennessee. *Public Health Rep* 1981;96:61–6.

22. Measles—Florida, 1981. MMWR Morb Mortal Wkly Rep 1981;30:593–6.

23. Vaccine Exemptions. Johns Hopkins Bloomberg School of Public Health—Institute for Vaccine Safety, 2008. (Accessed April 16, 2009, at www.vaccinesafety.edu/ccexem.htm.)

24. National Center for Immunization and Respiratory Diseases. School and childcare vaccination surveys. May 2007. (Accessed April 13, 2009, at www.cdc.gov/vaccines/stats-surv /schoolsurv/default.htm.)

25. School Status Data Reports. Washington State Department of Health, 2009. (Accessed April 16, 2009, at //www.doh.wa.gov /cfh/Immunize/schools/schooldatarprts.htm.)

26. Omer SB, Enger KS, Moulton LH, Halsey NA, Stokley S, Salmon DA. Geographic clustering of nonmedical exemptions to school immunization requirements and associations with geographic clustering of pertussis. *Am J Epidemiol* 2008;168:1389–96.

27. Attitudes, networking and immunizations in a community with a high rate of religious exemptions. Presented at the 37th National Immunization Conference, Chicago, March 17–20, 2003. Abstract.

28. Salmon DA, Omer SB, Moulton LH, et al. Exemptions to school immunization requirements: the role of school-level requirements, policies, and procedures. *Am J Public Health* 2005;95:436–40. [Erratum, Am J Public Health 2005;95:551.]

29. Salmon DA, Moulton LH, Omer SB, et al. Knowledge, attitudes, and beliefs of school nurses and personnel and associations with nonmedical immunization exemptions. *Pediatrics* 2004;113(6):e552–e559.

30. Luman ET, Barker LE, Shaw KM, McCauley MM, Buehler JW, Pickering LK. Timeliness of childhood vaccinations in the United States: days undervaccinated and number of vaccines delayed. *JAMA* 2005;293:1204–11.

31. Luman ET, Shaw KM, Stokley SK. Compliance with vaccination recommendations for U.S. children. *Am J Prev Med* 2008;34:463–70. [Erratum, Am J Prev Med 2008:35:319.]

32. Cohen E. Should I vaccinate my baby? Cable News Network. 2008. (Accessed April 13, 2009, at www.cnn.com/2008 /HEALTH/family/06/19/ep.vaccines/index.html.)

33. Sears R. Dr. Bob's blog categories: alternative vaccine schedule. (Accessed April 13, 2009, at http://askdrsears.com/ thevaccinebook/labels/Alternative%20Vaccine%20Schedule .asp.)

34. Salmon DA, Haber M, Gangarosa EJ, Phillips L, Smith NJ, Chen RT. Health consequences of religious and philosophical exemptions from immunization laws: individual and societal risk of measles. *JAMA* 1999;282:47–53. [Erratum, JAMA 2000;283:2241.]

35. Feikin DR, Lezotte DC, Hamman RF, Salmon DA, Chen RT, Hoffman RE. Individual and community risks of measles and

pertussis associated with personal exemptions to immunization. *JAMA* 2000;284:3145–50.

36. Measles—United States. MMWR Morb Mortal Wkly Rep 1977;26:109–11.

37. Robbins KB, Brandling-Bennett D, Hinman AR. Low measles incidence: association with enforcement of school immunization laws. *Am J Public Health* 1981;71:270–4.

38. van Loon FP, Holmes SJ, Sirotkin BI, et al. Mumps surveillance—United States, 1988–1993. *MMWR CDC Surveill* 1995;44:1–14.

39. Williams IT, Milton JD, Farrell JB, Graham NM. Interaction of socioeconomic status and provider practices as predictors of immunization coverage in Virginia children. *Pediatrics* 1995;96:439–46.

40. Bisgard KM, Pascual FB, Ehresmann KR, et al. Infant pertussis: who was the source? *Pediatr Infect Dis J* 2004;23:985–9.

41. Deen JL, Mink CA, Cherry JD, et al. Household contact study of Bordetella pertussis infections. *Clin Infect Dis* 1995;21:1211–9.

42. Poehling KA, Talbot TR, Griffin MR, et al. Invasive pneumococcal disease among infants before and after introduction of pneumococcal conjugate vaccine. *JAMA* 2006;295:1668–74.

43. Bloch AB, Orenstein WA, Stetler HC, et al. Health impact of measles vaccination in the United States. *Pediatrics* 1985;76:524–32.

44. Orenstein WA, Papania MJ, Wharton ME. Measles elimination in the United States. *J Infect Dis* 2004;189:Suppl 1:S1–S3.

45. Measles—United States, January 1–April 25, 2008. MMWR Morb Mortal Wkly Rep 2008;57:494–8.

46. Update: measles—United States, January–July 2008. MMWR Morb Mortal Wkly Rep 2008;57:893–6.

47. Smith PJ, Chu SY, Barker LE. Children who have received no vaccines: who are they and where do they live? *Pediatrics* 2004;114:187–95.

48. Allred NJ, Wooten KG, Kong Y. The association of health insurance and continuous primary care in the medical home on vaccination coverage for 19- to 35-month-old children. *Pediatrics* 2007;119:Suppl 1:S4–S11.

49. Daniels D, Jiles RB, Klevens RM, Herrera GA. Undervaccinated African-American preschoolers: a case of missed opportunities. *Am J Prev Med* 2001;20:Suppl:61–68.

50. Luman ET, McCauley MM, Shefer A, Chu SY. Maternal characteristics associated with vaccination of young children. *Pediatrics* 2003;111:1215–8.

51. Smith PJ, Santoli JM, Chu SY, Ochoa DQ, Rodewald LE. The association between having a medical home and vaccination coverage among children eligible for the Vaccines for Children program. *Pediatrics* 2005;116:130–9.

52. Salmon DA, Moulton LH, Omer SB, Dehart MP, Stokley S, Halsey NA. Factors associated with refusal of childhood vaccines among parents of school-aged children: a case-control study. *Arch Pediatr Adolesc Med* 2005;159:470–6.

53. Humiston SG, Lerner EB, Hepworth E, Blythe T, Goepp JG. Parent opinions about universal influenza vaccination for infants and toddlers. *Arch Pediatr Adolesc Med* 2005;159:108–12.

54. Allred NJ, Shaw KM, Santibanez TA, Rickert DL, Santoli JM. Parental vaccine safety concerns: results from the National Immunization Survey, 2001–2002. *Am J Prev Med* 2005;28:221–4.

55. Gust DA, Strine TW, Maurice E, et al. Underimmunization among children: effects of vaccine safety concerns on immunization status. *Pediatrics* 2004;114(1):e16–e22.

56. Fredrickson DD, Davis TC, Arnould CL, et al. Childhood immunization refusal: provider and parent perceptions. *Fam Med* 2004;36:431–9.

57. Bardenheier B, Yusuf H, Schwartz B, Gust D, Barker L, Rodewald L. Are parental vaccine safety concerns associated with receipt of measles-mumps-rubella, diphtheria and tetanus toxoids with acellular pertussis, or hepatitis B vaccines by children? *Arch Pediatr Adolesc Med* 2004;158:569–75.

58. Salmon DA, Pan WK, Omer SB, et al. Vaccine knowledge and practices of primary care providers of exempt vs. vaccinated children. *Hum Vaccin* 2008;4:286–91.

59. Smith PJ, Kennedy AM, Wooten K, Gust DA, Pickering LK. Association between health care providers' influence on parents who have concerns about vaccine safety and vaccination coverage. *Pediatrics* 2006;118(5):e1287–e1292.

60. Freed GL, Clark SJ, Hibbs BF, Santoli JM. Parental vaccine safety concerns: the experiences of pediatricians and family physicians. *Am J Prev Med* 2004;26:11–4.

61. Flanagan-Klygis EA, Sharp L, Frader JE. Dismissing the family who refuses vaccines: a study of pediatrician attitudes. *Arch Pediatr Adolesc Med* 2005;159:929–34.

62. Diekema DS. Responding to parental refusals of immunization of children. *Pediatrics* 2005;115:1428–31.

63. Rota JS, Salmon DA, Rodewald LE, Chen RT, Hibbs BF, Gangarosa EJ. Processes for obtaining nonmedical exemptions to state immunization laws. *Am J Public Health* 2001;91:645–8.

64. Salmon DA, Siegel AW. Religious and philosophical exemptions from vaccination requirements and lessons learned from conscientious objectors from conscription. *Public Health Rep* 2001;116:289–95.

65. Luman ET, Barker LE, McCauley MM, Drews-Botsch C. Timeliness of childhood immunizations: a state-specific analysis. *Am J Public Health* 2005;95:1367–74.

66. Seward JF, Watson BM, Peterson CL, et al. Varicella disease after introduction of varicella vaccine in the United States, 1995–2000. *JAMA* 2002;287:606–11.

67. Wexler DL, Anderson TA. Websites that contain information about immunization. In: Plotkin S, Orenstein WA, Offit PA, eds. Vaccines. 5th ed. Philadelphia: Saunders, 2008:1685–90.

68. Vaccine safety websites meeting credibility and content good information practices criteria. Geneva: World Health Organization, September 2008.

69. National Center for Immunization and Respiratory Diseases. Centers for Disease Control and Prevention, 2009. (Accessed April 16, 2009, at www.cdc.gov/ncird/.)

Critical Thinking

1. Is vaccination more dangerous than getting the disease prevented by the vaccine?

2. Why do some parents refuse to have their children vaccinated? Are their reasons valid?

From the Hubert Department of Global Health, Rollins School of Public Health (S.B.O.), and the Emory Vaccine Center (S.B.O., W.A.O.), Emory University, Atlanta; the Department of International Health (S.B.O., D.A.S., N.H.) and the Institute for Vaccine Safety (N.H.), Johns Hopkins Bloomberg School of Public Health, Baltimore; the National Vaccine Program Office, Department of Health and Human Services, Washington, DC (D.A.S.); and Maternal and Child Health Assessment, Washington State Department of Health, Olympia (M.P.D.). Address reprint requests to Dr. Omer at the Hubert Department of Global Health, Rollins School of Public Health, Emory University, 1518 Clifton Rd. NE, Atlanta, GA 30322, or at somer@emory.edu.

Dr. Salmon reports serving on the Merck Vaccine Policy Advisory Board; Dr. Orenstein, receiving research funds from Novartis, Merck, and Sanofi Pasteur and a training grant from the Merck Foundation and serving on data and safety monitoring boards associated with GlaxoSmithKline and Encorium; and Dr. Halsey, receiving research funds from Wyeth and Berna, lecture fees from Sanofi, and payments for testimony to the Department of Justice regarding several vaccine compensation cases and serving on data and safety monitoring committees associated with Novartis and Merck. No other potential conflict of interest relevant to this article was reported.

We thank Tina Proveaux of the Johns Hopkins Bloomberg School of Public Health for reviewing an earlier version of the manuscript and Dr. Jane Seward of the Centers for Disease Control and Prevention for providing input on new measles cases.

Medical Tourism: What You Should Know

From international outsourcing to in-home visits, doctors and patients are reinventing the way medicine is viewed and practiced at home and around the world.

LORENE BURKHART AND LORNA GENTRY

In 2006, West Virginia lawmaker Ray Canterbury made headlines across the country when he introduced House Bill 4359, which would allow enrollees in the state government's health plan to travel to foreign countries for surgery and other medical services. In fact, not only would the bill allow for such a choice, it encourages it; those choosing to go to an approved foreign clinic for a procedure covered by the plan would have all of their medical and travel expenses (including those of one companion) paid, plus be given 20 percent of the savings they racked up by having the procedure done overseas, rather than here at home.

Canterbury's bill drew attention to a growing international boom in medical tourism—an industry with special appeal for many of America's 61 million uninsured or underinsured citizens. At prices as much as 80 to 90 percent lower than those here, hospitals in countries such as Costa Rica, Thailand, India, and the Philippines offer a wide range of healthcare procedures in accommodations equal to or even better than their American counterparts. Some estimate that 500,000 Americans went overseas for medical treatment in 2006 alone, and that medical tourism could become a $40 billion industry by 2010.

Overseas Surgery? What You Should Know

According to Canterbury and other proponents of medical service outsourcing, the idea is all about competition. Proponents believe the rate of healthcare inflation in this country, at almost four times the rate of overall inflation, has placed an unsustainable burden on the American economy.

"The best way to solve this problem is to rely on market forces," Canterbury writes. "My bills are designed to force domestic healthcare companies to compete for our business."

It's hard to argue with the economics of medical outsourcing. According to MedicalTourism.com, the cost of typical heart bypass surgery in the United States is $130,000. The same operation is estimated to cost approximately $10,000 in India, $11,000 in Thailand, and $18,500 in Singapore. A $43,000 hip replacement in an American hospital could be performed for $9,000 in India, or for $12,000 in either Thailand or Singapore. Even adding the costs of travel and lodging, consumers stand to save real money by traveling overseas for these and many other types of routine surgery, including angioplasties, knee replacements, and hysterectomies.

Of course, many people have serious concerns about the idea of shopping overseas for invasive medical procedures. What about the quality of the service? Followup care? And what happens if something goes terribly wrong? Those backing the business—including employers and lawmakers desperately seeking ways to cut the cost of employer-sponsored medical care—are quick to answer these concerns.

Most of the foreign medical facilities courting Western tourists are state-of-the-art facilities that offer luxurious accommodations and individual around-the-clock nursing attention. Thailand's Bumrungrad Hospital, for example, offers five-star hotel quality rooms, a lobby that includes Starbucks and other restaurants, valet parking, an international staff and interpreters, a travel agent, visa desk, and a meet-and-greet service at Bangkok's Suvarnabhumi Airport. In a 2007 report broadcast on NPR, an American woman told how when her doctor in Alaska announced that she needed double knee replacements at a cost of $100,000, she replied that she couldn't afford the treatment. Her doctor recommended that she wait four years, when she would be eligible for Medicare. Instead, the woman opted for treatment at Bumrungrad, where the two knee replacements cost $20,000 (including the services of two physicians, an anesthesiologist, and physical therapy), and she was able to recover in the hospital's luxurious surroundings with her husband at her side. Her husband, who underwent surgery in the United States the previous year, couldn't believe the amount of attention his wife received from her doctors and nurses, whom he said were in almost constant attendance.

Why is all of this lavish treatment and high-quality care so much cheaper abroad than here? We only need to look at all of the other services the United States has outsourced in the past decade to find the first part of the answer to that question: In places like Thailand and India—two popular destinations for cardiac, orthopedic, and cosmetic surgery—salaries are much lower than in the United States. Further, most services are provided under one roof, and patients select and pay for their medical services up front—no insurance billing. Medical malpractice liability insurance and claims caps in some foreign countries also help keep costs down.

But how safe are foreign medical facilities? Bumrungrad Hospital is accredited by the Joint Commission International (the same organization that accredits U.S. hospitals) and has over 200 U.S. board-certified physicians. And that hospital isn't unique in the world of international medicine. Increasing numbers of medical tourism facilities are staffed by American- and European-trained physicians and backed by well-funded research facilities. Dubai, already a luxury travel destination, is preparing to enter the business of international medical practice and research in a very serious way. Its 4.1 million square-foot Dubai Healthcare City is slated to open in 2010 and will offer academic medical research facilities, disease treatment, and wellness services backed by the oversight of a number of international partners, including a new department of the Harvard School of Medicine.

Good News for Patients Might Be Bad News for U.S. Hospitals

Most baby boomers love to travel, and many are only too happy to combine foreign travel experiences with low-cost and high-value medical procedures. And many insurance companies are eyeing medical outsourcing, too, as a way to cut costs for both enrollees and their employers. Blue Cross/Blue Shield of South Carolina, for example, has begun working with Bumrungrad to provide overseas alternatives for healthcare to its members.

Of course, one or two horrific medical mishaps alone could seriously damage the medical tourism industry. Most foreign countries don't support malpractice litigation to the extent that we do in the United States, and fears of the "what ifs" are keeping many private individuals and organizations from plunging in until they have a few more years to observe the medical outsourcing industry in action. For now, however, foreign medical facilities are eager to maintain standards high enough to avoid any claims of malpractice. And many Americans with our fondness for bargains and luxury are more than willing to give those facilities an opportunity to prove their worth.

Medical tourism is good news for patients, but it could pose consequences for America's already-ailing hospital system. If patients travel to foreign lands to avoid pricey surgeries at home, what kind of financial "hit" will American hospitals face? At 2007's International Medical Tourism Conference in Las Vegas, hospital physicians and administrators from around the globe

gathered to discuss the issues surrounding medical tourism and its impact on the healthcare industry. In an interview about the conference, Sparrow Mahoney, chief executive officer of MedicalTourism.com and conference co-chair, admitted that American medical facilities are now in direct competition with their foreign competitors. "Hospitals will feel a pinch," she said.

Yes, We Make House Calls

All of us have experienced the frustrating and sometimes frightening wait for medical care that we desperately need. We have a raging fever and are told that the doctor can see us in three days. If we choose instead to go to the emergency room of a nearby hospital, we may wait for hours in a roomful of equally ill and distressed people with their impatient spouses, parents, or screaming children, and the constant chiming of cell phones. If our doctor agrees to "work us in," we're faced with an only slightly less daunting process, requiring what might be an hour or so wait. When we finally see a doctor, we're rushed through a few minutes of evaluation, given a prescription, and sent on our way—typically worn out and much worse for the wear of the experience.

But many Americans are opting out of this tribal experience and choosing instead to pay an annual fee (typically, $3,000 to $30,000 above insurance costs) to retain the personalized, private care of a family physician. The "boutique" healthcare movement began in the early 1990s in Seattle, Washington, and has since spread to urban areas around the nation. Instead of waiting days, weeks, or even months for an appointment that fits the doctor's schedule, members of these plans schedule medical visits at their convenience.

Need a house call? Not a problem with most boutique or "concierge" plans. Members have their doctor's cell phone number and can simply call to arrange for the doctor to come to their home. If a plan member needs to see a specialist or go to the emergency room, he or she is accompanied by a plan physician—and no rushing through appointments.

Although many primary care physicians have caseloads of as many as 3,000 to 5,000 patients, doctors in boutique plans might have no more than a few hundred patients under their care; Seattle retainer medicine pioneer MD^2 (pronounced "MD Squared") limits its doctor loads to no greater than 50 patients.

Some retainer plans require that members also carry insurance, while others refuse to process insurance payments at all. In a 2005 report on boutique medicine by CBS5 News in California, one doctor complained that he had lost patience with insurance companies that require reams of tedious paperwork and billing regulations, then reimburse at 20 percent of his billing rate. "I went to medical school to be a doctor and take care of patients," says Dr. Jordan Shlain of the San Francisco group On Call. "I didn't take one class on billings, on insurance company shenanigans and the HMO grip."

Although some concierge medical services charge fees aimed squarely at the middle class, most admit that their fees put them out of the range of many people. FirstLine Personal Health Care, in Indianapolis, charges members an annual retainer of a few thousand dollars in return for 24-hour access to one of the plan's doctors, unlimited office visits, and a small keychain hard drive loaded with their medical records. Even though their fees are modest in comparison with some concierge medical services, FirstLine doctors Kevin McCallum and Timothy Story know that many patients they saw prior to forming the service won't be able to afford membership.

Like other doctors around the country, however, McCallum and Story believe that retainer medicine offers the only option for family medicine doctors trying to escape the grinding demands of escalating practice costs and patient caseloads. With many family physicians around the country retiring early and medical students avoiding the low pay and high demands of a typical family practice, retainer-fee medical groups might be the most viable way to keep the "good old family doctor" in business.

We have yet to see what will happen when the average American is financially excluded from most family medicine clinics and groups—a fate that may occur in the not-so-distant future. Dr. Kevin Grumbach of the University of California at San Francisco was in family practice for more than 20 years and now worries that the rush to boutique medical services is threatening our nation's system of medical care.

"I have grave concerns," he told the CBS5 news reporter, "that . . . we are as a profession abandoning the need of the vast majority of Americans . . . . It's the middle class people that are increasingly left behind in an increasingly inequitable system."

Critical Thinking

1. What is medical tourism?
2. Distinguish between the risks and benefits of medical tourism.

From *The Saturday Evening Post*, January/February 2008. Copyright © 2008 by Lorene Burkhart and Lorna Gentry. Reprinted by permission via Meitus Gelbert Rose LLP.

Bed Bugs: The Pesticide Dilemma

Rebecca Berg

"Six different companies have now found them in movie theaters," said Michael Potter, professor of entomology at the University of Kentucky. Potter works with pest control companies and their customers all over the country. Asked where bed bugs are cropping up, he rattled off a list that included everything from single-family homes to hospitals, libraries, schools ("obviously dormitories," he noted), and modes of transportation. The problem is particularly daunting in apartment buildings since people frequently move in and out with all their belongings.

"It's bad and getting worse," he said. "It's almost like an epizootic or a pandemic where somebody coughs and six more people get it."

He is not alone in sounding the alarm.

"I don't think we've hit anywhere near the peak," observed Jack Marlowe, president of Eden Advanced Pest Technologies. Eden Commercial I.P.M. Consultant Cody Pace, who was on the same call, added that before World War II, one in three homes were infested with bed bugs. "People dealt with it, and it was part of life. . . . I hope it doesn't get to the point where we're all just living with bed bugs."

A Logistical Nightmare

They are small. They can hide in any crack or crevice. (Think furniture joints, floorboards, baseboards, box springs, picture frames, closets full of clothing, personal belongings of almost any sort.) The early stages of infestations are hard to spot.

They can spread from room to room through duct work or false ceilings. They can be transported from venue to venue on clothing and belongings.

Their eggs are even smaller and almost transparent. They are attached to surfaces by means of a sticky substance.

You can't reduce infestations the way you might with cockroaches, by cleaning up food scraps, depriving them of shelter, and putting out bait. "You *are* their meal," said Elizabeth Dykstra, public health entomologist for the Zoonotic Disease Program of the Washington State Department of Health (WDOH).

And, she said, they can survive up to 18 months without a meal.

They have a history of developing resistance to pesticides. Potter and colleagues' research has shown widespread resistance to the pyrethroid insecticides that are currently the standard treatment (Romero, Potter, & Haynes, 2007).

They have idiosyncratic tastes—they're attracted by the heat and carbon dioxide that sleeping people generate, and they will feed only through a membrane. That means significant logistical challenges for trapping and baiting. (A Rutgers University Web page provides information on devising traps out of cat food bowls and dry ice—but only for diagnostic purposes. See njaes.rutgers.edu/pubs/publication .asp?pid=FS1117.)

None of the experts *JEH* spoke with saw any prospect of the bed bug problem spontaneously lessening in coming years.

Solutions from the Last Time Around

For half a century now, most Americans haven't had to worry about bed bugs. The problem previously reached its height in the 1920s and 1930s. Bed bugs had spread from port areas to major cities and eventually reached less populated rural areas.

Through the '40s and '50s, populations of the pest declined, primarily because DDT was widely available. Consumers could, for instance, buy DDT bug bombs in grocery stores. By the time bed bugs began developing resistance to DDT—which, inevitably, they did—organophosphates like diazinon and malathion were being used to clear up remaining infestations.

Larry Treleven, whose family has been in the pest control business for 84 years, said that his father and grandfather used to fumigate used furniture in their vaults. State laws required that the furniture be tagged as fumigated before it could be resold.

It was a different way of life, according to Potter. When people traveled, they knew to check their beds. When children came back from summer camp, their clothes and bedding had to be checked. He wondered whether people these days are prepared to exercise that kind of vigilance.

"And," he said, "people have a lot more clutter today, a lot more *stuff*. Which makes bed bug elimination more difficult."

Today, the hazards of pesticide treatment are also more widely recognized. Pesticide treatment options have narrowed for other reasons. DDT, for instance, is now illegal in the United States (U.S. Environmental Protection Agency [U.S. EPA], 1972). Besides, toward the end of the last epidemic, it had lost much of its effectiveness because bed bugs had developed resistance to it. Then other chemicals such as lindane and the organophosphates diazinon and malathion were used to mop up.

The Propoxur Proposal

On October 21, 2009, Matt Beal, acting chief of the Plant Industry Division of the Ohio Department of Agriculture (ODA), submitted a Section 18 request to the U.S. Environmental Protection Agency (U.S. EPA). The request was for an emergency exemption that would allow a pesticide called propoxur to be used by pest control professionals for treatment of bed bugs.

"For reasons nobody fully understands," Potter told *JEH,* "Ohio is really getting hammered."

Mystery Pesticide

Propoxur is a carbamate pesticide with a murky regulatory history. Currently it is used in some ant and cockroach baits, insecticidal strips, shelf paper, and pet collars. Although it is also labeled for use as a crack-and-crevice spray in food-handling establishments, U.S. EPA does not currently permit its use in locations where children may be present. That means no use in residential buildings and hotels.

But there's a loophole: products that were already in the channels of trade when current prohibitions went into effect may still be labeled for now prohibited uses. Strictly speaking, Beal said, use of those products is still legal. "The label is the law," as Jennifer Sievert, public health advisor for the WDOH Pesticide Program, put it. Indeed, because some of the labels allow consumers to use the product indoors, the permission that ODA is seeking (which would make propoxur available only to pest control professionals) would actually be *more* restrictive than the law as it now stands. That circumstance, according to Beal, has been a factor in the choice of propoxur for the Section 18 exemption request.

Of course, legality is not synonymous with safety. In 1988, U.S. EPA considered conducting a Special Review of propoxur "because of the potential carcinogenic risks to pest control operators and the general public during indoor and outdoor applications and risks to occupants of buildings treated with propoxur products" (U.S. EPA, 1997a, 1997b). In 1995, the agency decided *not* to initiate the Special Review because "the uses which posed the greatest concern had been eliminated through voluntary cancellation or label amendment" (U.S. EPA, 1997b). And in 2007, at the request of the registrant, it issued a final order terminating indoor use, according to the U.S. EPA document *Risk Management Decisions for Individual N methyl Carbamate Pesticides* (U.S. EPA, 2007).

Sievert interprets that history to mean that propoxur was withdrawn because of evidence suggesting it was not safe. Potter interprets the withdrawal as a business decision; he believes that the cost of refuting challenges to its safety would have been more than the product was worth to its manufacturers. Either way, there are now some gaps in the data on health effects.

U.S. EPA has placed propoxur in Toxicity Category II (the second-highest category) for oral exposure and Toxicity Category III for dermal and inhalation exposures. Propoxur is also classed as a "probable human carcinogen."

Why Propoxur?

A couple of years ago, Potter and colleagues at the University of Kentucky decided to test some older insecticides and compare their efficacy to that of pyrethroids. They tested propoxur and chlorpyrifos (an organophosphate) on five populations of bed bugs collected from the field. Four of those populations had proved to be highly resistant to pyrethroids. Both pesticides killed 100% of all populations within 24 hours—"and frankly," Potter told *JEH,* "within an *hour.*"

Ohio is not making its request in a vacuum. Beal has worked on this issue not only with Potter, but also with the Association of Structural Pest Control Regulatory Officials (ASPCRO). There were also some preliminary conversations with U.S. EPA, he said, and "there's a multitude of other states awaiting this decision."

What about the safety concerns? Beal told *JEH:* "Basically, our role here is that we have a serious situation at hand. . . . We feel that it's a reasonable request to ask the agency to take a look at this. Certainly I'm not a toxicologist, I'm not a physician. I'm in the area of pesticide regulation. So we felt it was a reasonable request."

Does that mean ODA is putting this request out as an open question to U.S. EPA? In other words, the gist is not: We think it's safe, and we definitely want to use it? Rather, the gist is: Will you check this out and see if it's safe?

"Exactly," Beal said. "That's what the process is."

What if U.S. EPA says no, it's not safe? Is there a plan B?

"That is an interesting dilemma," he said. "Then we stand back and we keep talking amongst the ASPCRO states. We talk with the professional management folks—the pest management professionals—and try to see if there are any other avenues for us to go down. Fortunately, we're not at that point right now."

Contra

Early this year, Dykstra and Sievert submitted the following comment to U.S. EPA: "We do not support the proposed health exemption request from the Ohio Department of Agriculture to use the pesticide propoxur . . . to treat indoor residential single or multiple unit dwellings, apartments, hotels, motels, office buildings, modes of transportation, and commercial industrial buildings to control bed bugs." They cited research showing that the pesticide "remains detectable in indoor air weeks after initial application" and that "use of propoxur exposes the developing fetus in pregnant women to the chemical."

Carbamate pesticides, of which propoxur is one, are neurotoxins. Like organophosphates, they inhibit cholinesterase, although poisoning with carbamates is more easily reversed with treatment, and there is a "greater span between symptom-producing and lethal doses," according to Reigart and Roberts's *Recognition and Management of Pesticide Poisonings* (Reigart & Roberts, 1999). Serious overexposure can cause death

Propoxur and the Regulatory Process: Information from U.S. EPA

In response to *JEH*'s request for an interview, U.S. EPA sent the following written statement about the regulatory history of propoxur and the process the agency is following in determining whether to grant ODA's Section 18 request:

Section 18 of Federal Insecticide, Fungicide, and Rodenticide Act (FIFRA) authorizes EPA to allow an unregistered use of a pesticide for a limited time if EPA determines that an emergency condition exists. EPA's review process for a Section 18 includes determining whether the use meets the applicable safety standard as well as whether the unregistered use meets the criterion of being an emergency. See www.epa.gov/opprd001/section18/for more information.

Propoxur is currently registered for use as follows:

- Indoor sprays in commercial buildings including food handling establishments to control roaches, ants, beetles, bees, etc. Labels explicitly exclude sprays in locations where children may be present (so no use in hotels, residential buildings, libraries, daycare facilities, schools). In food handling establishments, the use is restricted to crack and crevice application. Note that products in the channels of trade currently before the most recent labeling requirements may still be labeled for indoor residential use.
- Granular and gel baits for ants and cockroaches, some enclosed in bait stations.
- Impregnated insecticidal strips and shelf paper, to control cockroaches, bees, wasps, ants, etc.
- Pet collars to control fleas and ticks. Some are combination products with other active ingredients.

Information about historical use/regulation is available in the Propoxur Reregistration Eligibility Decision (1997), which can be accessed at www.epa.gov/pesticides/reregistration/propoxur/.

But the fact that propoxur is classed as a probable carcinogen is of concern for people of any age.

Dykstra and Sievert think pest control professionals should pursue alternative treatments. Such treatments might not, Dykstra acknowledged, completely eliminate the problem. But they would reduce it to tolerable levels.

"Instead of poisoning yourself or your children or whoever lives in the house," Sievert said. "That's really being played down here by propoxur proponents. In fact, there's basically no mention of it, that I can see."

Other Options

Marlowe of Eden Advanced Pest Technologies told *JEH* he is not a "fan" of the Ohio request: "From a *business* standpoint, it seems like we're headed in the wrong direction, to use a product like that around people's beds and in their bedrooms." Pesticides in sleeping quarters, he noted, are a potential liability for a company: "Even if it was made available to us, I'd probably stay with some of the other, lighter chemistries that we already have in the toolbox."

Eden uses steam heat to kill bedbugs, in combination with cedar oil and some other essential oils. Since these methods kill bed bugs only upon direct contact, Eden also applies diatomaceous earth to cracks, crevices, and any area bed bugs might be likely to crawl across. Diatomaceous earth abrades the exoskeleton, so that bodily fluids leak out and the insect eventually dries up.

Everyone agreed that diatomaceous earth is effective and that it shares an important advantage with propoxur: the ability to act residually. That is, it will act on any bugs not killed by direct-contact treatments, as well as on any bugs that get reintroduced after a treatment. A drawback, however, is that it works slowly. Potter also noted that application is tricky because it requires an extremely fine dusting, and applicators are not readily available to consumers. Pest control professionals have to be called in, and that means expense. Of course, the same would also be true of propoxur.

Another alternative, used by Treleven's company, Sprague Pest Solutions, is volumetric heating, which involves "superheating" an entire room to around 140F. Probes are used to ensure that the internal temperatures of objects in the room also reach temperatures high enough to kill the bugs. In addition, Sprague has dogs trained to sniff out any bed bugs that might remain. Unfortunately, this approach is expensive. The cost of equipping a single pest control team with a heater and generator approaches $50,000, and the setup and breakdown work make treatment an all-day, labor-intensive affair. Treleven estimated that treating a 1,700 square foot townhouse could cost a couple thousand dollars. Any conjoined units might then also have to be treated. Room-by-room treatment of multi-unit buildings could be a daunting prospect.

Treleven does recommend heat, combined with diatomaceous earth and canine detection, as a first, best treatment choice. But, he said, "If they can't afford the heating and the alternatives and things, it would be nice to have propoxur. I mean, I'm not going to lie to you. Because it is an alternative that would work."

by cardiorespiratory depression. Early symptoms include malaise, sweating, muscle weakness, headache, dizziness, and gastrointestinal symptoms. Other symptoms of acute toxicity are coma, hypertension, trouble breathing, blurred vision, lack of coordination, twitching, and slurring of speech.

The biggest concern is with chronic (or acute) exposure to small children and developing fetuses, according to Wayne Clifford, who manages the Pesticide Illness and Zoonotics Disease Surveillance and Prevention program in WDOH's Office of Environmental Health. Children are not small adults, he reminded *JEH;* their neurological pathways are developing. "There's so much going on there biologically that *isn't* happening in full-grown adults, and they are much more sensitive. That's the primary population that we're trying to protect."

Conclusion

In the case of bed bugs, none of the options are ideal. All can take a bite, figuratively speaking, out of someone's life.

Let's start with pesticides. Cancer risk, developmental detriments, and central nervous system effects can all subtract from longevity, fruitfulness, and life satisfaction. According to U.S. EPA's *R.E.D. Facts,* a reference dose (RfD) of 0.004 mg/kg/day is not expected to cause adverse effects over a 70-year lifetime (U.S. EPA, 1997). But as Clifford of WDOH put it, "there is not really a safe level of exposure to a carcinogen," because effects are cumulative and people may have exposures from other sources, such as residue on food. Propoxur treatments in areas where people sleep could entail extended exposures, especially since the pesticide has been demonstrated to volatilize in the air and be absorbed into the blood weeks after application (Whyatt et al., 2003).

But absent an effective pesticide, the need for relentless vigilance just as assuredly takes a bite out of life. Potter told *JEH* that he's had residents call him in tears when infestations have persisted after months of vigilant laundering and vacuuming. Added to the many stresses contemporary Americans already face, that kind of constant pressure can have a cumulative effect. Nor is money a negligible concern: the need for repeated expensive treatments can further contribute to financial insecurity—which in turn has its own, well-documented, health impacts.

Individual consumers could well come to different conclusions depending on personal circumstances, and making propoxur available could add to their choices.

But there are a couple of problems with casting this issue as a straightforward risk-benefit decision for individuals.

First, the impacts of neurotoxins on developing brains are difficult to sort out, much less document and quantify—which doesn't mean they're not happening. As Colborn writes: "Unlike obvious birth defects, most developmental effects cannot be seen at birth or even later in life. Instead, brain and nervous system disturbances are expressed in terms of how an individual behaves and functions, which can vary considerably from birth through adulthood" (2006, p.10).

Second, there's the question of whose risk and whose benefit. It's one thing for homeowners to weigh risks and benefits on their own and their families' behalf. Apartment buildings and other rental properties represent a different scenario. How many landlords, given the choice between repeated expensive heat treatments and a quick, inexpensive treatment with a U.S EPA approved pesticide, can be expected to choose the former? Perhaps a few. But it seems likely that in most cases, the decision will be a foregone conclusion. In the end, apartment dwellers could be subject, involuntarily and perhaps unknowingly, to extended exposures.

Nobody *JEH* interviewed thinks propoxur holds all the answers. ODA's exemption request is just a way of looking for something to, as Beal said, "help us through this critical time right now that we're seeing until something else further down the road can be developed to try to take care of the problem."

But will something else be developed "down the road"? Or will propoxur simply become the default treatment—at least until bed bugs develop resistance to it, too?

References

Colborn, T. (2006). A case for revisiting the safety of pesticides: A closer look at neurodevelopment. *Environmental Health Perspectives, 114*(1), 10-17.

Reigart, J.R., & Roberts, J.R. (1999). *Recognition and management of pesticide poisonings* (5th ed.). Washington, DC: U.S. EPA. Retrieved March 3, 2010, from www.epa.gov/pesticides/safety / healthcare/handbook/Chap05.pdf

Romero, A., Potter, M.F., & Haynes, K.F. (2007, July). Insecticide-resistant bed bugs: Implications for the industry. *Pest Control Technology.* Retrieved April 6, 2010, from www.pctonline.com /Article.aspx?article%5fid=37916

U.S. Environmental Protection Agency. (1972). *DDT ban takes effect.* Retrieved April 5, 2010, from www.epa.gov/history/topics /ddt/01.htm

U.S. Environmental Protection Agency. (1997a). *Reregistration eligibility decision (RED): Propoxur.* Retrieved April 5, 2010, from www.epa.gov/oppsrrd1/REDs/2555red.pdf

U.S. Environmental Protection Agency. (1997b). *R.E.D. facts: Propoxur* (U.S. EPA document # EPA-738-F-97-009). Retrieved April 5, 2010, from www.epa.gov/oppsrrd1/REDs /factsheets/2555fact.pdf

U.S. Environmental Protection Agency. (2007). *Risk management decisions for individual N-methyl carbamate pesticides.* Retrieved April 3, 2010, from epa.gov/oppsrrd1/cumulative /carbamate_ risk_mgmt.htm#propoxur

Whyatt, R.M., Barr, D.B., Camann, D.E., Kinney, P.L., Barr, J.R., Andrews, H.F., Hoepner, L.A., Garfinkel, R., Hazi, Y., Reyes, A., Ramirez, J., Cosme, Y., & Perera, F.P. (2003). Contemporary-use pesticides in personal air samples during pregnancy and blood samples at delivery among urban minority mothers and newborns. *Environmental Health Perspectives, 111*(5), 749–756.

Critical Thinking

1. What are the health risks, if any, associated with bed bugs?

Is Your Food Contaminated?

New approaches are needed to protect the food supply.

MARK FISCHETTI

Given the billions of food items that are packaged, purchased and consumed every day in the U.S., let alone the world, it is remarkable how few of them are contaminated. Yet since the terrorist attacks of September 11, 2001, "food defense" experts have grown increasingly worried that extremists might try to poison the food supply, either to kill people or to cripple the economy by undermining public confidence. At the same time, production of edible products is becoming ever more centralized, speeding the spread of natural contaminants, or those introduced purposely, from farms or processing plants to dinner tables everywhere. Mounting imports pose yet another rising risk, as recent restrictions on Chinese seafood containing drugs and pesticides attest.

Can the tainting of what we eat be prevented? And if toxins or pathogens do slip into the supply chain, can they be quickly detected to limit their harm to consumers? Tighter production procedures can go a long way toward protecting the public, and if they fail, smarter monitoring technologies can at least limit injury.

Tighten Security

Preventing a terrorist or a disgruntled employee from contaminating milk, juice, produce, meat or any type of comestible is a daunting problem. The food supply chain comprises a maze of steps, and virtually every one of them presents an opportunity for tampering. Blanket solutions are unlikely because "the chain differs from commodity to commodity," says David Hennessy, an economics professor at Iowa State University's Center for Agricultural and Rural Development. "Protecting dairy products is different from protecting apple juice, which is different from protecting beef."

Even within a given supply chain there are few technology-based quick fixes. Preventing contamination largely comes down to tightening physical plant security and processing procedures at every turn. Each farmer, rancher, processor, packager, shipper, wholesaler and retailer "has to identify every

possible vulnerability in the facility and in their procedures and close up every hole," says Frank Busta, director of the National Center for Food Protection and Defense at the University of Minnesota. The effort begins with standard facility access controls, which Busta often refers to as "gates, guns and guards," but extends to thoroughly screening employees and carefully sampling products at all junctures across the facility at all times.

That advice seems sound, of course, but the challenge for operators is how best to button down procedures. Several systems for safeguarding food production have been rolled out in recent years. Though these are not required by any regulatory agency, Busta strongly recommends that producers implement them. In the U.S., that impetus has been made stronger by legislation such as the 2002 Bioterrorism Act and a 2004 presidential directive, both of which require closer scrutiny of ingredient suppliers and tighter control of manufacturing procedures.

The primary safeguard systems Busta recommends borrow from military practices. The newest tool, which the FDA and the U.S. Department of Agriculture are now promoting, carries the awkward name of CARVER + Shock. It is being adapted from Defense Department procedures for identifying a military service's greatest vulnerabilities. "CARVER + Shock is essentially a complete security audit," says Keith Schneider, associate professor at the University of Florida's department of food science and human nutrition. The approach analyzes every node in the system for factors that range from the likely success of different kinds of attacks to the magnitude of public health, economic and psychological effects (together, the "shock" value) that a given type of infiltration could cause.

Track Contaminants

No matter how tightly procedures are controlled, determined perpetrators could still find ways to introduce pathogens or poisons. And natural pathogens such as salmonella are always a

Detect, Track and Trace

If a natural pathogen, or a perpetrator, contaminates food, lives will be saved if the tainted product can be quickly detected, then traced back to its point of origin so the rest of the batch can be tracked down or recalled. The following technologies, in development, could help:

- **Microfluidic Detectors**—Botulinum bacteria produce the most poisonous toxin known. They and similar agents, such as tetanus, could be detected during food processing by microfluidic chips—self-contained diagnostic labs the size of a finger. The University of Wisconsin–Madison is crafting such a chip, lined with antibodies held in place by magnetic beads, that could detect botulism during milk production. The chip could sample milk before or after it was piped into tanker trucks that leave the dairy and before or after it was pasteurized at a production plant. Other chips could detect other toxins at various fluid-processing plants, such as those that produce apple juice, soup or baby formula.

- **Active Packaging**—*E. coli,* salmonella and other pathogens could be detected by small windows in packaging, such as the cellophane around meat or the plastic jar around peanut butter. The "intelligent" window would contain antibodies that bind to enzymes or metabolites produced by the microorganism, and if that occurred the patch would turn color. The challenge is to craft the windows from materials and reactants that can safely contact food. Similar biosensors could react if the contents reached a certain pH level or were exposed to high temperature, indicating spoilage. And they could sense if packaging was

tampered with, for example, by reacting to the pressure imposed by a syringe or to oxygen seeping in through a puncture hole.

- **RFID Tags**—Pallets or cases of a few select foods now sport radio-frequency identification (RFID) tags that, when read by a scanner, indicate which farm or processing plant the batch came from. Future tokens that are smaller, smarter and cheaper could adorn individual packages and log every facility they had passed through and when. The University of Florida is devising tags that could be read through fluid (traditional designs cannot) and thus could be embedded inside the wall of sour cream or yogurt containers. The university is also developing active tags that could record the temperatures a package had been exposed to.

- **Edible Tags**—Manufacturers often combine crops from many growers, such as spinach leaves, into a retail package, so tags affixed to bags might not help investigators track contamination back to a specific source. ARmark Authentication Technologies can print microscopic markers that indicate site of origin directly onto a spinach leaf, apple or pellet of dog food using a spray made from edible materials such as cellulose, vegetable oil or proteins. Also, the tiny size would be hard for terrorists to fake, making it harder for them to sneak toxin-laced counterfeit foods past inspectors and into the supply. As an alternative, DataLase can spray citrus fruits or meats with an edible film in a half-inch-diameter patch that is then exposed to a laser beam that writes identification codes within the film.

concern. Detecting these agents, tracing them back to the spot of introduction, and tracking which grocery stores and restaurants ended up with tainted products are therefore paramount. Putting such systems in place "is just as important as prevention," Schneider says.

Here new technology does play a major role, with various sensors applied at different points along the chain. "You can't expect one technology to counter all the possible taintings for a given food," notes Ken Lee, chairman of Ohio State University's department of food science and technology.

A variety of hardware is being developed [see box on top of this page], although little has been deployed commercially thus far. Radio-frequency identification (RFID) tags are furthest along, in part because the Defense Department and Wal-Mart have required their main suppliers to attach the tokens to pallets or cases of foodstuffs. The Metro AG supermarket chain in Germany has done the same. The ultimate intent is for automated readers to scan the tags at each step along the supply chain—from farm, orchard, ranch or processor, through

packaging, shipping and wholesale—and to report each item's location to a central registry. That way if a problem surfaces, investigators can quickly determine where the batch originated and which stores or facilities might have received goods from that batch and when. Retailers can also read the tags on their items to see if they have received a product later identified as suspicious.

As RFID tags get smaller and cheaper, they will be placed directly on individual items—on every bag of spinach, jar of peanut butter, container of shrimp and sack of dog food. "That way if a recall is issued, the items can be found as they run past a scanner at the checkout counter," says Jean-Pierre Émond, professor of agricultural and biological engineering at the University of Florida.

Universities and companies are developing all kinds of other tags, some that are very inexpensive and others that cost more but supply extensive information. Some tokens, for example, can sense if food has been exposed to warm temperatures and thus might be more likely to harbor *Escherichia coli* or

Intentional Poisonings

U.S., 1984,
salmonella in salad bars, by Rajneeshees cult,
751 sickened

China, 2002,
rat poison in breakfast foods, by competitor to the vendor,
400 sickened, over 40 killed

U.S., 2002,
nicotine sulfate in ground beef, by disgruntled worker,
111 sickened

salmonella. Other tags could track how long items spent in transit from node to node in the supply chain, which could indicate unusually long delays that might raise suspicion about tampering. So-called active packaging could detect contamination directly and warn consumers not to eat the product they are holding.

The big impediment for any marker, of course, is the price. "Right now it costs 25 cents to put an RFID tag on a case of lettuce," Émond notes. "But for some growers, that equals the profit they're going to make on that case."

To be embraced widely, therefore, he says tags will have to provide additional value to suppliers or buyers. His university has been conducting an ongoing project with Publix Super Markets and produce suppliers in Florida and California to assess the possibilities. In initial trials, tags tracked crates and pallets that were shipped from the growers to several of Publix's distribution centers. Information gleaned from scanning tags at various points was available to all the companies via a secure Internet site hosted by VeriSign, the data security firm. The compilation allowed the participants to more quickly resolve order discrepancies, to log how long food sat idle, and to reveal ways to raise shipping efficiency. The group plans to extend the test to retail stores.

The U.S. imports 50 percent more food than it did just five years ago.

Control Suppliers

Costs will not drop until new technologies are widely deployed, but food defense analysts say adoption is unlikely to occur until clear, streamlined regulations are enacted. That prospect, in turn, will remain remote until the highest levels of government are reformed. "There are more than a dozen different federal agencies that oversee some aspect of food safety," Lee points out, noting that simple coordination among

Making Imports Safer

Alarming warnings about Chinese products in recent months have shown how dangerous imported edibles can be. In March some 100 brands of pet food were recalled after they were found to contain melamine, a toxic chemical used as a cheap replacement for wheat gluten. Then in June the U.S. Food and Drug Administration issued alerts about five types of seafood that contained antibiotic residues, pesticides and salmonella.

After the seafood scare, Senator Charles Schumer of New York declared that the federal government should establish an import czar. He blamed poor control of imports on a lack of inspection and poor regulation, telling the *Washington Post* that "neither the Chinese or American government is doing their job."

Regardless of how safe domestic production is, "imports are our Achilles' heel," says Ken Lee, chairman of Ohio State University's department of food science and technology. "There is no global food regulator. If the Chinese want to put an adulterant into food, they can do it until they get caught. I'll wager it will happen again, because it's driven by the profit motive."

Realistically, no technology can ensure that imports are safe. The food in every shipping container entering a U.S. port or border crossing could be pulled and irradiated, and some comestibles such as spices are already processed this way. But industry says the step would add significant cost for producers and shipping delays for middlemen. And the public continues to be wary of the technology. Furthermore, although irradiation would kill pathogens, it would have no effect on poisons or adulterants.

Inspecting all incoming food would also require vast increases in FDA and U.S. Department of Agriculture budgets; the agencies currently inspect a meager 1 percent of imports. As a partial alternative, in June the FDA said it intended to conduct more inspections of products from countries it deems to have poorer food-safety controls, such as China, offset by fewer inspections of products from countries with stronger standards, such as Britain and Canada. The agency also said it might require importers and U.S. manufacturers that use imported ingredients to provide more detailed information about production processes at foreign suppliers.

The best recourse, Lee says, is for companies to insist that suppliers impose strict standards and that the companies send inspectors overseas to verify compliance. Other experts agree, adding that government edicts are not as effective. "Too often import requirements are used as trade barriers, and they just escalate," says David Hennessy, an economics professor at Iowa State University. "The food companies themselves have a lot to lose, however. When they source a product in a country, they ought to impose tough procedures there."

—M.F.

The Vigilant Kitchen

If contaminated food does make it into your grocery bag, smart appliances could still prevent it from reaching your mouth. Innovations that could reach commercial introduction are described here by Ken Lee of Ohio State University. "None of this technology would be visually obtrusive," he says, "and all of it would be easy to clean."

Pulsed Light

When homeowners are asleep, fixtures underneath cabinets emit pulses of ultraviolet light that kill germs on counter-tops and other surfaces.

Microwave

An infrared sensor gauges internal food temperature and compares it with safety guidelines, indicating when the proper value has been reached. Instead of entering a cooking time, a user enters the food type or target temperature.

Refrigerator

A built-in reader scans RFID tags on food and checks for recalls over a wireless Internet connection. (A homeowner could hold nonrefrigerator items under it, too.) The reader also notes expiration dates written into the tags and tracks when containers such as milk cartons are removed and put back, to see if they have been out for too long and therefore might be spoiled. A red light warns of trouble.

---

them is difficult enough, and efficient approval of sensible requirements is even harder to come by. The FDA regulates pizza with cheese on it, but the USDA regulates pizza if it has meat on it, quips Jacqueline Fletcher, professor of entomology

and plant pathology at Oklahoma State University. "The requirements for organic farmers are different from those for nonorganic farmers."

Spurred by recent recalls, members of Congress have called for streamlining the regulation system. Illinois Senator Richard Durbin and Connecticut Representative Rosa DeLauro are advocating a single food-safety agency, but turf wars have hampered any progress toward that goal.

Concerned that more effective government is a long shot, experts say the responsibility for improved vigilance falls largely on food suppliers. "The strongest tool for stopping intentional contamination is supply-chain verification," says Shaun Kennedy, deputy director of the National Center for Food Protection and Defense. That means a brand-name provider such as Dole or a grocery store conglomerate such as Safeway must insist that every company involved in its supply chain implement the latest security procedures and detection, track and trace technologies or be dropped if it does not. The brand company should also validate compliance through inspections and other measures. The impetus falls on the brand-name provider because it has the most to lose. If a natural or man-made toxin is found in, say, a bag of Dole spinach or a container of Safeway milk, consumers will shun that particular label. "If a brand-name company wants to protect its products," Kennedy says, "it should validate every participant in the chain, all the way back to the farm."

Critical Thinking

1. What is the purpose of CARVER + Stock audit technique? Which government agencies/departments are supporting the use of this technique in the U.S. food supply chain?

2. What is RFID? How could the use of this technology be beneficial to the food supply?

3. Why is food safety more of a concern now than 50 years ago?

Hazardous Health Plans

Coverage gaps can leave you in big trouble.

Many people who believe they have adequate health insurance actually have coverage so riddled with loopholes, limits, exclusions, and gotchas that it won't come close to covering their expenses if they fall seriously ill, a *Consumer Reports* investigation has found.

At issue are so-called individual plans that consumers get on their own when, say, they've been laid off from a job but are too young for Medicare or too "affluent" for Medicaid. An estimated 14,000 Americans a day lose their job-based coverage, and many might be considering individual insurance for the first time in their lives.

But increasingly, individual insurance is a nightmare for consumers: more costly than the equivalent job-based coverage, and for those in less-than-perfect health, unaffordable at best and unavailable at worst. Moreover, the lack of effective consumer protections in most states allows insurers to sell plans with "affordable" premiums whose skimpy coverage can leave people who get very sick with the added burden of ruinous medical debt.

Just ask Janice and Gary Clausen of Audubon, Iowa. They told us they purchased a United Healthcare limited benefit plan sold through AARP that cost about $500 a month after Janice lost her accountant job and her work-based coverage when the auto dealership that employed her closed in 2004.

"I didn't think it sounded bad," Janice said. "I knew it would only cover $50,000 a year, but I didn't realize how much everything would cost." The plan proved hopelessly inadequate after Gary received a diagnosis of colon cancer. His 14-month treatment, including surgery and chemotherapy, cost well over $200,000. Janice, 64, and Gary, 65, expect to be paying off medical debt for the rest of their lives.

For our investigation, we hired a national expert to help us evaluate a range of real policies from many states and interviewed Americans who bought those policies. We talked to insurance experts and regulators to learn more. Here is what we found:

- Heath insurance policies with gaping holes are offered by insurers ranging from small companies to brand-name carriers such as Aetna and United Healthcare. And in most states, regulators are not tasked with evaluating overall coverage.
- Disclosure requirements about coverage gaps are weak or nonexistent. So it's difficult for consumers to figure out in advance what a policy does or doesn't cover, compare plans, or estimate their out-of-pocket liability for a medical catastrophe. It doesn't help that many people who have never been seriously ill might have no idea how expensive medical care can be.
- People of modest means in many states might have no good options for individual coverage. Plans with affordable premiums can leave them with crushing medical debt if they fall seriously ill, and plans with adequate coverage may have huge premiums.
- There are some clues to a bad policy that consumers can spot. We tell you what they are, and how to avoid them if possible.
- Even as policymakers debate a major overhaul of the health-care system, government officials can take steps now to improve the current market.

Good Plans vs. Bad Plans

We think a good health-care plan should pay for necessary care without leaving you with lots of debt or high out-of-pocket costs. That includes hospital, ambulance, emergency-room, and physician fees; prescription drugs; outpatient treatments; diagnostic and imaging tests; chemotherapy, radiation, rehabilitation and physical therapy; mental-health treatment; and durable medical equipment, such as wheelchairs. Remember, health insurance is supposed to protect you in case of a catastrophically expensive illness, not simply cover your routine costs as a generally healthy person. And many individual plans do nowhere near the job.

For decades, individual insurance has been what economists call a "residual" market—something to buy only when you have run out of other options. The problem, according to insurance experts we consulted, is that the high cost of treatment in the U.S., which has the world's most expensive health-care system, puts truly affordable, comprehensive coverage out of the reach of people who don't have either deep pockets or a generous employer. Insurers tend to provide this choice: comprehensive coverage with a high monthly premium or skimpy coverage at a low monthly premium within the reach of middle- and low-income consumers.

More consumers are having to choose the latter as they become unemployed or their workplace drops coverage. (COBRA, the federal program that allows former employees to continue with the insurance from their old job by paying the full monthly premium, often costs $1,000 or more each month for family coverage. The federal government is temporarily subsidizing 65 percent of those premiums for some, but only for a maximum of nine months.) *Consumer Reports* and others label as "junk insurance" those so-called affordable individual plans with huge coverage gaps. Many such plans are sold throughout the nation, including policies from well-known companies.

Decent insurance covers more than just routine care.

Aetna's Affordable Health Choices plans, for example, offer limited benefits to part-time and hourly workers. We found one such policy that covered only $1,000 of hospital costs and $2,000 of out-patient expenses annually.

The Clausens' AARP plan, underwritten by insurance giant United Health Group, the parent company of United Healthcare, was advertised as "the essential benefits you deserve. Now in one affordable plan." AARP spokesman Adam Sohn said, "AARP has been fighting for affordable, quality health care for nearly a half-century, and while a fixed-benefit indemnity plan is not perfect, it offers our members an option to help cover some portion of their medical expenses without paying a high premium."

Nevertheless, AARP suspended sales of such policies last year after Sen. Charles Grassley, R-Iowa, questioned the marketing practices. Some 53,400 AARP members still have policies similar to the Clausens' that were sold under the names Medical Advantage Plan, Essential Health Insurance Plan, and Essential Plus Health Insurance Plan. In addition, at least 1 million members are enrolled in the AARP Hospital Indemnity Insurance Plan, Sohn said, an even more bare-bones policy. Members who have questions should first call 800-523-5800; for more help, call 888-687-2277. (Consumers Union, the nonprofit publisher of *Consumer Reports,* is working with AARP on a variety of health-care reforms.)

United American Insurance Co. promotes its supplemental health insurance as "an affordable solution to America's health-care crisis!" When Jeffrey E. Miller, 56, of Sarasota, Fla., received a diagnosis of prostate cancer a few months after buying one of the company's limited-benefit plans, he learned that it would not cover tens of thousands of dollars' worth of drug and radiation treatments he needed. As this article went to press, five months after his diagnosis, Miller had just begun treatment after qualifying for Florida Medicaid. A representative of United American declined to comment on its products.

Even governments are getting into the act. In 2008, Florida created the Cover Florida Health Care Access Program, which Gov. Charlie Crist said would make "affordable health coverage available to 3.8 million uninsured Floridians." But many of the basic "preventive" policies do not cover inpatient hospital treatments, emergency-room care, or physical therapy, and they severely limit coverage of everything else.

7 Signs a Health Plan Might Be Junk

Do Everything in Your Power to Avoid Plans with the Following Features:

Limited benefits. Never buy a product that is labeled "limited benefit" or "not major medical" insurance. In most states those phrases might be your only clue to an inadequate policy.

Low overall coverage limits. Health care is more costly than you might imagine if you've never experienced a serious illness. The cost of cancer or a heart attack can easily hit six figures. Policies with coverage limits of $25,000 or even $100,000 are not adequate.

"Affordable" premiums. There's no free lunch when it comes to insurance. To lower premiums, insurers trim benefits and do what they can to avoid insuring less healthy people. So if your insurance was a bargain, chances are good it doesn't cover very much. To check how much a comprehensive plan would cost you, go to *ehealthinsurance.com,* enter your location, gender, and age as prompted, and look for the most costly of the plans that pop up. It is probably the most comprehensive.

No coverage for important things. If you don't see a medical service specifically mentioned in the policy, assume it's not covered. We reviewed policies that didn't cover prescription drugs or outpatient chemotherapy but didn't say so anywhere in the policy document—not even in the section labeled "What is not covered."

Ceilings on categories of care. A $900-a-day maximum benefit for hospital expenses will hardly make a dent in a $45,000 bill for heart bypass surgery. If you have to accept limits on some services, be sure your plan covers hospital and outpatient medical treatment, doctor visits, drugs, and diagnostic and imaging tests without a dollar limit. Limits on mental-health costs, rehabilitation, and durable medical equipment should be the most generous you can afford.

Limitless out-of-pocket costs. Avoid policies that fail to specify a maximum amount that you'll have to pay before the insurer will begin covering 100 percent of expenses. And be alert for loopholes. Some policies, for instance, don't count co-payments for doctor visits or prescription drugs toward the maximum. That can be a catastrophe for seriously ill people who rack up dozens of doctor's appointments and prescriptions a year.

Random gotchas. The AARP policy that the Clausens bought began covering hospital care on the second day. That seems benign enough, except that the first day is almost always the most expensive, because it usually includes charges for surgery and emergency-room diagnostic tests and treatments.

The Wild West of Insurance

Compounding the problem of limited policies is the fact that policyholders are often unaware of those limits—until it's too late.

"I think people don't understand insurance, period," said Stephen Finan, associate director of policy at the American Cancer Society Cancer Action Network. "They know they need it. They look at the price, and that's it. They don't understand the language, and insurance companies go to great lengths to make it incomprehensible. Even lawyers don't always understand what it means."

Case in point: Jim Stacey of Fayetteville, N.C. In 2000, Stacey and his wife, Imelda, were pleased to buy a plan at what they considered an "incredible" price from the Mid-West National Life Insurance Co. of Tennessee. The policy's list of benefits included a lifetime maximum payout of up to $1 million per person. But after Stacey learned he had prostate cancer in 2005, the policy paid only $1,480 of the $17,453 it cost for the implanted radioactive pellets he chose to treat the disease.

"To this day, I don't know what went wrong," Stacey said about the bill.

We sent the policy, along with the accompanying Explanation of Benefit forms detailing what it did and didn't pay, to Karen Pollitz, research professor at the Georgetown University Health Policy Institute. We asked Pollitz, an expert on individual health insurance, to see whether she could figure out why the policy covered so little.

"The short answer is, 'Beats the heck out of me,'" she e-mailed back to us. The Explanation of Benefit forms were missing information that she would expect to see, such as specific billing codes that explain what treatments were given. And there didn't seem to be any connection between the benefits listed in the policy and the actual amounts paid.

Contacted for comment, a spokeswoman for HealthMarkets, the parent company of Mid-West National, referred us to the company website. It stated that the company "pays claims according to the insurance contract issued to each customer" and that its policies "satisfy a need in the marketplace for a product that balances the cost with the available benefit options." The spokeswoman declined to answer specific questions about Stacey's case, citing patient privacy laws.

One reason confusion abounds, Pollitz said, is that health insurance is regulated by the states, not by the federal government, and most states (Massachusetts and New York are prominent exceptions) do not have a standard definition of what constitutes health insurance.

"Rice is rice and gasoline is gasoline. When you buy it, you know what it is," Pollitz said. "Health insurance—who knows what it is? It is some product that's sold by an insurance company. It could be a little bit or a lot of protection. You don't know what is and isn't covered. Nothing can be taken for granted."

How to Protect Yourself

Seek out comprehensive coverage. A good plan will cover your legitimate health care without burdening you with oversized debt.

Want Better Coverage? Try Running for Congress

President Barack Obama says Americans should have access to the kind of health benefits Congress gets. We detail them below. Members of Congress and other U.S. government employees can receive care through the Federal Employees Health Benefits Program. Employees choose from hundreds of plans, but the most popular is a national Blue Cross and Blue Shield Preferred Provider Organization plan. Employee contributions for that plan are $152 per person, or $357 per family, per month.

Plan Features
- No annual or lifetime limits for major services
- Deductible of $300 per person and $600 per family
- Out-of-pocket limit of $5,000 per year with preferred providers, which includes most deductibles, co-insurance, and co-payments

Covered Services
- Inpatient and outpatient hospital care
- Inpatient and outpatient doctor visits
- Prescription drugs
- Diagnostic tests
- Preventive care, including routine immunizations
- Chemotherapy and radiation therapy
- Maternity care
- Family planning
- Durable medical equipment, orthopedic devices, and artificial limbs
- Organ and tissue transplants
- Inpatient and outpatient surgery
- Physical, occupational, and speech therapy
- Outpatient and inpatient mental-health care

"The idea of 'Cadillac' coverage vs. basic coverage isn't an appropriate way to think about health insurance," said Mila Kofman, Maine's superintendent of insurance. "It has to give you the care you need, when you need it, and some financial security so you don't end up out on the street."

What you want is a plan that has no caps on specific coverages. But if you have to choose, pick a plan offering unlimited coverage for hospital and outpatient treatment, doctor visits, drugs, and diagnostic and imaging tests. When it comes to lifetime coverage maximums, unlimited is best and $2 million should be the minimum. Ideally, there should be a single deductible for everything or, at most, one deductible for drugs and one for everything else. And the policy should pay for 100 percent of all expenses once your out-of-pocket payments hit a certain amount, such as $5,000 or $10,000.

If you are healthy now, do not buy a plan based on the assumption that you will stay that way. Don't think you can safely

The Real Cost of Illness Can Be Staggering . . .

Few Americans realize how much care costs. Coverage gaps can leave you in debt.

Condition	Treatment	Total Cost
Late-stage colon cancer	124 weeks of treatment, including two surgeries, three types of chemotherapy, imaging, prescription drugs, hospice care.	$285,946
Heart attack	56 weeks of treatment, including ambulance, ER workup, angioplasty with stent, bypass surgery, cardiac rehabilitation, counseling for depression, prescription drugs.	$110,405
Breast cancer	87 weeks of treatment, including lumpectomy, drugs, lab and imaging tests, chemotherapy and radiation therapy, mental-health counseling, and prosthesis.	$104,535
Type 2 diabetes	One year of maintenance care, including insulin and other prescription drugs, glucose test strips, syringes and other supplies, quarterly physician visits and lab, annual eye exam.	$5,949

. . . and Out-of-Pocket Expenses Can Vary Widely

With its lower premium and deductible, the California plan at right would seem the better deal. But because California, unlike Massachusetts, allows the sale of plans with large coverage gaps, a patient there will pay far more than a Massachusetts patient for the same breast cancer treatments, as the breakdown below shows.

Massachusetts Plan	California Plan
Monthly premium for any 55-year-old: $399	**Monthly premium for a healthy 55-year-old:** $246
Annual deductible: $2,200	**Annual deductible:** $1,000
Co-pays: $25 office visit, $250 outpatient surgery after deductible, $10 for generic drugs, $25 for nonpreferred generic and brand name, $45 for nonpreferred brand name	**Co-pays:** $25 preventive care office visits
	Co-insurance: 20% for most covered services
Co-insurance: 20% for some services	**Out-of-pocket maximum:** $2,500, includes hospital and surgical co-insurance only.
Out-of-pocket maximum: $5,000, includes deductible, co-insurance, and all co-payments	**Exclusions and limits:** Prescription drugs, most mental-health care, and wigs for chemotherapy patients not covered. Outpatient care not covered until out-of-pocket maximum satisfied from hospital/surgical co-insurance.
Exclusions and limits: Cap of 24 mental-health visits, $3,000 cap on equipment	
Lifetime benefits: Unlimited	**Lifetime benefits:** $5 million

Service and Total Cost	Patient Pays	Patient Pays
Hospital	$0	$705
Surgery	$981	$1,136
Office visits and procedures	$1,833	$2,010
Prescription drugs	$1,108	$5,985
Laboratory and imaging tests	$808	$3,772
Chemotherapy and radiation therapy	$1,987	$21,113
Mental health care	$950	$2,700
Prosthesis	$0	$350
Total $104,535	$7,668	$37,767

Source: Karen Pollitz, Georgetown University Health Policy Institute, using real claims data and policies. Columns of figures do not add up exactly because all numbers are rounded.

go without drug coverage, for example, because you don't take any prescriptions regularly today. "You can't know in advance if you're going to be among the .01 percent of people who needs the $20,000-a-month biologic drug," said Gary Claxton, a vice president of the nonprofit Kaiser Family Foundation, a health-policy research organization. "What's important is if you get really sick, are you going to lose everything?"

Consider trade-offs carefully. If you have to make a trade-off to lower your premium, Claxton and Pollitz suggest opting for a higher deductible and a higher out-of-pocket limit rather than fixed dollar limits on services. Better to use up part of your retirement savings paying $10,000 up front than to lose your whole nest egg paying a $90,000 medical bill after your policy's limits are exhausted.

What Lawmakers Need to Do Next

Consumers Union, the nonprofit publisher of *Consumer Reports,* has long supported national health-care reform that makes affordable health coverage available to all Americans. The coverage should include a basic set of required, comprehensive health-care benefits, like those in the federal plan that members of Congress enjoy. Insurers should compete for customers based on price and the quality of their services, not by limiting their risk through confusing options, incomplete information, or greatly restricted benefits.

As reform is developed and debated, Consumers Union supports these changes in the way health insurance is presented and sold:

Clear terms. All key terms in policies, such as "out-of-pocket" and "annual deductible," should be defined by law and insurers should be required to use them that way in their policies.

Standard benefits. Ideally, all plans should have a uniform set of benefits covering all medically necessary care, but consumers should be able to opt for varying levels of cost-sharing. Failing that, states should establish a menu of standardized plans, as Medicare does for Medigap plans. Consumers would then have a basis for comparing costs of plans.

Transparency. Policies that insurers currently sell should be posted in full online or available by mail upon request for anyone who wants to examine them. They should be the full, legally binding policy documents, not just a summary or marketing brochure. In many states now, consumers can't see the policy document until after they have joined the plan. At that point, they're legally entitled to a "free look" period in which to examine the policy and ask for a refund if they don't like what they see. But if they turn the policy back in, they face the prospect of being uninsured until they can find another plan.

Disclosure of costs. Every plan must provide a standard "Plan Coverage" summary that clearly displays what is—and more important, is not—covered. The summary should include independently verified estimates of total out-of-pocket costs for a standard range of serious problems, such as breast cancer treatment or heart bypass surgery.

Moreover, reliable information should be available to consumers about the costs in their area of treating various medical conditions, so that they have a better understanding of the bills they could face without adequate health coverage.

With such a high deductible, in years when you are relatively healthy you might never collect anything from your health insurance. To economize on routine care, take advantage of free community health screenings, low-cost or free community health clinics, immediate-care clinics offered in some drugstores, and low-priced generic prescriptions sold at Target, Walmart, and elsewhere.

Look for a plan that doesn't cap your coverage.

If your financial situation is such that you can afford neither the higher premiums of a more comprehensive policy nor high deductibles, you really have no good choices, Pollitz said, adding, "It's why we need to fix our health-care system."

Check out the policy and company. You can, at least, take some steps to choose the best plan you can afford. First, see "7 Signs a Health Plan Might Be Junk" to learn to spot the most dangerous pitfalls and the preferred alternatives.

Use the Web to research insurers you're considering. The National Association of Insurance Commissioners posts complaint information online at www.naic.org.

Entering the name of the company and policy in a search engine can't hurt either. Consumers who did that recently would have discovered that Mid-West National was a subsidiary of HealthMarkets, whose disclosure and claims handling drew many customers' ire. Last year, HealthMarkets was fined $20 million after a multi-state investigation of its sales practices and claims handling.

Don't rely on the salesperson's word. Jeffrey E. Miller, the Florida man whose policy failed to cover much of his cancer treatment, recalls being bombarded with e-mail and calls when he began shopping for insurance. "The salesman for the policy I bought told me it was great, and I was going to be covered, and it paid up to $100,000 for a hospital stay," he said. "But the insurance has turned out to pay very little."

Pollitz advises anyone with questions about their policy to ask the agent and get answers in writing. "Then if it turns out not to be true," she said, "you can complain."

Critical Thinking

1. What should consumers look for when choosing health insurance?
2. What constitutes inadequate health care coverage?

The Rough Road to *Dreamland*

Sleep needs and patterns might be unique to each individual, but the typical thieves of restful slumber are not.

MICHAEL J. BREUS

Sleep affects how we work, relate to other people, and make decisions, as well as how we feel. The idea that we need to "sleep on it" when faced with a big decision is scientifically proven. A Dutch study shows that people make "better" decisions by letting the "unconscious" mind during sleep chum through the options presented. We know that sleep helps us think better and stronger, as well as prepare our minds for optimal functionality, but getting a good night's rest is difficult for many.

Sleep as a topic has gotten a lot of attention recently—and for good reason. Inadequate amounts have been shown to create poorer health, obesity, lower productivity on the job (including the occupation of being a full-time parent), more danger on the roads, a less vibrant sex life, and a lower quality of existence.

Research is not the only thing alerting us to the dangers of sleep deprivation, as the results of a series of polls taken by the National Sleep Foundation demonstrate the extent of the issue. About 75 percent of Americans frequently have a sleep problem symptom, including repeated waking during the night or snoring, and 25 percent maintain that their daily activities are affected by this lack of sleep, and that includes sexual relationships in which respondents say they have been having less sex or have lost interest in sex entirely. Sixty percent have driven while drowsy in the past year, and about four percent have had an accident or close call because of drowsiness or actually falling asleep at the wheel.

On average, adults are sleeping 6.8 hours a night on weekdays and 7.4 hours on weekends. Twenty-six percent of adults say they have "a good night's sleep" only a few nights a month or less. On average, people maintain they need a minimum of 6.5 hours of sleep a night to function at their best during the day. In general, men report needing less (6.2 hours) than women (6.8 hours). On average, it takes about 23 minutes to fall asleep on most nights.

When an individual is suffering from a lack of sleep, reaction time and the ability to think clearly and quickly slow down. A person is more likely to make poor decisions, become irritable and moody, be low on stamina, and have a compromised ability to fight off disease and weight gain. A chronic lack of sleep may put individuals at greater risk for type 2 diabetes.

When you consider how much of your life depends on others making good decisions—physicians, industrial workers, pilots, air-traffic controllers, drivers, train conductors, presidents, world leaders, and so on—you soon realize that sleep deprivation is not just about you, but everybody.

Scientists only are beginning to understand disordered sleep and how to treat it. We sleep less today than ever before. In the last 100 years, Americans have cut their sleep time by about 20%. How we sleep has had a few major changes over the centuries based on some interesting historical developments. The introduction of the light bulb in 1879 suddenly altered how long people could work. Another issue was the mainstreaming of caffeine (in consumable drinks) as an alerting agent, which prevents sleep, or at least replaces it for a short while. The concept of overtime also has molded sleep habits. Our lifestyles leave little time for sleep, and our society motivates people to work and play more while sleeping less. As humans in a modern society, we endure a great deal of stress, and that morphs into psychological problems such as anxiety, nervousness, depression, and, ultimately, lost sleep.

Measuring sleep deprivation is difficult without knowing exactly how many hours you need daily. Not everyone is created equal. Some people require seven hours to feel refreshed and alert all day long, whereas others might need nine hours, or only 6.5. Sleep needs might vary depending on what is going on in your life. You may require more sleep during times of acute stress, grief, hard work, physical training, illness, or depression. Your sleep habits also can change with age.

Is it possible to sleep too much? If you sleep more than nine hours a night, for instance, should you aim to cut back on your sleep time? Some studies have documented that there are health risks of sleeping too long. One found long sleepers had a 50% greater risk of stroke than did those who slept six to eight hours a night. They also may have higher rates of cardiovascular disease and possibly an increased risk for diabetes. A large Japanese study found that those who sleep more than 7.5 hours a day have a greater risk of death than those who get less than 6.5 hours—but do not be alarmed. These studies cannot make any definitive conclusions yet because the explanations behind the results are not clear, and there are just as many other studies to complicate some of this new evidence. For instance, research suggests that women who are, in fact, longer sleepers may have a lower risk of breast cancer.

There is no magical number for sleep that covers everybody's needs. Sleep requirements are individual. If you are a long sleeper who feels lethargic much of the day, you might benefit from restricting your time in bed. The point is to find which number of hours makes you feel the best and then aim to sleep that number every night. Thus, if you know you need eight hours a night and you only get seven hours for eight straight days, then you have lost one full night's sleep during that span. You probably know if you are chronically sleep deprived without having to take a test. It is not rocket science. Much like being thirsty, your body tells you when you are missing something it wants.

Who needs more sleep, men or women? From a clinical perspective, women tend to confess more about sleep issues than men. As a gender, women appear to bear more stresses seeking balance in their multiple roles as moms, wives, employees, chauffeurs, cooks, cleaners, entrepreneurs, family managers, caretakers, etc. One would think that, since women and men are physiologically different, they would have different sleep needs, but women from adolescence to post-menopause are underrepresented in studies of sleep and its disorders even though sleep complaints are twice as prevalent in females. Some studies show that women may be at greater risk for insomnia, or have a predisposition due to their sex, but explaining this from a purely scientific standpoint is not entirely possible at present.

Compounding this question is the fact that age can have more to do with sleep needs and experiences than gender. For instance, younger women may build up sleep debt more easily than older women, allowing the latter to function better with fewer hours of sleep. Whether or not this is true, however, is up for debate. In fact, plenty of sleep studies result in controversial and inconclusive data.

What we do know about sleep and aging is that the older you get, the more likely you are to suffer from interrupted sleep. Older individuals still need roughly the same number of sleep hours as they got when they were younger (it may deviate by 30 minutes to an hour over a lifetime), but the architecture of their sleep shifts. They do not get as much deep (delta) sleep, so they easily are awakened by noise, light, or even their own pain from a chronic medical condition. Sleep becomes more fragmented and inefficient, so the actual time spent sleeping is less than the time spent in bed.

Another influential aspect to aging that can affect sleep is circadian rhythm, the patterns of repeated activity associated with the environmental cycles of day and night. Our internal rhythms repeat roughly every 24 hours. A lot of people's sleep dilemmas can be attributed to an internal clock that has become out of sync or mismatched with the day-night cycle. Everyone's circadian pacemaker ticks at a different rate but, as you age, your pacemaker speeds up or slows down, thus altering how the body responds to that 24-hour cycle. Later on in life, our clocks speed up so the body does not match so well with the 24-hour day. It wants to go to bed early and get up super-early.

What is more important: the amount of minutes an individual gets or the quality of those minutes? If you wake up after seven to eight hours of sleep and still feel unrefreshed, your problem may not be about quantity, but quality. The quality of sleep is as vitally important to health and well-being as the quantity. Our sleep has a complex pattern, or architecture, which consists of five stages that run through various cycles during the night. During certain stages and times of the sleep cycles, we secrete hormones and other substances that help regulate our metabolism and support our general health. What happens in our brains during REM sleep is how we retain information, organize our memories, and prepare to learn something new or perform a special task. If our sleep patterns are altered, it may leave us feeling unrefreshed, tired, and sleepy, as well as put us at risk for a host of minor or even serious medical conditions.

Disturbed or Disordered?

Could a person have disordered sleep and not a sleep disorder? Wake up to this simple fact: you are not supposed to be sleepy, with your feet dragging and lids lagging during the day. If you literally are asleep before your head hits the pillow, it probably is not a good sign. Do not let the notion that "I have always been this way" fool you into thinking it is okay. You should awaken feeling relatively refreshed and remain alert throughout the day—every day. If you do not, it could be the result of one of two problems: a sleep disorder or simply disordered sleep. What is the difference? The distinction is important. Think of sleep disorders as formal syndromes with definitive criteria, which repeat time after time. They can be primary sleep disorders, which are not attributed to other conditions, or secondary sleep disorders, which arise due to an underlying physical or mental condition.

The criteria that define disorders are developed and agreed upon by national researchers and societies to help the medical field understand how to identify a particular set of circumstances. Once a disorder has been identified, the goal is to develop systematically a therapy to avert the symptoms associated with it, or cure the underlying situation. There are more than 85 recognized sleep disorders, with the most diagnosed being insomnia, apnea, narcolepsy, and restless leg syndrome. These and others may manifest themselves in various ways.

Disordered sleep refers to everything else that relates to sleep but does not qualify as a disorder. One's symptoms might not quite meet the disorder criteria based on severity or frequency, or there might be an external behavioral factor that is affecting sleep, such as a cat in the bed or too much heat in the room. Disordered sleep also can reflect the value we place on sleep, or the quality of sleep we get.

For the vast majority of people, disordered sleep is the biggest culprit. In fact, sleep problems often occur as the result of poor "sleep hygiene"—bad habits that do not support a good sleep experience. These entail a range of practices and environmental factors, many of which are under your control. They include things such as smoking; alcohol and caffeine intake; exercise; eating large amounts before bed; jet lag; and psychological stressors (deadlines, exams, marital conflict, job crises, etc.) that intrude on one's ability to fall or stay asleep. Designing and sticking with a good sleep hygiene program should alleviate these types of difficulties, or at least give you a disciplined way to handle them so that they affect your sleep minimally.

The most common type of disordered sleep I see in my practice is nonrefreshing. Patients will come in and say they have been waking up after enough sleep, but feels as if they have slept poorly. This can be caused by several things: poor diet, stress, environment, genetics. My job is to figure out which of these, if not a combination, is the culprit and take action. The most common treatments include behavioral and relaxation techniques, environmental tips, and suggestions for medications or supplements.

Sleep needs and patterns might be unique to each individual, but the typical thieves of restful slumber are not. Clinicians hear time and time again the same complaints and discover that the roots of the problems—of disordered sleep—typically fall under one of six categories: anxiety, stress, and nervousness; caffeine consumption; parenting; bed partners; hormonal fluctuations (culprits or either the X or Y chromosome); and traveling, especially business travel.

Of course, you might have issues with more than one of these culprits. For instance, you might be a working mother who uses caffeine to stay alert through the day, struggles to juggle work and home life, has a husband whose sleep habits do not jibe with your own, and experiences severe hormonal fluctuations through the month that impact your sleep-wake cycle. The surprising part is that most people, when asked what they would do if they thought they had a sleep problem, would not speak with a physician about it—and about two in 10 would just assume the problem will go away, so they would opt to do nothing. Maybe it will go away, but chances are it will not.

Critical Thinking

1. Why are humans getting less sleep these days?
2. What are the health implications of sleep deprivation?

MICHAEL J. BREUS is a clinical psychologist, dipolomate of the American Board of Sleep Medicine, and the author of *Good Night: The Sleep Doctor's 4 Week Program to Better Sleep and Better Health.*

From *USA Today Magazine,* January 2010, pp. 58–60. Copyright © 2010 by Society for the Advancement of Education, Inc. Reprinted by permission.

The *Surprising Reason* Why Heavy Isn't Healthy

It's not just because fat ups your risk of disease. How much you weigh can keep you from getting the same health care everyone else gets. Our *special report* looks at a growing problem in women's health.

GINNY GRAVES

It's shocking, but it's true: Being a woman who's more than 20 pounds overweight may actually hike your risk of getting poor medical treatment. In fact, weighing too much can have surprising—and devastating—health repercussions beyond the usual diabetes and heart-health concerns you've heard about for years. A startling new *Health* magazine investigation reveals that if you're an overweight woman you:

- may have a harder time getting health insurance or have to pay higher premiums;
- are at higher risk of being misdiagnosed or receiving inaccurate dosages of drugs;
- are less likely to find a fertility doctor who will help you get pregnant;
- are less likely to have cancer detected early and get effective treatment for it.

What's going on here? Fat discrimination is part of the problem. A recent Yale study suggested that weight bias can start when a woman is as little as 13 pounds over her highest healthy weight. "Our culture has enormous negativity toward overweight people, and doctors aren't immune," says Harvard Medical School professor Jerome Groopman, MD, author of *How Doctors Think.* "If doctors have negative feelings toward patients, they're more dismissive, they're less patient, and it can cloud their judgment, making them prone to diagnostic errors." With nearly 70 million American women who are considered overweight, the implications of this new information is disturbing, to say the least. Here, what you need to know to get the top-quality health care you deserve—no matter what you weigh.

How Weight Gets in the Way

When Jen Seelaus, from Danbury, Connecticut, went to her doc's office because she was wheezing, she expected to get her asthma medication tweaked. Instead, she was told she'd feel better if she'd just lose some weight. "I didn't go to be lectured about my weight. I was there because I couldn't breathe," says the 5-foot-3, 195-pound woman. "Asthma can be dangerous if it gets out of control, and the nurse practitioner totally ignored that because of my weight."

Seelaus's nurse made a classic diagnostic error, according to Dr. Groopman. "It's called attribution, because your thinking is colored by a stereotype and you attribute the entire clinical picture to that stereotype. Because obesity can cause so many health problems, it's very easy to blame a variety of complaints, from knee pain to breathing troubles, on a patient's weight. That's why doctors—and patients—need to constantly ask, 'What else could this be?'"

There aren't statistics on how many diagnostic errors are due to weight, but the data for the general population is disturbing enough. "Doctors make mistakes in diagnosing 10 to 15 percent of all patients, and in half of those cases it causes real harm," Dr. Groopman says. Based on anecdotal evidence—patients who've told her that their doctors are often too quick to blame symptoms on weight—Rebecca Puhl, PhD, director of Research and Weight Stigma Initiatives at the Rudd Center for Food Policy and Obesity at Yale University, suspects that being heavy could further increase the odds of being misdiagnosed.

Even if doctors are aware of the potential traps they can fall into when diagnosing an overweight patient, extra body fat can literally obscure some illnesses, including heart disease and different types of cancer. "It's more difficult to hear heart and lung sounds in heavy people," says Mary Margaret Huizinga, MD, MPH, director of the Johns Hopkins Digestive Weight Loss Center. "I use an electronic stethoscope, which works well, but I'm very aware of the issues that can crop up in overweight patients. Not all doctors have these stethoscopes—or are aware they need one."

Jeffrey C. King, MD, professor and director of maternal-and-fetal medicine at the University of Louisville School of Medicine, says that "the more tissue between the palpating hand and what you're trying to feel, the harder it is to detect a mass." That may be what happened to Karen Tang [not her real name], a 5-foot-8, 280-pound woman who went to the doctor for pelvic pain. Her doc palpated her uterus but didn't feel anything. "By the time I was referred to a gynecologist, I had a fibroid the size of a melon—so large it was putting pressure on my bladder," she recalls.

Even a routine pelvic exam can be tricky, especially if you've had children. "The vaginal walls become lax and collapse into the middle, obscuring the cervix," Dr. King says. Larger or modified speculums can help, but not all docs have them and they can make the exam more uncomfortable, says Lynda Wolf, MD, a reproductive endocrinologist at Reproductive Medicine Associates of Michigan.

That may explain the disturbing finding that obese women are less likely to get Pap smears than normal-weight women. But doctors may be partly to blame for the screening lapse, too. A University of Connecticut study of more than 1,300 physicians found that 17 percent were reluctant to do pelvic exams on obese women and that 83 percent were hesitant if the patient herself seemed reluctant.

Physical exams aren't the only things hampered by obesity. Large patients may not fit into diagnostic scanning machines—computed tomography (CT) and magnetic resonance imaging (MRI), for instance—and X-rays and ultrasounds may not be as effective, says Raul N. Uppot, MD, a radiologist in the Division of Abdominal Imaging and Intervention at Massachusetts General Hospital in Boston. "Ultrasound is the approach that's the most limited by body fat, because the beams can't penetrate the tissue if you have more than 8 centimeters of subcutaneous fat," he says.

This affects women, in particular, because ultrasound is used to diagnose uterine tumors and ovarian cysts and to evaluate the mother's and baby's health during pregnancy. Just last May, researchers at the University of Texas Southwestern Medical Center at Dallas reported a 20 percent decrease in the ability to detect problems in fetuses of obese women with ultrasound. In another study, obese women were 20 percent more likely to have false-positive results from mammograms—readings that can lead to unnecessary biopsies and anxiety.

Too much body fat can *obscure organs on scans,* giving doctors fuzzy results.

While CT scans are less affected by body fat, getting clear images in heavy patients typically requires a lot more radiation than with normal-weight patients, making it riskier, especially if numerous CT scans are required. But trying to diagnose a health problem without proper imaging is like driving blindfolded. Doctors are sometimes left with little to go on except symptoms and intuition, especially in the emergency room, where physicians make life-and-death decisions in minutes. "If we can't get the imaging because of a patient's weight, and we are concerned about a pulmonary embolism or appendicitis, for example, we have to go ahead and treat based on our clinical impression," says Archana Reddy, MD, a Chicago-area ER physician.

A Big, Fat Health Insurance Problem

Need to lose weight? That's not going to make your insurance company happy. If you're overweight or obese it probably costs them more. Even if you're in an employer's health insurance plan, you may all have to pay higher premiums if there are overweight people in the office filing more health claims.

But the real challenge is for those women who are trying to get private insurance—finding affordable health coverage can be difficult, if not impossible, if you're overweight. Rules vary by insurance company. But, in general, heavier women are likely to take a financial hit. For instance, a woman who is 5 feet 4 inches tall and has no other health problems will likely need a medical exam and pay higher premiums if she weighs more than around 180 or 190 pounds, says John Barrett of Health Insurance Brokers in Pasadena, California. Rates may range from 20 to 100 percent higher, depending on the carrier. And if that 5 foot 4 woman weighs more than around 220? She could be automatically declined coverage.

Women who try to lose weight don't get much help, either. "Weight counseling and early preventive treatment of obesity aren't covered by many plans," says John Wilder Baker, MD, president of the American Society for Metabolic and Bariatric Surgery. And insurance plans often won't cover bariatric surgery or other obesity treatments.

Being overweight can get in the way of effective cancer treatment, too, experts say. The problem: underdosing. "Oncologists usually base chemo on patients' ideal weight rather than their true weight, partly because chemo is so toxic and partly because drug trials typically include only average women, so we don't know the correct dose for bigger women," says Kellie Schneider, MD, a gynecologic oncologist at the University of Alabama at Birmingham. "But underdosing can mean the difference between life and death."

Doctors have long known that obese women are more likely to die of ovarian and breast cancers, but when Dr. Schneider and her colleagues recently gave a group of overweight ovarian cancer patients chemotherapy based on their *actual* weights, they found that the women were as likely to survive the illness as thinner patients. "Doctors aren't intentionally under-treating overweight women," Dr. Schneider says. "We're just working with limited information."

Why Heavy Patients Can't Find Help

There are no studies on how often doctors refuse to treat patients because of their weight. But Sondra Solovay, an Oakland, California, attorney and author of *Tipping the Scales of*

Justice: Fighting Weight-Based Discrimination, says she hears enough anecdotes to believe it's commonplace.

Because of recent studies about various complications, A.J. Yates Jr., MD, associate professor in the Department of Orthopaedic Surgery at the University of Pittsburgh Medical Center, says there are legitimate concerns about operating on patients with a very high body mass index (BMI). But Dr. Yates also notes that some surgeons are reluctant to offer surgery to very overweight patients because the operations are more difficult and time-consuming.

And because data on surgical-complication rates is often calculated without accounting for the higher risk of an obese patient, even a few patients with complications can make the surgeon or hospital look bad to insurance companies. "If hospitals feel they're not looking good they could put subtle pressure on surgeons to avoid risky patients," Dr. Yates says. His concern is that overweight people could be increasingly discriminated against because of this.

Suzy Smith, a 5-foot-3, 400-pound woman from Colonial Beach, Virginia, believes she was one of those people. When her doctor found a large tumor on her kidney, she struggled to find a surgeon who would treat her. Her urologist said that the hospital where he practiced didn't have a table sturdy enough to hold her, and he referred her to a surgeon several hours away. "As soon as that doctor walked in the room, I could tell something was wrong by the look on his face," she says. "He told me he wouldn't operate. He wouldn't risk it," she says. Instead, he offered her cryoablation—a technique that freezes and removes tissue but is less effective than surgery for large tumors.

"I was so shocked," Smith says. "He was basically telling me he wouldn't do the thing that was the most likely to save my life." Finally, in early-December 2008, a doctor removed the tumor. The surgery, after all the preceding drama, was anticlimactic. "It went fantastically well," Smith says. "My doctors were really pleased." But the overall experience, she says, was degrading and disheartening. "Here I was trying to deal with a diagnosis of cancer, worrying that the cancer might spread with every day that went by, and the medical field was closing doors on me left and right."

Infertile couples who are told they can't have in vitro fertilization (IVF) because of the woman's weight also feel doors shutting. Most fertility clinics have stringent rules. "I'd say 95 percent won't do IVF on a woman with a BMI higher than 39 [5-foot-4, weighing 228 pounds, for example], and they usually require an electrocardiogram (EKG) and blood tests if it's higher than 34, because being overweight reduces your chance of getting pregnant and having a healthy pregnancy," says Laurence Jacobs, MD, of Fertility Centers of Illinois. In most cases, he can't accept a patient with a BMI of 40, even if she has no other health issues, because IVF typically takes place in an outpatient setting that's not set up for the higher anesthesia risks associated with obese patients. "No anesthesiologist is going to take that risk for someone who's not willing to make the effort to lose weight," Dr. Jacobs says.

Even more worrisome, a study from Duke University found that obese patients were less likely to receive procedures like cardiac catheterization that can help diagnose and treat heart

How to Get the Care You Deserve

Here, ways women can speak out for better care and more respectful treatment—and get the help they need to reach a healthier weight:

- **Find a physician who isn't fatphobic.** Ask for referrals from heavier friends. Doctors who have struggled with their own weight may be more understanding.
- **Take a friend with you.** "A clinician is much less likely to treat someone badly when there's a witness," says Pat Lyons, RN, co-developer of *A Big Woman's Passport to Best Health,* a guide to overcoming barriers to health care.
- **Be your own advocate.** Have your doc run your numbers so you have all of your measures of health, from body mass index (BMI) to cholesterol and blood sugar. Ask for an assessment of your health based on the big picture.
- **Ask for tools.** Tell your doctor you're interested in sustainable health habits, like walking and eating right. Request a reasonable healthy weight and BMI range so you have goal.
- **Dig deeper.** If you've tried and tried and still can't lose weight, insist that your doc give you more help. For some people there's a medical reason for weight gain that goes beyond lifestyle choices, including medications or conditions that might cause weight gain. "We're trying to educate doctors so they provide obese women with more sensitive and in-depth care," says Keith Bachman, MD, a weight-management expert with Kaiser Permanente's Care Management Institute. The goal: to help doctors see the whole patient and look for all the possible causes of weight gain.
- **Stick to your symptoms.** During your visit say, "Here are the symptoms I'm concerned about. I know some health problems can be caused by weight, but I'd like you to focus on the symptoms I'm here to see you about."
- **Get the doctor you deserve.** If you feel your doctor isn't giving you the kind of care you deserve, find a new one. "When I asked physicians what they would do if they perceived a negative attitude from their doctor, each one said he or she would find another doctor," says Harvard's Jerome Groopman, MD. It's your right to do the same.

disease, perhaps because doctors are concerned about potential complications, says lead author William Yancy Jr., MD, an associate professor at Duke and a staff physician at the VA Medical Center in Durham, North Carolina. Because of the high risk of heart disease in obese patients, the benefits of catheterization may outweigh the risks, he says. "But if the tests aren't performed, heavy patients may not receive appropriate therapy."

Even organ transplants may be withheld because of weight. Patients with BMIs higher than 35—if you're, say, 5 feet

4 inches tall and weigh 205 pounds—are typically less likely to be given a kidney or liver transplant because of the increased risk of postsurgery complications, including infections, blood clots, and pneumonia.

"It's a very difficult issue," says Shawn Pelletier, MD, surgical director of liver transplants at the University of Michigan Health System in Ann Arbor. "We have an obligation to use donor organs in a responsible way. But this is lifesaving surgery, and we don't want to turn people away. Obese kidney-transplant patients may not survive as long as thinner patients, but they live an average of three times longer than if they didn't get the transplant. That's a big benefit, even if there are risks."

Many experts believe the issue goes beyond the strictly medical and into the arena of ethics. "Doctors need to ask themselves, 'Is this obese person less deserving of medical care than the same person would be after weight-loss surgery?'" says Barbara Thompson, vice-chair of the Obesity Action Coalition, a nonprofit advocacy group. "How do we determine whether a person's weight somehow justifies withholding needed medical care or whether bias by providers is the reason treatment is denied?" Yale's Rebecca Puhl asks. "It's an extremely important question with significant implications."

Fat People Get No Respect

When Celina Reeder, a 5-foot-5, 185-pound woman with a torn ligament in her right knee, was told by her surgeon she needed to stop eating so much fast food before he would schedule surgery, the Woodacre, California, woman was astounded. "I left his office feeling ashamed," she recalls. "And I don't even eat fast food! The more I thought about it, the madder I got. So I switched surgeons. Anybody who thinks doctors treat heavy women the same as thin women has obviously never had a weight problem. I really felt like my doctor didn't respect me."

She may have been right. University of Pennsylvania researchers found that more than 50 percent of primary care physicians viewed obese patients as awkward, unattractive, and noncompliant; one third said they were weak-willed, sloppy, and lazy. In addition, researchers at Rice University and the University of Texas School of Public Health in Houston found that as patient BMI increased doctors reported liking their jobs less and having less patience and desire to help the patient.

Whether they know it or not, doctors' attitudes may actually encourage unhealthy behavior. Feeling dissed about their weight can make some women turn to food for comfort. "Stigma is a form of stress, and many obese women cope by eating or refusing to diet," Puhl says. "So weight bias could actually fuel obesity."

Studies have also found that overweight women are more likely to delay doctors' appointments and preventive care, including screenings for cancer, because they don't want to face criticism. "It can be frustrating to treat obese patients,"

admits Lee Green, MD, MPH, a professor of family medicine at the University of Michigan in Ann Arbor. "I spend most of my time treating the consequences of unhealthy lifestyles instead of actual illnesses. People come in complaining of foot or knee pain, and I'm thinking, *Do you not see that you're in pain because you're 60 pounds overweight?* I don't say that, of course. I try to encourage them to lose weight."

Seeing heavy patients was *a waste of time*, doctors admitted in one survey.

Dr. Green seems to be in the minority when it comes to focusing on weight-loss solutions. One study found that just 11 percent of overweight patients received weight-loss counseling when they visited a family-practice doctor.

A Healthy-Weight Wakeup Call

Without a doubt, the medical community needs to take a hard look at the secret biases that may be coloring how they care for overweight women. But some progress is being made. The National Institutes of Health has been encouraging researchers to start identifying and fixing the barriers heavy people face when trying to get health care, says Susan Yanovski, MD, co-director of the Office of Obesity Research at the National Institute of Diabetes and Digestive and Kidney Diseases. And some hospitals are adding larger surgical instruments, wheelchairs, and other equipment.

There's an even bigger problem, though: when heavy women are ignored, the obesity epidemic is ignored, too—and that has to stop, experts say. "Being mistreated or dismissed by your doctor because of your weight is unacceptable. But what's just as important is that doctors are missing an opportunity to help their patients lose weight and improve their health," says Dr. Huizinga of Johns Hopkins. "Doctors and patients need to be able to speak openly about weight-related issues, whether it's the diseases caused by excess weight or the reasons why a patient overeats. That level of conversation requires a certain degree of comfort, and the basis for that is mutual respect, plain and simple," she says. "That's how we can help *all* women get healthier."

Critical Thinking

1. Why are overweight women less likely to receive quality health care?

2. How can being overweight affect your health insurance?

3. How can a doctor's attitude encourage unhealthy behavior?

UNIT 10
Contemporary Health Hazards

Unit Selections

Learning Outcomes

After reading this unit, you should be able to:

- Describe traumatic brain injury (TBI) and posttraumatic stress disorder (PTSD) and explain why these conditions can be difficult to diagnose.

- Explain the risks associated with the "choking game."

- Explain the health impact of chemicals in plastic water bottles.

- Explain why manufacturers continue to use bisphenol A (BPA) despite the potential health concerns.

- Contrast chronic and acute AIDS.

- Discuss reasons why some people continue to engage in high-risk behaviors that increase their susceptibility to contracting HIV.

- Explain the risks associated with contracting MRSA.

- Discuss who is most likely to contract MRSA.

- Describe the diseases that are most likely to have an environmental link.

- Discuss the health risks that typically occur after an earthquake.

- Describe the health challenges Haitians faced after the 2010 earthquake.

- Discuss the risks related to radiation exposure.

Student Website

www.mhhe.com/cls

Internet References

Centers for Disease Control: Flu
www.cdc.gov/flu
Environmental Protection Agency
www.epa.gov

Food and Drug Administration
www.fda.gov
www.epa.gov
World Health Organization
www.who.org

This unit examines a variety of health hazards that Americans face on a daily basis. Topics ranging from environmental health issues to newly emerging or, rather, reemerging infectious illnesses are included.

During the 1970s and 1980s, Americans became deeply concerned about environmental changes that affect the air, water, and food we take in. While some improvements have been observed in these areas, much remains to be done, as new areas of concern continue to emerge.

Global warming is responsible for climatic changes, including an increase in the number of earthquakes, hurricanes, and other natural disasters. In "Post-Earthquake Public Health in Haiti," author Stan Deresinski addresses the serious health concerns that remain in that poor country following a deadly earthquake in early 2010. Denise Grady addresses radiation concerns following another natural disaster, the earthquake and tsunami that occurred in Japan in the spring of 2011.

Another area of concern has to do with the potential health dangers of bisphenol A, an issue addressed by Valerie Jablow in "Chemical in Plastic Bottles Fuels Science, Concern—and Litigation."

We face newly recognized diseases such as Methicillin-Resistant *Staphlococcus aureus*, (MRSA) Avian Flu, Severe Acute Respiratory Syndrome (SARS), AIDS, West Nile virus, and mad cow disease. Some diseases may have their causes rooted in environmental factors. Environmental author Zach Patton discusses the changes in the way AIDS is treated and perceived in "HIV Apathy." In "MRSA: Hospitals Step Up Fight," author Julius A. Karash addresses the growing health problem related to this drug-resistant bacterial infection. It is a particular

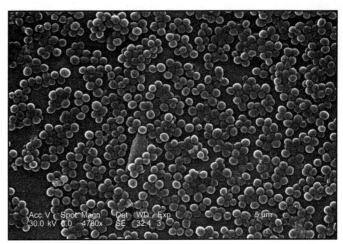

© CDC/Janice Carr

concern among the institutionalized elderly and in any place where many people are in close contact with each other.

While this unit focuses on exogenous factors that influence our state of health, it is important to remember that health is a dynamic state representing the degree of harmony or balance that exists between endogenous and exogenous factors. This concept of balance applies to the environment as well. Due to the intimate relationship that exists between people, animals, and their environment, it is impossible to promote the concept of wellness without also safeguarding the quality of our environment, both the physical and the social.

The Warrior's Brain

One family's terrifying medical mystery could represent the military's next big crisis.

ANDREW BAST

Brooke Brown, the wife of Marine Lance Cpl. David Brown, explains how her life changed after her young husband returned home from Iraq with mild Traumatic Brain Injury and PTSD.

The worst was the day Brooke Brown came home to find her husband with a shotgun in his mouth. But there had been plenty of bad days before that: after he returned from a deployment in Iraq, Lance Cpl. David Brown would start shaking in crowded places. Sitting down for a family meal had become nearly impossible: in restaurants he'd frantically search for the quickest exit route. He couldn't concentrate; he couldn't do his job. The Marine Corps placed him on leave prior to discharging him. Brooke quit her job to care for him and the children. The bills piled up.

It sounds like another troubling story of a war vet struggling with PTSD. But Brown's case is more complicated. In addition to the anxiety, he suffered a succession of mild seizures until a devastating grand mal episode sent him to the hospital covered in his own blood, vomit, and excrement. There were also vision problems and excruciating headaches that had plagued him since he'd been knocked to the ground by a series of mortar blasts in Fallujah four years earlier.

Brown, now 23, didn't have any visible injuries, but clearly the man who left for Iraq was not the same man who returned. "Our middle son clings to David; he knows something is wrong," Brooke, 22, explained late this summer. "Our 4-year-old doesn't know what caused it, but he knows Daddy's sick and he needs help."

But what kind of help does Corporal Brown need? His case perplexed civilian doctors and the Department of Veterans Affairs. The headaches and seizures suggest that he is suffering from the aftereffects of an undiagnosed concussion—or, in the current jargon, mild traumatic brain injury (TBI). But some of his symptoms seem consistent with a psychological condition, posttraumatic stress disorder (PTSD). Or could it be both—and if so, are they reinforcing one another in some kind of vicious cycle? The person who knows David better than anyone, his wife, thinks it was hardly a coincidence that one of his worst seizures came on the day last year that his best friend was deployed with the Second Battalion, Eighth Marines, as part of President Obama's surge into Afghanistan.

David Brown's symptoms have placed him at the vanguard of military medicine, where doctors, officials, and politicians are puzzling out the connection between head injuries and PTSD, and the role each plays in both physical and psychological post-combat illness.

Invisible Wounds

The military reports that 144,453 service members have suffered battlefield concussions in the last decade; a study out of Fort Carson argues that that number misses at least 40 percent of cases. By definition, a concussion is a shaking of the brain that results from a blow to the head. Typical symptoms include headache, memory loss, and general confusion. For decades, head injuries were a challenge mainly for civilian doctors, who studied the results of auto accidents and football injuries. The best treatment, it was generally thought, was rest and time. And in the great majority of these civilian cases, the brain heals by itself in as little as a week.

Concussions sustained on the battlefield are another matter, and a vexing one. According to the Department of Veterans Affairs, symptoms such as vision, memory, and speech problems, dizziness, depression, and anxiety last far longer in men and women returning from combat. Why? Doctors suspect that the high-stress combat environment stifles the kind of recovery that would normally occur. More often than not, those unlucky enough to suffer a concussion in Afghanistan, or especially in Iraq, do so in stifling heat, "which can make the effects of a concussion worse," says David Hovda, director of the UCLA Brain Injury Research Center. Then there's the question of reinjury before full recovery. If an injured fighter reports symptoms that match the concussion watch list, he or she is pulled from action for 24 hours. (There's currently no test for a concussion besides self-diagnosis, though the military is actively pursuing biomarker tests that could be done on site.) But in a macho military culture, admitting unseen symptoms that can take you out of the action doesn't happen as often as it should. "If you ain't bleeding, you ain't hurt," says Brooke of the military culture around head injuries.

Blood or not, evidence is mounting that battlefield concussions from these two long-running wars could result in decades of serious and expensive health-care issues for a significant number of veterans. After all, TBI is a relatively new problem of modern warfare. Thanks to technological advances, warriors are surviving what once would have been fatal blasts—but the long-term consequences of the impact are still unknown. Two years ago, the RAND Corporation published a comprehensive study, "The Invisible Wounds of War," which highlighted brain injuries as a massive, and little-understood, mental-health issue for returning combat veterans. This summer the nonprofit journalism site ProPublica chronicled challenges in diagnosis of head trauma and breakdowns in care within the military medical system. Around the same time, the Senate Armed Services Committee called the brass from each of the military branches and the Department of Veterans Affairs to testify on the topic, and at the hearing senators expressed concern that head trauma may be a factor in service-member suicide.

The military's concerns have arisen during something of a boom in concussion research in civilian institutions, and new research in sustained head trauma in athletes shows that repeated concussions can lead to a condition called chronic traumatic encephalopathy. This disorder, which can present 10 to 15 years after the initial trauma, is linked to depression and suicidal thoughts, as well as Parkinson's, dementia, and even a devastating neurological condition resembling Lou Gehrig's disease. Another study found that those who abused drugs and alcohol after a TBI had drastically increased rates of suicide attempts.

Suicide is a serious threat to the military: an August 2010 report by the Department of Defense showed that the military suicide rate comes to one death every 36 hours. In the past, suicide has been associated with PTSD—an issue armed forces across the world have been struggling with for years. "Nostalgia" afflicted Napoleon's troops fighting his endless campaigns far from home. "Traumatic neurosis" and "shell shock" overcame British troops in the trenches of World War I. Col. John Bradley, head of psychiatry at Walter Reed Army Medical Center, describes today's PTSD as the inability to dial back on the instincts necessary for survival in combat even long after one is out of danger. "If you go back to your family and you still feel like you're in mortal danger, that creates a problem," says Bradley. A common estimate inside the military is that 20 percent of veterans in combat experience symptoms of posttraumatic stress. Some 2.1 million service members have been deployed to Iraq and Afghanistan—implying more than 400,000 potential cases.

Connecting the Dots

But in Iraq and Afghanistan, the symptoms of PTSD are often complicated by TBI—a condition seen as a consequence of the fact that, thanks to better battlefield technology and medical care, more soldiers are surviving blasts that proved deadly in previous wars. Figuring out what's caused by PTSD and what's the result of a head injury isn't easy, especially since the symptoms of TBI overlap with those of PTSD. "You may have been injured, may have lost a buddy during an attack," says Bradley. "Traumatic brain injury has both a physical and psychological component, and so does PTSD." After a concussion, one is almost certain to have headaches, but headaches are also common among people with a mental-health disorder. Concussions cause trouble sleeping—and so can PTSD. Difficulty concentrating is common to both. "It's very difficult to determine if it's a psychological problem or the results of an organic brain injury," says Terry Schell, a behavioral scientist at RAND.

The Road Home

Scientists are just starting to understand if and how the two are connected. It's been shown in animal models that a head trauma can make one more susceptible to PTSD. "Minor traumatic brain injury does not necessarily cause PTSD, but it puts the brain in a biochemical and metabolic state that enhances the chances of acquiring posttraumatic stress disorder," says UCLA's Hovda, who is part of a civilian task force of doctors and scientists commissioned by the military to assess how PTSD and TBI affect troops. They'll meet in December to discuss whether troops suffering from both should receive special medical treatment. Hovda also played a key role in the development of the National Intrepid Center of Excellence, a military medical facility in Bethesda, Md., devoted to the care of returning vets who suffer from PTSD and/or head trauma. "When they get to Bethesda, or get home, a lot of times individuals will be suffering from symptoms related to these multiple concussions," he says. "They don't understand that it's related to a brain injury, and they become very depressed and confused."

Murray Stein, a neurologist at the University of California, San Diego, is leading a consortium of doctors and specialists through several clinical trials investigating the long-term effects of concussions mixed with high-stress situations. Stein suspects there's more to the long-term effects of battlefield brain injuries than we now understand. "Right now it's extremely controversial," he says. "It's simply too simplistic to suggest [TBI] and emotional symptoms can't be linked."

There's not a lot research as of yet. Early on in the Iraq War, Col. Charles Hoge, then the director of mental-health research at Walter Reed Army Medical Center, surveyed some 2,700 soldiers about battlefield concussions and PTSD, as well as the extent of their injuries and the state of their current mental and physical health (relying on self-reported measures like days of work missed). In 2008, *The New England Journal of Medicine* published Hoge's findings: battlefield concussions existed, perhaps in significant numbers, but "cognitive problems, rage, sleep disturbance, fatigue, headaches, and other symptoms" that had become commonplace among service members back home resulted almost entirely from PTSD. Hoge argued that attributing postcombat symptoms to the effect of concussions, which "usually resolve rapidly," could lead to a large number of military personnel receiving treatment for the wrong problem—treatment that could actually make things worse for the patient and put undue strain on the health-care system.

In an interview with NEWSWEEK, Hoge agreed that there was a connection between the two conditions. "PTSD and battlefield concussions are interrelated, and they have to be treated as such," he said. But he's also standing by his findings that one should not be confused for the other. In his new book, Once a Warrior, Always a Warrior, published earlier this year as a mental-health handbook for veterans and their families, Hoge reiterates that "concussions/TBIs have also become entangled and confused with PTSD." Battlefield concussions, he writes, are best diagnosed at the time of injury, and the more time that elapses, the more difficult it becomes to link symptoms to the incident.

That much is true: with shoddy records of brain injuries from the early parts of the wars in Iraq and Afghanistan, many veterans who could be afflicted by the long-term effects of battlefield concussions will have little—if any—documentation to rely on in their claims for disability benefits. And as evidenced by Lance Cpl. David Brown, in some cases those men and women could require a significant amount of ongoing care.

The Path Ahead

There's another, unsettling reality, of course: that PTSD and TBI are far from the only culprits for Brown's mystery symptoms. "Headaches are almost useless as a diagnostic," says Barry Willer, professor of psychology at the University of Buffalo and an expert on concussions. He notes that headaches present for a large number of illnesses. And depression, anxiety, and trouble sleeping? Those are often the result of living with an unexplainable illness. In reality, the troops are coming home with myriad medical issues, some new, like TBI; some,

like PTSD, as old as war itself; and some a hybrid of the two. The question is whether we have the tools and treatments to figure out which is which.

Brown finally found some respite thanks to Tim Maxwell, a fellow Marine, who was pierced in the skull with shrapnel in Iraq and later lost his leg to mortar fire. Maxwell has established a quiet network of wounded warriors and maintains a Web site on the topic, SemperMax. Earlier this year, he got wind of Brown's struggle and helped get him back into the Marines and into the TBI ward at the National Naval Medical Center in Bethesda. Today, Brown's back at Camp Lejeune, readmitted to the Marines and working to get medically retired. "I spend most of my time over at the wounded-warrior tent doing rehab," he says. He's taking Topamax, a drug usually prescribed to epileptics to stave off seizures, and it seems to be effective, despite the side effects. "He's lost his speech for 30 minutes a couple of times," Brooke says, but he hasn't had any more grand mal seizures. His wife is fighting for him at every turn. "I'm going to stand by my man," she said in August, and then stiffened her spine. "He stood for me over in Iraq. The least I can do is stand by him now."

Critical Thinking

1. What are the symptoms of traumatic brain injury (TBI) and posttraumatic stress disorder (PTSD)? Why is difficult to differentiate between these two conditions?

Discovering Teenagers' Risky "Game" Too Late

PAULINE W. CHEN, MD

The patient was tall, with legs that extended to the very end of the operating table, a chest barely wider than his 16-year-old hips and a chin covered with pimples and peach fuzz.

He looked like any number of boys I knew in high school, I reflected. And then the other transplant surgeons and I began the operation to remove the dead boy's liver, kidneys, pancreas, lungs and heart.

We knew the organs would be perfect. He had been a healthy teenager, and the cause of death was not a terrible, mutilating car or motorcycle crash.

The boy had hanged himself. He had been discovered early, though not early enough to have survived.

While I had operated on more than a few suicide victims, I had never come across someone so young who had chosen to die in this way. I asked one of the nurses who had spent time with the family about the circumstances. Was he depressed? Had anyone ever suspected? Who found him?

"He was playing the choking game," she said quietly.

I stopped what I was doing and, not believing I had heard correctly, turned to look straight at her.

"You know that game where kids try to get high," she explained. "They strangle themselves until just before they lose consciousness." She put her hand on the boy's arm and continued: "Problem was that this poor kid couldn't wiggle out of the noose he had made for himself. His parents found him hanging by his belt on his bedroom doorknob."

That image comes rushing back whenever I meet another victim or read about the grim mortality statistics associated with this "game." But one thing has haunted me even more in the years since that night. As a doctor who counts adolescents among her patients, I knew nothing about the choking game before I cared for a child who had died playing it.

Some try strangulation in the hopes of attaining a legal high.

Until recently, there has been little attention among health care professionals to this particular form of youthful thrill-seeking. What has been known, however, is that those ages 7 to 21 participate in such activities alone or in groups, holding their breath, strangling one another or dangling in a noose in the hopes of attaining a legal high.

Two years ago the Centers for Disease Control and Prevention reported 82 deaths attributable to the choking game and related activities. This year the C.D.C. released the results of the first statewide survey and found that 1 in 3 eighth graders in Oregon had heard of the game, while more than 1 in 20 had participated.

The popularity of the choking game may be due in part to the misguided belief that it is safe. In one recent study, almost half of the youths surveyed believed there was no risk associated with the game. And unlike other risk-taking behaviors like alcohol or drug abuse, where doctors and parents can counsel teenagers on the dangers involved, no one is countering this gross misperception regarding the safety of near strangulation.

Why? Because like me that night in the operating room, many of my colleagues have no clue that such a game even exists.

This month in the journal *Pediatrics,* researchers from the Rainbow Babies and Children's Hospital in Cleveland reported that almost a third of physicians surveyed were unaware of the choking game. These physicians could not describe any of the 11 warning signs, which include bloodshot eyes and frequent and often severe headaches. And they failed to identify any of the 10 alternative names for the choking game, startlingly benign monikers like "Rush," "Space Monkey," "Purple Dragon" and "Funky Chicken."

"Doctors have a unique opportunity to see and prevent this," the senior author of the study, Dr. Nancy E. Bass, an associate professor of pediatrics and neurology at Case Western Reserve University, said in an interview. "But how are they going to educate parents and patients if they don't know about it?"

In situations where a patient may be contemplating or already participating in choking activities, frank discussions about the warning signs can be particularly powerful. "The sad thing about these cases," Dr. Bass observed, "is that every parent says, 'If we had known what to look for, we probably could have prevented this.'" One set of parents told Dr. Bass that they had noticed knotted scarves and ties on a closet rod in their son's room weeks before his death.

"They had the telltale signs," Dr. Bass said, "but they never knew what to look for."

Broaching the topic can be difficult for parents and doctors alike. Some parents worry that talking about such activities will paradoxically encourage adolescents to participate. "But that's kind of a naïve thought," Dr. Bass countered. "Children can go to the Internet and YouTube to learn about the choking game." In another study published last year, for example, Canadian researchers found 65 videos of the choking game on YouTube over an 11-day period. The videos showed various techniques of strangulation and were viewed almost 175,000 times. But, added Dr. Bass, "these videos don't say that kids can die from doing this."

Few doctors discuss these types of activities with their adolescent patients. Only two doctors in Dr. Bass's study reported ever having tackled the topic because of a lack of time. "Talking about difficult topics is really hard to do," Dr. Bass noted, "when you just have 15 minutes to follow up."

But it is even harder when neither doctor nor patient has any idea of what the activity is or of its lethal consequences.

Based on the results of their study, Dr. Bass and her co-investigators have started programs that educate doctors, particularly those in training, about the warning signs and dangers of strangulation activities. "The choking game may not be as prominent as some of the other topics we cover when we talk with patients," Dr. Bass said, "but it results in death.

"If we don't talk to doctors about this issue, they won't know about the choking game until one of their patients dies."

Critical Thinking

1. Describe the risks associated with the "choking game."
2. What are some of the warning signs of strangulation activities, and what can be done to prevent adolescents from participating in them?

Chemical in Plastic Bottles Fuels Science, Concern—and Litigation

Valerie Jablow

A common chemical denominator in the stuff of modern life—helmets, CDs, baby bottles, sunglasses, cell phones, can coatings, and dental sealants—is the focus of increasing scientific and legislative scrutiny, as well as lawsuits. More than 20 cases have been filed, mostly since April, against manufacturers and sellers of baby and water bottles containing bisphenol A (BPA).

BPA, studied in the 1930s as an estrogen mimic, came into commercial use in the 1950s after scientists discovered that it could make clear, hard, yet not easily breakable plastic compounds called polycarbonates. These plastics, along with epoxy resin can linings containing BPA, have become ubiquitous in food uses, where they are prized for their durability. Today, more than 6 billion pounds of BPA is produced each year; the United States alone accounts for more than a third of worldwide production.

But BPA's association with food has attracted controversy. Although the FDA had maintained that the chemical did not leach out of containers made with it, in 1999 scientists began using more sensitive testing techniques, allowing them to measure very low levels of BPA.

Studies since then have measured the chemical in a variety of human tissues, including placenta, cord blood, fetal blood, and urine. The Centers for Disease Control and Prevention (CDC) found that nearly 93 percent of people tested had measurable levels of BPA in their urine, with children having the highest levels.

The Centers for Disease Control and Prevention found that nearly 93 percent of people tested had measurable levels of BPA in their urine, with children having the highest levels.

Scientists believe that most human exposure comes from diet, through the leaching of BPA from can linings and polycarbonate water bottles and baby bottles. Researchers have shown that leaching occurs at a higher rate when the bottles are heated, such as for warming milk or formula or for hot-water washing or sterilizing of baby bottles.

All of which may be cause for concern—depending on who you talk to.

In testimony before the House Subcommittee on Commerce, Trade, and Consumer Protection on June 10, Marian Stanley, senior director of the American Chemistry Council, a trade group for the plastics industry, concluded a presentation of BPA studies by noting that "no restriction on [BPA's] uses in current applications is warranted at this time." Stanley said studies showing low-dose effects of BPA in animals were "unvalidated."

But in April, a draft report on BPA by the National Toxicology Program (NTP) noted that such low doses produce in fetal and young animals changes in "behavior and the brain, prostate gland, mammary gland, and the age at which females attain puberty." Because those low doses are similar to human exposure levels, the report raised "some concern for neural and behavioral effects in fetuses, infants, and children at current human exposures" and "some concern" about how BPA exposure in young children might affect their prostate and mammary glands and the onset of puberty in females.

The NTP—a joint program of agencies within the FDA, CDC, and National Institutes of Health—concluded that "the possibility that bisphenol A may alter human development cannot be dismissed."

The NTP draft came in the wake of more than 150 low-dose BPA studies in animals showing harmful effects ranging from cancer to genital malformations to early puberty. Other studies found high levels of the chemical in human amniotic fluid and showed that fetuses cannot metabolize BPA.

After the NTP issued the draft report, Sen. Charles Schumer (D-N.Y.) proposed legislation banning BPA in children's products, and Reps. John Dingell (D-Mich.) and Bart Stupak (D-Mich.) asked four infant formula makers to stop using the chemical in their packaging. In June, Rep. Edward Markey (D-Mass.) proposed legislation to prohibit the use of BPA in all food and beverage containers.

Several polycarbonate bottle manufacturers, including Playtex and Nalgene, have said they will use alternatives to BPA, and Wal-Mart and Toys "R" Us are in the process of pulling BPA-containing items for babies from store shelves. The California senate in May passed a bill to ban BPA from food or beverage containers for children younger than three.

The FDA, which regulates containers that come into contact with food, is not yet raising alarm bells. Norris Alderson, an associate commissioner for science at the agency, testified at the June congressional hearing that the FDA is reviewing the use of BPA in food containers, but that currently it is satisfied that "exposure levels to BPA from these materials . . . are below those that may cause health effects."

The FDA has been criticized for relying on two studies, both funded by the chemical industry, to arrive at this conclusion. Dingell and Stupak are investigating that connection.

Class Actions

Lawsuits against the makers of polycarbonate baby bottles and covered "sippy" cups for toddlers (including Gerber, Avent, and Playtex) have been filed in several states, including Arkansas, California, Connecticut, Illinois, Kansas, Missouri, and Washington. Most have been filed in federal court and claim that the sale of products containing BPA violates various state consumer protection acts. None of the claims allege personal injury.

Other claims include breach of express and implied warranties, defective design, failure to warn, false and misleading advertising, fraudulent concealment, intentional and negligent misrepresentation, unfair and deceptive business practices, and unjust enrichment. The cases seek reimbursement to consumers who bought the products, in addition to punitive and actual damages.

Although most of the BPA lawsuits emerged earlier this year, the first—a California class action against makers and retailers of plastic baby bottles and cups—was filed in 2007. (*Ganjei v. Ralphs,* No. 367732 (Cal., Los Angeles Co. Super. filed Mar. 12, 2007).) The lead plaintiffs are five children with varying disorders—including congenital genital injury, attention deficit hyperactivity disorder, premature puberty, and Down syndrome—who used polycarbonate baby bottles and cups. Although the complaint does not say that BPA caused the children's disabilities, it alleges that most of their conditions are associated with exposure to BPA.

Stephen Murakami, a Jericho, New York, lawyer who is handling the class action, said proving specific causation is not yet possible. But, he noted, "the primary suspect group are infants and children, who are most susceptible to the dose of estrogen-like chemical [BPA] during critical times during their development. It changes them permanently. They're not equipped to handle that level of estrogen that affects their brain and sexual development."

The first class action concerning the use of BPA in water bottles was filed in April, also in California. The lead plaintiff, a mother of two daughters who also used the bottles, claims that the company violated the California Business and Professions Code by "omitting, suppressing, and withholding material information regarding the bottles' BPA-related risks," according to the complaint. (*Felix-Lozano v. Nalge Nunc Intl. Corp.,* No. 08-cv-854 (E.D. Cal. filed Apr. 22, 2008).)

The defendant, Nalge Nunc International, notes on its website that it believes that its water bottles containing BPA "are safe for their intended use." Meanwhile, the company is phasing out the use of the chemical in its bottles because of consumer requests for alternative materials, it says.

In May, a group of plaintiff attorneys asked the district court in the Northern District of Illinois to consolidate 13 similar class actions filed in seven federal districts. One of the lawyers, Scott Poynter of Little Rock, Arkansas, noted that the classes would be hard to certify if they included personal injury claims.

Cause and Effect

Causation—and BPA's effects in humans—is a point of frequent debate. In 1987, the EPA said a BPA exposure level of 50 micrograms per kilogram per day (micrograms/kg/day) was safe in humans, based on animal experiments then available showing that 1,000 times that amount in rodents caused weight loss.

Today, the BPA level known to cause birth defects in pregnant mice is 2.4 micrograms/kg/day. But the level in humans that is harmful remains uncertain and contentious, in large part because few human studies have been conducted.

And some studies have reached different conclusions about human and animal harm from BPA. Why the disparity? A 2005 review of many studies found that one factor may be the researchers' funding source. In 94 of 104 published studies on BPA funded by the government, researchers found that doses of less than 50 milligrams/kg/day had significant effects. But none of 11 industry-funded studies found significant effects at those doses.

Almost everyone involved in the issue agrees that further study of BPA in humans is needed. Meanwhile, the chemical's ubiquity will likely continue to cause powerful clashes. For instance, attempts to pass or enact legislation banning BPA in Maryland, Minnesota, and San Francisco have failed. The plastics industry even sued San Francisco when it attempted to enact its ban.

Some BPA critics say the industry's reach affects official government statements on the chemical as well. In 2007, the Center for the Evaluation of Risks to Human Reproduction, part of NTP, assembled a nonexpert panel to look at 500 BPA studies. But the company hired to compile the data was also doing work for Dow Chemical, a BPA maker.

Although the company was fired from the project, the panel concluded that most people were safe because exposure levels were below those set by the government. (It did note some concern for BPA in young children and fetuses.)

Then, in June, the NTP draft report on BPA underwent peer review by the program's Board of Scientific Counselors, made up of 19 researchers from academia, pharmaceutical companies, and biological research firms. One board member works for Dow Chemical, and all are appointed by the secretary of the Department of Health and Human Services.

The board voted to lower the concern expressed in the NTP draft—from "some concern" to "minimal concern"—for BPA's effects on young children's mammary glands and puberty onset in females. The NTP's final report is due at the end of the summer.

Critical Thinking

1. What are the risks associated with exposure to bisphenol A in plastic water bottles?

2. Why do water bottle manufacturers continue to use bisphenol A in their products?

HIV Apathy

New drugs have changed HIV from a terminal to a chronic illness. To counter complacency, health officials are pushing to make testing more widespread.

ZACH PATTON

On a rainy day last June, local officials in Washington, D.C., gathered under tents erected on a public plaza to be tested for HIV. The District of Columbia's health department was kicking off a sweeping new effort to encourage city residents to take action against the disease. With banners, music and mobile-testing units, officials hoped the launch event and the campaign would help raise local awareness about HIV—and help the city address its most pressing health concern.

Washington has the nation's highest rate of new AIDS cases, and the city's goal—HIV testing for every resident between the ages of 14 and 84, totaling over 400,000 people—was unprecedented in its scope. City officials said the campaign, which also included distributing an initial 80,000 HIV tests to doctors' offices, hospitals and health clinics, would enable them to get a better idea of how many residents are infected with HIV. And making such screenings routine, they hoped, would help erase the stigma against getting tested for the disease.

Six months later, though, the effort was faltering. Fewer than 20,000 people had been tested. Many of the HIV test kits expired before they were distributed, forcing the city to throw them away. Others were donated to the Maryland health department to use before they went bad. And the city still lacked a comprehensive plan for ensuring effective treatment for those residents who test positive for the disease.

It's not all bad news. The District nearly tripled the number of sites offering free HIV screenings, and the Department of Corrections began screening all inmates for HIV. And the city improved its disease-surveillance technique, recording information on behaviors and lifestyles, in addition to counting the number of new HIV cases.

But D.C.'s struggle to meet its goals underscores a challenge common to local health officials across the country. More than a million U.S. residents are infected with HIV, and one-quarter of them don't know it, experts estimate. Diagnosis rates of HIV have stabilized in recent years, but large cities continue to grapple with much higher rates. They're dealing with higher incidents of the risky behaviors—drug use and unprotected sex, particularly gay sex—that tend to spread the disease. But they're also trying to battle something less tangible: complacency. Antiretroviral drugs have largely changed HIV from a terminal illness into a chronic one. And the fears associated with AIDS have faded over the past

20 years. As health officials work to combat HIV, they're finding that their hardest fight is the one against apathy.

Testing Laws

The first test for the human immunodeficiency virus was licensed by the FDA in March 1985. It was quickly put into use by blood banks, health departments and clinics across the country. But HIV testing at that time faced some major obstacles, which would continue to thwart HIV policies for much of the following two decades. For one, it usually took two weeks to obtain lab results, requiring multiple visits for patients waiting to see if they had HIV. Many patients—in some places, as many as half—never returned for the second visit. Another barrier was that, at the time, a diagnosis of the disease was a death sentence. With no reliable drugs to slow the progression of HIV into AIDS, and with an attendant stigma that could decimate a person's life, many people just didn't want to know if they were HIV-positive. "The impact of disclosure of someone's HIV-positive status could cost them their job, their apartment and their social circle," says Dr. Adam Karpati, assistant commissioner for HIV/AIDS Prevention & Control for the New York City health department. "In a basic calculus, the value to the patient was questionable. Knowing their status could only maybe help them, but it could definitely hurt them."

Because of that stigma and the seriousness of a positive diagnosis, many cities and states developed rigorous measures to ensure that testing was voluntary and confidential, and that it included a full discussion of the risks associated with the disease. That meant requiring written consent in order to perform tests, and mandatory pre- and post-test counseling. "A lot of the laws were, appropriately, concerned with confidentiality and protecting people's rights," Karpati says.

Two major developments have since changed the method—and the purpose—of HIV testing. First, the development of antiretroviral drugs in the mid-1990s has lessened the impact of HIV as a fatal disease. And in the past two or three years, advancements in testing technology have effectively eliminated the wait time for receiving results. Rapid tests using a finger-prick or an oral swab can be completed in 20 minutes, meaning nearly everyone can receive results within a single visit.

Those changes, along with aggressive counseling and education about risk-prevention measures, helped stabilize the rate of HIV diagnosis. After peaking in 1992, rates of AIDS cases leveled off by 1998. Today, about 40,000 AIDS cases are diagnosed every year. Data on non-AIDS HIV infection rates are much harder to come by, but they seem to have stabilized as well.

The problem, however, remains especially acute in urban areas. While health experts take pains to stress that HIV/AIDS is no longer just a "big city" problem, the fact is that 85 percent of the nation's HIV infections have been in metropolitan areas with more than half a million people. "Urban areas have always been the most heavily impacted by the HIV epidemic, and they continue to be," says Jennifer Ruth of the Centers for Disease Control and Prevention. Intravenous drug use, risky sexual behavior and homosexual sex all contribute to higher HIV rates, and they are all more prevalent in urban areas. But cities face other complicating factors as well, including high poverty rates and residents with a lack of access to medical care, which exacerbate the challenges of HIV care.

Prevention Fatigue

Nowhere is that more evident than in Washington, D.C., where an estimated one in every 20 residents is HIV-positive. That's 10 times the national average. But that figure is only a rough guess. The truth is that health officials don't even know what the city's HIV rate is. Last year's campaign was supposed to change that. By setting a goal to test nearly all city residents, District health officials hoped to make HIV screening a routine part of medical care. In the process, the health department hoped it could finally get a handle on just how bad the crisis was. "We've had problems in the past, I'll be the first to say," says D.C. health department director Dr. Gregg A. Pane. "But we have galvanized interest and action, and we've highlighted the problem in a way it hasn't been before."

The effort stumbled, though. The Appleseed Center for Law and Justice, a local public advocacy group, has issued periodic report cards grading the District's progress on HIV. The most recent assessment, published six months into last year's testing push, found mismanagement and a lack of coordination with the medical community. The District was testing substantially more people than it had been, but the number was still falling far short of officials' goal. "D.C. took a great step forward, but it takes more than just a report announcing it," says Walter Smith, executive director for the Appleseed Center. "You have to make sure there's a plan."

What D.C. did achieve, however, was a fundamental shift in the way health officials perceive the HIV epidemic. "This is a disease that affects everyone," says Pane. "It's our No. 1 public health threat, and treating it like a public health threat is the exact right thing to do."

That paradigm change has been happening in health departments across the country. Last year, the CDC made waves when it announced new recommendations for treating HIV as an issue of public health. That means testing as many people as possible, making HIV testing a routine part of medical care, and removing the barriers to getting tested. Washington was the first city to adopt the CDC's recommendations for comprehensive testing, but other cities have also moved to make testing more routine. San Francisco health officials dropped their written-consent and mandatory-counseling requirements for those about to be tested. New York City has been moving in a similar direction, although removing the written-consent rule there will require changing state law. Many health officials think that since testing has become so easy and social attitudes about the disease have shifted, the strict testing regulations adopted in the 1980s are now cumbersome. The protections have become barriers.

Officials also are moving away from "risk-assessment testing," in which doctors first try to identify whether a patient falls into a predetermined high-risk category. "What has evolved is that, with an epidemic, risk-based testing is not sufficient," says New York City's Karpati. "Now there's a general move toward comprehensive testing." Privacy advocates and many AIDS activists oppose the shift away from individual protections. Yes, the stigma isn't what it used to be, they say, but it still exists. HIV isn't like tuberculosis or the measles, so they believe health officials shouldn't treat it like it is.

But even if officials could strike the perfect balance between public health and private protection, there's another factor that everyone agrees is thwarting cities' efforts to combat HIV. Call it burnout or complacency or "prevention fatigue." In an age when testing consists of an oral swab and a 20-minute wait, and an HIV-positive diagnosis means taking a few pills a day, health officials are battling a growing sense of apathy toward the disease. "The very successes we've made in the past 20 years have hurt us, in a sense," Karpati says. "We don't have hospital wards full of HIV patients. We don't have people dying as much. There's a whole new generation of folks growing up who don't remember the fear of the crisis in the 1980s."

That casual attitude toward the disease can lead to riskier behavior and, in turn, more infections. With HIV and AIDS disproportionately affecting low-income residents, any increase in infections places an additional burden on governments. And while prescription drugs have made the disease more manageable, the fact is that 40 percent of the new HIV diagnoses in the nation are still made within a year of the infection's progressing to AIDS—which is usually too late for medicine to do much good. As cities try to fight HIV complacency through refined testing policies and a focus on comprehensive testing, residents will have increasingly widespread access to tests for the disease. But for health officials, the greatest challenge will be getting the right people to care.

Critical Thinking

1. Distinguish between chronic and acute AIDS.

2. Why do some individuals continue to engage in risky behaviors that increase their chance of contracting HIV?

ZACH PATTON can be reached at zpatton@governing.com.

From *Governing*, February 2007, pp. 48–50. Copyright © 2007 by Governing. Reprinted by permission.

MRSA: Hospitals Step Up Fight. Will It Be Enough?

Julius A. Karash

The drug-resistant bacterial infection MRSA has become so commonplace among the American populace in the last several years that most clinicians now diagnose and treat it as routinely as they do the flu. Still, tens of thousands of Americans with MRSA die each year, putting intense pressure on providers to do more.

Hospitals have instituted a multipronged approach. Certain strategies, like mandating and monitoring frequent hand washing by doctors and staff, are universally accepted, if not universally implemented. Others, such as testing all incoming patients, are much more controversial.

MRSA full name methicillin-resistant *Staphylococcus aureus*—was first identified 50 years ago, but newly compiled data paints an alarming picture. For instance, a June study in the journal Pediatrics found that the number of children hospitalized with MRSA was 10 times higher in 2008 than in 1999, surging from two cases per 1,000 admissions to 21 cases per 1,000 admissions. All told, 30,000 children were hospitalized with MRSA during that 10-year period and 374 died.

Most of the infections were acquired in a community setting, not hospitals, according to the study, led by Jason Newland, M.D., an infectious-disease physician at Children's Mercy Hospitals and Clinics in Kansas City, Mo. The emergence of CA-MRSA—acquired in public places such as playgrounds and health dubs as opposed to health care settings—-complicates experts' efforts to get their arms around the problem.

"What's new of late is we're seeing a blending of these strains," says Russ Olmsted, an epidemiologist at Saint Joseph Mercy Health System in Ann Arbor and president-elect of the Association for Professionals in Infection Control and Epidemiology. "As patients with community-acquired MRSA get admitted to hospitals, those strains are getting transmitted or are adapting to the environment and becoming more like health care-associated MRSA."

The Conundrum

At the same time, hospitals are making progress on certain fronts. For example, researchers led by Deron C. Burton, M.D., reported in the Feb. 18, 2009, issue of *The Journal of the American Medical Association* that central-line catheter-associated bloodstream infections of MRSA declined significantly from 2001 through 2007 in all types of intensive care units except pediatric units, where rates remained static.

"There is some encouraging news," says John Jernigan, M.D., deputy chief of the Prevention and Response Branch of the Division of Healthcare Quality Promotion at the Centers for Disease Control and Prevention. "We have begun to see, using various parameters, some movement in the right direction."

No one disputes that more needs to be done, but infection specialists worry that too much emphasis on MRSA may deflect attention from other drug-resistant infections, such as *Clostridium difficile* and *Acinetobacter.*

Jernigan says MRSA cases represent about 8 percent of the health care-acquired infections reported to the CDC's National Healthcare Safety Network surveillance system. "That means 92 percent are caused by other pathogens, and we don't want to forget about those other problems," he says.

"It is important to remember that MRSA is only one of the important challenges that we face," Jernigan says. "It's a poster child of a large group of problems that we have to deal with in hospitals every day in the United States."

Also complicating matters is a lack of consensus on two key issues: the value of universal MRSA testing of hospital patients, and whether it's fair for Medicare and private insurers to classify health care-acquired infections as "never events" and refuse to pay to treat them.

Amid all the controversy, hospitals have instituted stringent hand-washing campaigns and taken many other measures to keep MRSA and other infections at bay. Far from being complacent, hospital officials know that much work lies ahead of them in this ongoing struggle to protect the health of their patients.

Epidemic or Not?

Health care-acquired infections such as MRSA killed 48,000 Americans in 2006 and cost more than $8 billion to treat, according to a study released in February by Ramanan Laxminarayan, a visiting scholar at Princeton University, and Anup Malani, a professor at the University of Chicago.

MRSA most commonly attacks hospital patients via central-line-related bloodstream infections, urinary catheter-induced infections, ventilator-related pneumonia and surgical-site infections. The billions of dollars in added costs are mostly the result of longer lengths of stay, especially for patients in intensive care units.

A new report by the Centers for Disease Control and Prevention "demonstrates that the steps we're taking to reduce these often-preventable infections are working."

—Kathleen Sebelius, HHS Senretary

Most MRSA cases are not life-threatening, consisting mainly of skin lesions that can be treated with a regimen of antibiotics that are carefully considered so as not to increase resistance. But the bacteria is never fully expunged from the body and infections are likely to recur.

But is MRSA a growing epidemic?

"The qualified answer is, it depends," Olmsted says. "In the U.S. in general, I wouldn't say we have an epidemic, but we have a high endemic rate, which means the background frequency is high compared to other countries."

Olmsted says the prevalence of MRSA among American hospital patients may be three to four times higher than among Canadian hospital patients. "In addition, trends over time that look at frequency of MRSA infections in the entire U.S. population, and not just those in hospitals, indicate significant increases of MRSA over the past 10 years," he says.

"The good news is we still have reasonable susceptibility of MRSA strains to vancomycin, the antibiotic of choice, especially for very serious infection," Olmsted says. "The real concern on the horizon is called vancomycin-resistant *Staph Aureus,* or VRSA. Those are more difficult to treat."

Hospitals Take Up the Challenge

Hospitals have been escalating the fight against MRSA. For example, the person who passes you in a corridor at Truman Medical Centers could very well be a designated observer watching to see if staff members wash their hands when entering and leaving a patient's room.

"Our infection control practitioners are out and about," says Mark Steele, M.D., chief medical officer at Truman Medical Centers in Kansas City, Mo. "We monitor the compliance of all segments of the hospital, with immediate feedback. We also educate the patients. One of the strategies is to have the patients participate in observation and speak up."

Other infection prevention practices at Truman include:

- Cleaning patient rooms and operating rooms with germ-killing bleach.
- Cleaning patients' skin before central-line catheters are inserted.

Enlisting IT in MRSA War

As in any war, the battle against MRSA requires reliable information about the enemy's position. And the faster you can obtain that information and act on it, the better.

That's why more and more hospitals are adding information technology to their arsenal of anti-MRSA weapons.

"Clearly, we think this is a big need for hospitals," says Nicole Latimer, executive director of business intelligence at the Advisory Board Co. "When you have a 30-year history of performing infection prevention through a paper and pencil process or through an Excel spreadsheet process, this is a big change."

The Advisory Board, a for-profit company and think tank based in Washington, D.C., is one of a number of organizations that advocate a major role for IT in the war on MRSA. Another is Advisory Board's technology partner, Vecna Technologies Inc. of Cambridge, Mass. Funded by a National Institutes of Health grant, Vecna developed QC PathFinder software, which went on the market in 2007.

The software is designed to quickly alert hospital staffers when it is determined that a patient is infected, thus enabling a quick response.

"We wanted it to go from a search-and-find exercise, where someone is thumbing through hundreds of pages of microbiology results, to an alert system," Latimer says. "Operational response of the hospital is now within 10 to 15 minutes, rather than within 24 to 48 hours."

Other players in this market include ICNet software. On its website, England-based ICNet says its system is "designed to automate the collection of data as required by the infection control team, thus-providing real-time alerts, reports and analytical tools, which saves considerable ICT [information and communications technology] time and helps to target action more effectively."

—JULIUS KARASH

- Elevating the heads of ventilator patients by at least 30 degrees.
- Isolating patients known to be colonized with MRSA.

Truman also has made adjustments in the antibiotics it uses to treat infections. Keflex and oxacillin have been replaced by Bactrim or clindamycin for outpatients, and sicker patients requiring hospitalization are likely to be given vancomycin.

"I don't think it's becoming significantly more difficult to treat," Steele says, while acknowledging, "It's obviously less easy for hospitals to deal with what's being caught in the community."

In a 2006 report published in the *New England Journal of Medicine,* a team led by Gregory J. Moran, M.D., wrote that "the high prevalence of MRSA among patients with community-associated skin and soft-tissue infections has implications for hospital policies regarding infection control. Our results suggest that strategies used for patients with confirmed MRSA infections should be considered for all patients with purulent skin and soft-tissue infections in areas with a high prevalence of MRSA."

Which strategies work best?

"We see many patients in the emergency department with cutaneous abscesses," Steele says. "Roughly three-quarters of those will be infected with MRSA. Fortunately, most of those are self-limited and amenable to treatment, the primary treatment being incision and drainage. We don't know if antibiotics help these to heal faster or not. That's the subject of an ongoing study I'm involved with now."

Olmsted says hospitals are employing infection prevention "bundles," such as a series of steps to follow when inserting a central-Me catheter. He rites one study that says standardized use of CDC recommendations for centralline insertion has been shown to reduce bloodstream infections by 66 to 70 percent.

But knowing what best practices are and malting sure they are implemented are two different things. "Many hospitals have the right polities in place," Jernigan says. "But we have learned that just having the right policy in place doesn't necessarily translate into effective implementation. Many of the gains we've been seeing have been achieved through better implementation of existing recommendations."

But Is It Enough?

Despite all the efforts being put forth, not everyone thinks hospitals are doing enough to stop MRSA. Several states have passed laws requiring hospitals to screen high-risk patients.

"If hospitals won't take meaningful steps to stop drug-resistant infections, then we'll pass legislation to make sure they do," Washington State Rep. Tom Campbell told the Seattle Times last year.

APIC and the Society for Healthcare Epidemiology of America in 2007 issued a joint statement opposing MRSA screening mandates, saying they are too costly and limit the flexibility of hospital infection-control efforts.

Olmsted says universal MRSA screening legislation represents "a very cement approach to a problem that is fairly fluid and changing all the time. Detection of MRSA on admission is not a one-size-fits-all. You need to use your facility-specific data and decide what measures make sense. It varies considerably by facility."

Steele says "the jury is still out" on the effectiveness of universal MRSA screening. "Our infectious disease experts and infection control people have not felt that, based on the level of evidence we currently have, that's something we should do at this particular time."

Overall, Olmsted cautions that overly stringent measures could result in overtreatment with antibiotics, which would create yet more resistant strains.

Twenty-seven states now require public reporting of hospital-acquired infection rates. Olmsted says he originally was skeptical of public reporting requirements. "However, I will say that it has raised awareness significantly throughout the United States of the problem of health care-acquired infections. In that regard it's been a positive initiative."

In response to concerns about imposing a "severe burden" on hospitals, the CDC on May 7 notified hospitals that it had reversed course and would no longer require them to submit MRSA data to the Buccaneer Data Systems Clinical Data Abstraction Center that they previously reported to the CDC.

Never Ever?

In 2008, the battle against MRSA took on a new dimension when Medicare implemented its "never events" policy. The policy states that Medicare will no longer pay hospitals for treatment of complications such as vascular catheter-associated infections, catheter-associated urinary tract infections and certain surgical-site infections.

"This is really about making hospitals and the health system just a safer place to be," former CMS Acting Administrator Kerry Weems said at the time.

Private insurers are following Medicare's example, but the policy continues to stir debate.

"Somebody who gets the wrong blood type, there's really no gray to that, that should be 100 percent preventable," Steele says. "But infections are a different deal, because there are different susceptibilities to infection. It's not dear that one can prevent 100 percent of infections."

Nonpayment should be decided on a case-by-case basis, Olmstead says, noting that while infections can be prevented in most usages of central-line and urinary-tract catheters, he says it is much more difficult to prevent ventilator-associated pneumonia.

The Road Ahead

Experts agree that a hard road lies ahead in the drive against MRSA and other drug-resistant infections. In its April report, AHRQ stated, "It is unfortunate that HAI rates are not declining. It is evident that more attention devoted to patient safety is needed to ensure that health care does not result in avoidable patient harm."

On the other hand, AHRQ earlier reported that the quality of care delivered in hospitals is improving faster than in any other care setting, and patients are more likely to receive quality of care in a hospital than in any other setting.

Olmsted says hospitals and epidemiologists will "continue to be challenged by new organisms. We can't culture every patient every day while they're in the hospital. If we put our resources into interrupting transmission, with good hand hygiene and cleaning the environment and the patient, that's going to give us a leg up and we'll be ready for whatever organism comes up next."

"There's a lot of work to be done," Jernigan says. "But I think we have come a long way."

Federal policymakers concur. In May, the CDC released *The First State-Specific Healthcare-Associated Infections Summary Data Report*. The report "demonstrates that the steps we're taking to reduce these often-preventable infections are working," Health & Human Services Secretary Kathleen Sebelius said. Citing the 18 percent reduction in the national CLABSI incidence rate, she said HHS, AHRQ and the CDC will work with hospital associations and others "to further reduce bloodstream infection rates through initiatives such as 'On the CUSP: Stop BSI.'"

The American Hospital Association is "committed to improving quality and sharing relevant information with the field," says spokesman Matthew Fenwick, adding, "infection control is a top priority." Though there are "no silver bullets here, we recognize that hospitals need to do more and we are focused upon areas where we can make the most difference," he says.

Critical Thinking

1. What are the risks associated with MRSA?

2. Who is most at risk for contracting MRSA?

Post-Earthquake Public Health in Haiti

At a depth of 13 km, and just 25 km from Port-Au-Prince, Haiti, a fault system along the boundary separating the North American and Caribbean plates abruptly experienced a rapid acceleration of its usual super-slow motion lateral strike slip faulting. On January 12, 2009, at 16:53 local time, the result was the devastation of portions of the western third of the island of Hispaniola by an earthquake of magnitude 7.0 on the Richter scale. This was not the first earthquake to strike Haiti—Port-Au-Prince was largely destroyed by one in 1770—but it appears to be the strongest recorded. It has been estimated that the number of deaths directly resulting from the event exceeds 50,000, perhaps by many tens of thousands. The injured must be dealt with and the population provided water and food. The conditions created by the devastation, particularly in a country that some considered a disaster before the earthquake, will produce a colossal public health challenge. WHO has posted a preliminary statement aimed at facilitating the response to the challenges presented by this calamity.

STAN DERESINSKI

Haiti, with a 2007 population of 9.7 million, is the poorest country in the Western Hemisphere, with 55% of households earning less than one U.S. dollar a day. Before the earthquake, 45% of the population lacked access to safe water and 83% lacked access to adequate sanitation. Most health care is provided by traditional healers. Malnutrition is commonplace, and multiple infectious diseases, including HIV and tuberculosis, are endemic. Vaccination rates are inadequate (see Table 1).

Traumatic injuries, including crushes and burns, are common after earthquakes. These obviously necessitate the availability of surgical facilities and intensive care—which will require evacuation to medical facilities in other countries. These will also result in infections, including gangrenous ones. The limited vaccination coverage of the population makes tetanus an important risk, as was seen in Aceh after its tsunami. The injuries and infections, as well as the lack of drinking water in a hot tropical climate, will lead to many cases of acute renal failure, necessitating dialysis.

The lack of safe drinking water is not likely to be solved by rain since, during the winter dry season, there are only an average of three days with measurable rainfall, yielding a total of 32 mm in the month of January. Water that is available is often not safe, putting the population at risk of water-borne diseases, such as typhoid, hepatitis A, and hepatitis E. Leptospirosis is endemic in Haiti but, fortunately, cholera is not. Polio has been eliminated from Haiti.

Resettlement of displaced individuals to camps often results in crowding (although crowding in urban Haiti existed already), with resultant transmission of a number of respiratory infections, including measles, diphtheria, pertussis, and a variety of

Table 1 Vaccine Coverage at One Year of Age, 2007

Antigen	Coverage
BCG	75%
DPT, 3rd dose	53%
Measles	58%
Polio, 3rd dose	52%

respiratory viral infections. Of note is that pandemic influenza A (H1N1) 2009 is currently circulating in Haiti. Meningococcal disease also may spread under these conditions. Of great concern in conditions of crowding is tuberculosis, which, in 2007, had an incidence of 147 cases per 100,000 population. Approximately 4,000 patients were receiving treatment for tuberculosis in Port-Au-Prince at the time of the earthquake. Many with tuberculosis are coinfected with HIV.

Vector-borne diseases also may pose a risk, especially with the population abandoning their homes for fear of aftershocks and living in the streets. West Nile virus has been detected in Haiti. All four dengue types are endemic in Haiti, where transmission mainly occurs during April through November. Malaria, however, is transmitted year round throughout the country. Only *Plasmodium falciparum* is present; it has been considered to always be susceptible to chloroquine, and failures of treatment with this drug have not been reported. However, mutations in the *pfcrt* gene associated with chloroquine resistance were recently identified in some isolates obtained in the

Artibonite Valley.[1] Lymphatic filariasis is common. Zoonoses of concern include leptospirosis and rabies. A program of mass rabies vaccination of dogs was in progress at the time of the earthquake.

WHO has enunciated a set of priority interventions for immediate implementation (see Table 2).

An element to consider with regard to essential emergent medical and surgical care is appropriate triage. Contaminated or infected wounds or those present for more than six hours should not be closed. Patients with wounds should be given tetanus prophylaxis. Standard infection control precautions should be maintained. Post-exposure prophylaxis should be available for health care, rescue, and other workers. Protection of the blood supply must be maintained. Measures must be taken to prevent interruption of treatment of patients with tuberculosis, HIV, and chronic non-infectious diseases, such as diabetes mellitus. Provisions for mental health and psychosocial support must be made available.

Measles vaccination is an immediate priority for children aged 6 months to 14 years living in crowded or camp settings, regardless of previous vaccination or disease history. Supplementation with vitamin A should be administered to children six months through 59 months of age. Mass tetanus vaccination is not indicated. Hepatitis A vaccination can be considered, and typhoid vaccination may be useful for control of outbreaks.

Large numbers of medical and other workers are entering Haiti to provide relief services. Guidance regarding personal measures for individuals planning on volunteering are addressed in this WHO document, but a more extensive set of recommendations has been posted by CDC.[2]

A medical correspondent on CNN warned of the danger of unburied corpses. As it has indicated before, WHO states, "It is important to convey to all parties that corpses do not represent

Table 2   Immediate Priorities

- Ensuring access to surgical, medical and emergency obstetric care and proper case management, particularly trauma, wound, and burn care
- Shelter and site planning
- Provision of sufficient and safe water and sanitation
- Priority immunizations, including for measles
- Communicable disease surveillance and response, including outbreak

a public health threat. When death is due to the initial impact of the event and not because of disease, dead bodies have not been associated with outbreaks. Standard infection control precautions are recommended for those managing corpses."

References

1. Londono BL, et al. Chloroquine-resistant haplotype *Plasmodium falciparum* parasites, Haiti. *Emerg Infect Dis.* 2009;15:735–740.

2. CDC. Guidance for Relief Workers and Others Traveling to Haiti for Earthquake Response. http://wwwnc.cdc.gov/travel/content/news-announcements/relief-workers-haiti.aspx

Critical Thinking

1. What are the diseases that are most likely to have an environmental link?

2. What health risks typically occur after a natural disaster?

3. What challenges did the Haitian people face after the 2010 earthquake?

Countering Radiation Fears with Just the Facts

Denise Grady

As soon as David J. Brenner heard about the undersea earthquake and subsequent tsunami that devastated northern Japan on March 11, he checked a map of the region's nuclear power plants. One, because of its coastal location and reactor design, looked particularly vulnerable: Fukushima Daiichi. He hoped he was wrong.

Less than a day later, ominous reports of failed cooling systems and radiation leaks at that plant began to emerge. Dr. Brenner, director of the Center for Radiological Research at Columbia University—the oldest and largest such center in the world—found himself called on repeatedly to explain what was happening with the failed reactors and to assess the radiation risk to public health, both in Japan and around the world.

Dr. Brenner, 57, a native of Liverpool, England, is a physicist who has spent his career studying the effects of radiation on human health. He has published research showing that CT scans increase the cancer risk in children, and he recently testified before Congress, saying that the widespread use of whole-body X-ray scanners at airports would produce 100 extra cases of cancer each year in the United States.

He thinks CT scanners and the people who use them need more regulation to make sure the scans are medically needed and the doses of radiation as low as possible. He believes that even low doses increase the risk of cancer, and that there is no "safe" level or threshold below which the risk does not rise—even if that risk cannot be measured statistically.

But for all his concern about potential harm from radiation, he does not foresee a public health disaster resulting from the crisis at Fukushima Daiichi.

From the start, he has spoken with a scientist's caution, respect for facts and numbers, and keen appreciation of how much is simply not known or, at this point, even knowable. The situation changes constantly, and the path to the truth can be dicey, twisting through parties with passionate agendas for or against nuclear power, information meted out by government and industry, and public fears of radiation that many scientists consider wildly exaggerated.

How to explain the facts without scaring people needlessly? How to reassure without seeming to sugar-coat or patronize?

The last thing people want, Dr. Brenner said, is a guy like him in a white coat on TV smugly telling them everything is fine.

"People are very worried, which is not surprising," he said. "We want people to be able to make some kind of realistic assessment."

In the week or so after the earthquake, he did about 30 interviews with reporters, he said, "some good, some dreadful."

Some interviewers tried to push him to say the danger was much greater than he believed it to be. He resisted, and canceled one appearance when he realized that the host group had a strong anti-nuclear agenda.

"I try to keep my political views separate from my academic life," he said.

Asked whether he was for or against nuclear power, he paused, then said, "I think there is a role for safe nuclear power."

From the beginning of the troubles at Fukushima Daiichi, he has said that the Japanese plant is not, and will not become, Chernobyl. The Soviet reactor, which had no real containment structure, blew up in 1986 and spewed its contents far and wide. The Japanese reactors, though damaged, do have containment vessels, and the government acted quickly to evacuate people from the areas around the plant.

But he thinks the events in Japan should be a call to action for the United States. "This country and Japan have a fleet of aging nuclear reactors," he said.

Early on, Dr. Brenner said that Fukushima Daiichi would probably turn out to be similar to the 1979 Three Mile Island accident in the United States, which has never been found to have effects on public health. As conditions deteriorated at the Japanese plant, he said he thought the outcome would be somewhat worse than that at Three Mile Island, but not much worse.

But he expects cases of radiation sickness among the workers at the contaminated plant, and, he added, "I fear there will be fatalities."

He said it was possible that there would be some cases of thyroid cancer—probably too few to prove a connection statistically—years from now among people exposed as children to milk, water or produce contaminated with radioactive iodine.

So far, it seems unlikely that the accident will create a vast uninhabitable zone in Japan like the one that Chernobyl left in what is now Ukraine, Dr. Brenner said. Extensive fall-out of radioactive cesium occurred at Chernobyl, and it takes many years to decay to safe levels. That kind of fallout has not occurred in Japan.

Over all, he said he thought the Japanese government was doing a good job of providing reliable information to the public—but that it has not always done so. At first, there was a delay in releasing radiation readings around the plant. And when officials announced that radioactive iodine had been found in milk and vegetables, and yet initially declared them safe, Dr. Brenner said, he "screamed loud" and spoke out to reporters about it. There was simply no reason to risk consuming them, he said.

Radioactive iodine is taken up by the thyroid gland, particularly in children, and a vast majority of the 6,000 cases of thyroid cancer caused by the Chernobyl accident occurred because people were not told to stop giving their children local milk. The milk was contaminated because it was produced by cows grazing on grass coated with fallout.

Potassium iodide pills are widely recommended to protect the thyroid gland from radioactive iodine, but Dr. Brenner said it was better just to stop drinking milk until the threat had passed.

His message changed, however, when radioactive iodine turned up in tap water in Tokyo. Though the public was advised that babies, children and pregnant women should not drink the water, Dr. Brenner conceded that some exposure might still be hard to avoid, and that using potassium iodide was a reasonable precaution.

"I've been maybe a little overstrong in saying that potassium iodide doesn't have a role to play," he said. "But usually the problem is milk. To me, the levels in water came as a surprise."

In recent years Dr. Brenner's research has focused on responses to terrorism. He finds himself in the odd position of having directed the development of a machine that he hopes will never be used, the Rapid Automated Biodosimetry Tool, or Rabit. Its purpose is to test blood samples—up to 30,000 a day—for signs that people have been exposed to a significant dose of radiation.

The Rabit was meant to be used in the event of a terrorist attack—a dirty bomb, for instance—in which large numbers of people fearing they had been exposed to radiation might overwhelm clinics and emergency rooms. Small blood samples could be drawn at many locations and sent to the Rabit; people with signs of exposure could be monitored and treated if necessary.

The radiation releases in Japan so far have been much lower than what the Rabit was designed for.

He may have inherited his knack for industrial design from his maternal grandfather, a mechanical engineer who was one of the inventors of the Kit Kat candy bar and the machinery to mass-produce it.

His office holds two prized possessions: a 1961 photograph of John Lennon and George Harrison with Stuart Sutcliffe, the Beatles' original bass player; and the desk used by the first director of the Columbia radiological center, in 1915. It came with a drawerful of tobacco pipes.

On a recent afternoon, the venerable desk was strewn with maps and graphs of radiation levels around the Fukushima plant. Unable to find the one he wanted, Dr. Brenner accused a colleague of having made off with it, and was cheerfully rebuffed. Television interviews were scheduled and a photographer was on the way; he winced and said that lately he had had no time for a haircut.

Critical Thinking

1. What are the risks related to radiation exposure?

Test-Your-Knowledge Form

We encourage you to photocopy and use this page as a tool to assess how the articles in *Annual Editions* expand on the information in your textbook. By reflecting on the articles you will gain enhanced text information. You can also access this useful form on a product's book support website at www.mhhe.com/cls.

NAME: DATE:

_____

TITLE AND NUMBER OF ARTICLE:

_____

BRIEFLY STATE THE MAIN IDEA OF THIS ARTICLE:

_____

LIST THREE IMPORTANT FACTS THAT THE AUTHOR USES TO SUPPORT THE MAIN IDEA:

_____

WHAT INFORMATION OR IDEAS DISCUSSED IN THIS ARTICLE ARE ALSO DISCUSSED IN YOUR TEXTBOOK OR OTHER READINGS THAT YOU HAVE DONE? LIST THE TEXTBOOK CHAPTERS AND PAGE NUMBERS:

_____

LIST ANY EXAMPLES OF BIAS OR FAULTY REASONING THAT YOU FOUND IN THE ARTICLE:

_____

LIST ANY NEW TERMS/CONCEPTS THAT WERE DISCUSSED IN THE ARTICLE, AND WRITE A SHORT DEFINITION:

We Want Your Advice

ANNUAL EDITIONS revisions depend on two major opinion sources: one is our Advisory Board, listed in the front of this volume, which works with us in scanning the thousands of articles published in the public press each year; the other is you—the person actually using the book. Please help us and the users of the next edition by completing the prepaid article rating form on this page and returning it to us. Thank you for your help!

ANNUAL EDITIONS: Health 12/13

ARTICLE RATING FORM

Here is an opportunity for you to have direct input into the next revision of this volume.
We would like you to rate each of the articles listed below, using the following scale:

1. **Excellent: should definitely be retained**
2. **Above average: should probably be retained**
3. **Below average: should probably be deleted**
4. **Poor: should definitely be deleted**

Your ratings will play a vital part in the next revision.
Please mail this prepaid form to us as soon as possible.
Thanks for your help!

RATING	ARTICLE
	1. Crimes of the Heart
	2. The Perils of Higher Education
	3. Carrots, Sticks, and Health Care Reform—Problems with Wellness Incentives
	4. The Depressing News about Antidepressants
	5. "I Can't Let Anything Go": A Case Study with Psychological Testing of a Patient with Pathologic Hoarding
	6. Internet Addiction
	7. Antioxidants: Fruitful Research and Recommendations
	8. Keeping a Lid on Salt: Not So Easy
	9. Fruit Loopiness
	10. F.D.A. Panel to Consider Warnings for Artificial Food Colorings
	11. Phys Ed: Why Wii Fit Is Best for Grandparents
	12. Defeating Childhood Obesity
	13. Eat Like a Greek
	14. Dieting on a Budget
	15. In Obesity Epidemic, What's One Cookie?
	16. Great Drug, but Does It Prolong Life?
	17. Caffeinated Alcohol in a Can, Four Loko Does the Job, Students Agree
	18. The New Quitter
	19. The Thoroughly Modern Guide to Breakups
	20. The Conservative Case for Gay Marriage
	21. Is Pornography Adultery?

RATING	ARTICLE
	22. Sex, Drugs, Prisons, and HIV
	23. New Mammogram Guidelines Raise Questions
	24. Who Still Dies of AIDS, and Why
	25. A Mandate in Texas: The Story of a Compulsory Vaccination and What It Means
	26. Pharmacist Refusals: A Threat to Women's Health
	27. The Cost Implications of Health Care Reform
	28. Myth Diagnosis
	29. The *Case for* Killing Granny
	30. Incapacitated, Alone and Treated to Death
	31. Vaccine Refusal, Mandatory Immunization, and the Risks of Vaccine-Preventable Diseases
	32. Medical Tourism: What You Should Know
	33. Bed Bugs: The Pesticide Dilemma
	34. Is Your Food Contaminated?
	35. Hazardous Health Plans
	36. The Rough Road to *Dreamland*
	37. The *Surprising Reason* Why Heavy Isn't Healthy
	38. The Warrior's Brain
	39. Discovering Teenagers' Risky "Game" Too Late
	40. Chemical in Plastic Bottles Fuels Science, Concern—and Litigation
	41. HIV Apathy
	42. MRSA: Hospitals Step Up Fight. Will It Be Enough?
	43. Post-Earthquake Public Health in Haiti
	44. Countering Radiation Fears with Just the Facts

BUSINESS REPLY MAIL
FIRST CLASS MAIL PERMIT NO. 551 DUBUQUE IA

POSTAGE WILL BE PAID BY ADDRESSEE

McGraw-Hill Contemporary Learning Series
501 BELL STREET
DUBUQUE, IA 52001

ABOUT YOU

Name   Date

Are you a teacher? ❑ A student? ❑
Your school's name

Department

Address   City   State   Zip

School telephone #

YOUR COMMENTS ARE IMPORTANT TO US!

Please fill in the following information:
For which course did you use this book?

Did you use a text with this ANNUAL EDITION? ❑ yes ❑ no
What was the title of the text?

What are your general reactions to the Annual Editions concept?

Have you read any pertinent articles recently that you think should be included in the next edition? Explain.

Are there any articles that you feel should be replaced in the next edition? Why?

Are there any World Wide Websites that you feel should be included in the next edition? Please annotate.

May we contact you for editorial input? ❑ yes ❑ no
May we quote your comments? ❑ yes ❑ no

NOTES

NOTES

NOTES

NOTES